INDEPENDENT PRESS IN D.C. AND VIRGINIA

INDEPENDENT PRESS IN D.C. AND VIRGINIA

AN UNDERGROUND HISTORY

DALE M. BRUMFIELD | Foreword by Katya Sabaroff Taylor

THE History PRESS

Published by The History Press
Charleston, SC 29403
www.historypress.net

Front cover: *Washington Free Press*, February 1–15, 1968; *Alice*, April 1969 issue; *Quicksilver Times*, July 3–13, 1970 issue; *The Gay Blade*, August 1971 issue.

Back cover: *Bread Box*, undated volume 1, number 1; *Voice from the Mother Country*, April 28–May 8, 1970 issue; *Alice*, February 1970 issue; *Left Face*, October 1, 1969 issue.

First published 2015

Manufactured in the United States

ISBN 978.1.62619.906.4

Library of Congress Control Number: 2015932375

CONTENTS

Foreword: Why?, by Katya Sabaroff Taylor 7
Author's Note: Why Not? 11
Acknowledgements 13
List of Abbreviations 15

1. Washington, D.C., and Northern Virginia 17
2. Charlottesville and Central Virginia 111
3. The Shenandoah Valley and Southwest Virginia 133
4. Tidewater 161
5. Virginia's GI Underground Press: 1968–72 173

Epilogue: Now What? 193
Bibliography 195
Index 201
About the Author 207

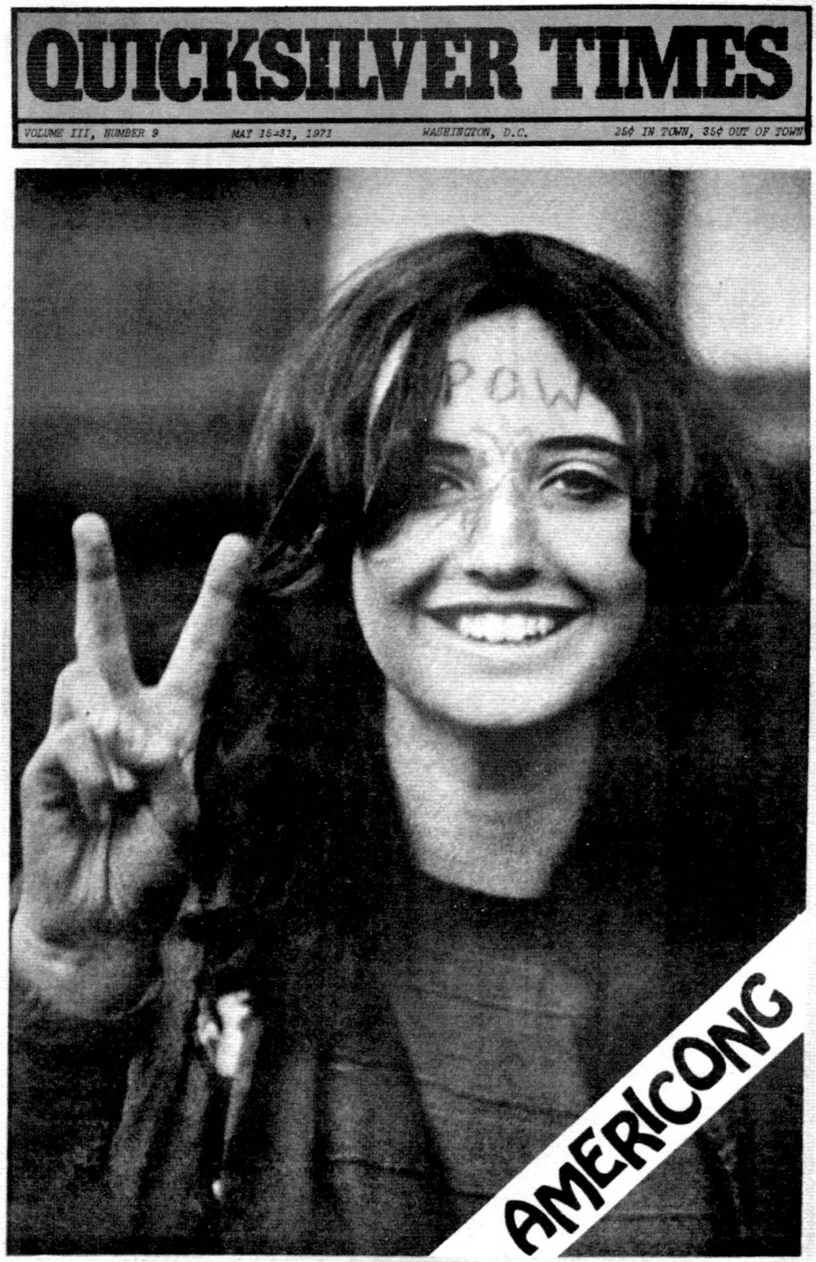
QUICKSILVER TIMES

VOLUME III, NUMBER 9 MAY 15-31, 1971 WASHINGTON, D.C. 25¢ IN TOWN, 35¢ OUT OF TOWN

Quicksilver Times, May 15, 1971. *Courtesy Paul Collinge.*

FOREWORD

WHY?

The late 1960s and early '70s—what a time in American history! Civil rights, the anti–Vietnam War movement, Haight-Ashbury's summer of love, Black Power, Sisterhood is Powerful, GIs rebelling against an "Imperialist" war, striking grape workers, Venceremos, turning on and dropping out, collectives, Students for a Democratic Society, Weathermen, V signs, clenched fists, free love, drugs and rock-and-roll.

But without the hundreds of underground newspapers that sprang up during this era to report on these radical movements and challenge the coverage of the "straight media," this era would never have achieved its far-ranging goals or raised the consciousness of American youth. The newspapers helped end the war in Vietnam; exposed the roots of racism and sexism; fought for student's, women's and gay rights; and revealed the brutal repression of citizens who dared to exercise their constitutional rights to assemble and protest.

In early 2012, I received an e-mail from Dale Brumfield asking me if I was the Nina Sabaroff who had worked on the *Richmond Chronicle* underground newspaper in 1969. I was amazed that he had found me; after all, I was now Katya Taylor, and it had been more than forty years since I'd left Richmond. But I am now not the least surprised that he located me; he shows himself to be a master sleuth in uncovering the history of the free press in Washington, D.C., and Virginia in this detailed account of the passionate and tumultuous years between 1965 and 1972. He shares his research on each underground paper in turn, uncovering stories that have heretofore never been told.

FOREWORD

If you participated in the demonstrations or actually worked on an underground paper during this time, you will be flooded with memories of "the way it was"—the fervency and camaraderie, the endless meetings, communal meals, late nights around the layout table, making headlines from press-type, the anger over the endless repression by the powers that be, the celebration over the people's victories, college students beaten with clubs, the tears shed over the killings of students at Kent State and Jackson State and the murders of Black Panthers Fred Hampton and Bobbie Hutton.

For nonparticipants who want to understand that era, this book will give you a guided tour of the dozens of papers and hundreds of dedicated individuals in Virginia and D.C. who lent their efforts twenty-four-seven to the causes of the day, who banded together with like-minded others to question authority and fight injustice, creating new modes of living and working, exploring self-empowerment and the moral imperatives that could no longer be swept under the rug.

Open the door into the offices of *Quicksilver Times*, *Off Our Backs*, the *Gay Blade*, *Hard Times*, *Open Sights* and many others. Learn about the students who challenged both the war and outmoded dress codes at their universities. Celebrate with women who stepped out of the shadows, away from the typewriter, and got behind the camera or wrote their own stories; the gay pioneers who dared to use their real names; the GIs who spoke up under threat of court-martial.

Brumfield told me, "This is a history few know, and the people who do know are rapidly disappearing." I know, because I was there, working as an editor for the *Richmond Chronicle*, working for Liberation News Service, which, long before the Internet, sent twice-weekly packets out to the hundreds of underground newspapers. I'm still here, and I'm moved by the stories of these bygone days, days that led to advances we could only have dreamed of back then.

Step back into 1965, two years before it became legal for blacks and whites to wed, one year after civil rights legislation ended Jim Crow laws. Step into the history of a people's transformative era, laid out before you now.

KATYA SABAROFF TAYLOR
November 20, 2014

KATYA SABAROFF TAYLOR is a former member of the Liberation News Service and was America's first female underground newspaper editor, serving at the

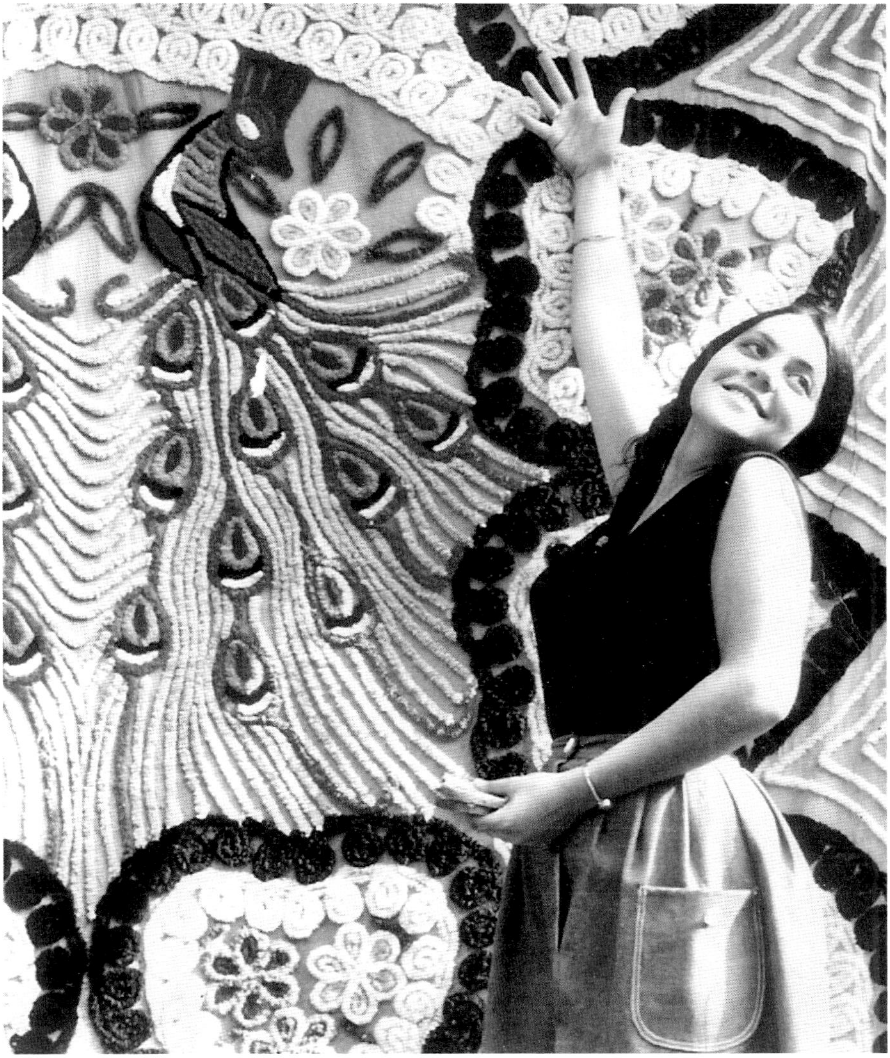

Nina Sabaroff, 1965. *Courtesy Katya Sabaroff Taylor.*

Richmond Chronicle from August 1969 until February 1970. She was such a fast and thorough typist that Yippie leader Abbie Hoffman asked her in 1969 to be his personal assistant. She declined.

She currently lives and teaches writing in Tallahassee, Florida.

AUTHOR'S NOTE

WHY NOT?

A modern phenomenon which has evolved in the last three or four years is the vast growth of the Underground Press. Underground means of mass communication utilized to avoid suppression by legal authority and/or attribution is not new to this age, but its volume and the apparent freedom and ease in which filth, slanderous and libelous statements, and what appears to be almost treasonous anti-establishment propaganda is allowed to circulate is difficult to rationalize.
—CIA Operation Resistance memo, 1968

When the above memo was issued in 1968, I was a nine-year-old living in Waynesboro, Virginia, experiencing only peripherally the tumult of the times through the lens of Walter Cronkite's nightly news; TV shows like *All in the Family*, *Laugh-In* and *Room 222*; and *Mad* magazine. I recall casually flipping through photo after photo of the Vietnam War in subscription copies of *Life* magazine, unable to comprehend such a confusing conflict a world away. I froze, however, on the famous photo taken by Gerald Upsham of Columbia University student David Shapiro sitting at university president Grayson Kirk's desk during the student takeover, wearing sunglasses and smoking one of Kirk's cigars.

That picture terrified me, because to this nine-year-old, the uprising was suddenly not in a rice paddy eight thousand miles away but in my backyard. It dawned on me that America was exploding. I have carried the significance of that rude awakening with me my whole life, trying to make sense of the influence the '60s, the radical young people and the underground free press had not just on me but on the American consciousness.

As a result, in 1981, I co-founded—with Peter Blake, Bill Pahnelas and others—an alternative arts and culture magazine called *ThroTTle* in

Richmond, Virginia, that carried on the do-it-yourself traditions handed to us by the pioneers of the '60s underground media. "DIY wasn't some trendy logo on a pre-ripped, pre-faded t-shirt at Hot Topic," Richmond culture junkie Ron Thomas Smith said in 2012. "You either did it yourself or it didn't get done. Money wasn't the primary motivation; just getting heard, just getting on the menu, just reaching your target audience and connecting with them was what it was all about."

While the exploits of the larger D.C. underground papers might be more well known, dissident papers from rural Virginia towns and college campuses, and especially those published at the state's military bases during that blistering period of history, are today virtually forgotten. Although they frequently embraced the editorial fire of the larger metro papers, they sometimes lacked the resources, audience or manpower to affect the large-scale change they sought. They might have assumed, however, that their suppression by college administrators and local law enforcement were signs they were considered a threat to the status quo and thus realizing similar goals as their larger, more urban counterparts.

As Smith said, their stories deserve to be put on the menu.

You will not find Richmond's underground papers here. For a complete history of Richmond's underground and alternative press, read my book *Richmond Independent Press: A History of the Underground Zine Scene*, also published by The History Press in 2013.

And David Shapiro, if you read this, I'm still angry at you for scaring me, but I also thank you for opening my eyes.

DALE M. BRUMFIELD

December 26, 2014

ACKNOWLEDGEMENTS

The author would like to thank the following individuals and institutions for their invaluable assistance in compiling this history: Joyce De Baggio; Francesco De Baggio; Bonnie Atwood; William Blum; Dorothy Koppelman; Ron Thomas Smith; Allen Young; David Fenton; Thomas Saunders; Susan Tichy; Michael Kazin; Charles McGuigan; Katya Sabaroff Taylor; Ken Wachsberger; Martha Mattus; Bill Shaefer; Bruce Smith; Susan Brumfield; Robert Sumner; Stan Flouride; Michael Wong; Robert Whalen; Peter Galuszka; Hal Muskat; Marilyn Webb; Carol Anne Douglas; Will Vaus; Diana Woodall; Paul Collinge; Steve Wise; Mary Lyons; Joan E. Biren; James Sheldrake; the Rainbow Project; Gary Nordlinger; Richard King; James Danky; John McMillian; Bryan Ackler; Edward H. Peeples; Orlan Cannon; Howard Romaine; Thomas Gardner; Sean Stewart, babylonfalling.tumblr.com; Craig Simpson, washingtonspark.wordpress.com; Beau Collier, darwinscans.com; and CRMVET.com.

Extra special thanks to: Lynn Eaton and staff at the Special Collections and Research Services, Carrier Library, James Madison University, Harrisonburg, Virginia; Chris Miller and Bud Bennett at the Radford University Special Collections, McConnell Library, Radford University, Radford, Virginia; special collections and archives, Newman Library, Virginia Polytechnic and State University, Blacksburg, Virginia; Alderman Library and Small Special Collections, University of Virginia Library, Charlottesville, Virginia; special collections and university archives, Patricia W. and J. Douglas Perry Library, Old Dominion University, Norfolk, Virginia; Bergis Jules, university archivist, and the great and patient staff at the Special Collections Research Center, Estelle and Melvin Gelman Library, George Washington University, Washington, D.C.; Dominique Dery, Megan O'Connell and Sarah Carrier at the David M. Rubenstein Rare Book and Manuscript Library, Duke University, Chapel Hill, North Carolina; Nichole Calero at the Sophia Smith Collection, college archives, Smith College, Northampton, Massachusetts; Ariel Myers, public services librarian, Knight-Capron Library, Lynchburg College, Lynchburg, Virginia; and John Ulmschneider, Wesley Chenault, Ray Bonis and the amazing, accommodating staff at the special collections and archives, James Branch Cabell Library, Virginia Commonwealth University, Richmond, Virginia.

LIST OF ABBREVIATIONS

ACLU: American Civil Liberties Union
AP: Associated Press
ASU: American Servicemen's Union
AU: American University
BLAC: Black Liberation Action Council
CADA: Campus Americans for Democratic Action
CARIC: Committee for Action/Research on the Intelligence Community
CIA: Central Intelligence Agency
CO: conscientious objector
COINTELPRO: Counterintelligence Program (FBI)
FBI: Federal Bureau of Investigation
GWU: George Washington University
IU: University of Indiana–Bloomington
LNS: Liberation News Service
NAACP: National Association for the Advancement of Colored People
NFO: Norfolk FBI field office
NOW: National Organization of Women
NPAC: National Peace Action Coalition
NSA: National Student Association
ODC: Old Dominion College (now University)
ONI: Office of Naval Intelligence
OOB: *Off Our Backs*
PCPJ: People's Coalition of Peace and Justice

LIST OF ABBREVIATIONS

PFP: Peace and Freedom Party
QT: *Quicksilver Times*
RSU: Radical Student Union
RYM: Revolutionary Youth Movement
SAC: (FBI) Special Agent in Charge
SDS: Students for a Democratic Society
SF: San Francisco
SMC: Student Mobilization Committee
SNCC: Student Nonviolent Coordinating Committee
SRC: Southern Regional Council
SSA: Students for Social Action
SSOC: Southern Students Organizing Committee
UPS: Underground Press Syndicate
VPI: Virginia Polytechnic Institute
VPP: Virginia Progressive Party
VSCRC: Virginia Students' Civil Rights Committee
VVAW: Vietnam Veterans against the War
WFO: Washington, D.C. FBI field office
WFP: *Washington Free Press*
WITCH: Women's International Terrorist Conspiracy from Hell
WU: Weather Underground
yippie: Youth International Party member
YSA: Young Socialist Alliance

1
WASHINGTON, D.C., AND NORTHERN VIRGINIA

UNDERGROUND
1966–67

We didn't think [Underground] was that bad. It wasn't filthy. It was all so normal for us.
—Joyce De Baggio, wife of Underground *founder Thomas De Baggio, May 2014*

The newspaper is just plain filthy.
—American University Physical Plant director Donald Dedrick, about Underground, *December 1966*

The concept of underground newspapers was so new in Virginia and D.C. in the fall of 1966 that a new tabloid called *Underground* was described as a "Beat" newspaper by the American University student paper the *Eagle*. "You can't really say what a newspaper is," founder and publisher Tom De Baggio told the *Eagle* in December 1966. "*Underground* is dedicated to free speech and press. We foster kooks and nuts, but we have something for others too."

Six months in the making, Virginia and D.C.'s "most banned, most maligned, most talked of new paper in town" and first true underground newspaper appeared on October 5, 1966, in an edition of twelve pages and three thousand copies. At the time, it was the only underground tabloid paper in existence between New York and Austin, Texas.

And it didn't even realize it was an underground paper—in fact, the only resemblance *Underground* shared with the more commonly known papers of the underground press was its name and membership in the Underground Press Syndicate. "Tom didn't think he could get a job at a legitimate paper, and he was enamored with being a reporter," said Tom's wife, Joyce De Baggio, in May 2014, of her husband's motivations for starting *Underground*. "[There was] no model that I know of, no influence by other underground papers. He just wanted his own paper."

According to Joyce, Thomas was a 1959 graduate of Washington-Lee High School in Arlington and attended the University of Arizona for about one month. "The ROTC guys were going to get him, so he left." In that one month, however, he met and befriended Robert Hurwitt, who would later become a valuable contributor to his paper.

Thomas was working as a picture framer at an Arlington, Virginia art store when he and Joyce created *Underground* at their house at 6100 North Twenty-sixth Street in Arlington to "disseminate information that is usually not believed by editors and most readers."

"It's open to experimentation in journalistic form," Tom told AU journalist Ann Beattie. "The schools have taught journalism as a profession and debased it."

But De Baggio was not a fan of the "sex & drugs" advocacy journalism practiced by underground papers that came at the end of the decade, desiring more balance in his paper's coverage, even if he found the topic personally distasteful. "He wasn't interested in the sex and drugs, although we did print articles about them," said Joyce, adding that was why he wasn't particularly interested in getting in touch with others who were starting newspapers. "And he believed in having different views in the paper. He had a pro-Vietnam column, which a lot of friends reamed him out about, but he said, 'That is what I want to do, I want to have all views.'"

Despite De Baggio's distance to other underground press papers, the De Baggio family and *Underground* still butted heads with the administration of D.C.'s American University when attempting distribution. The dispute highlighted the disconnect between the paper, the students and some of the more liberal faculty members against the conservative university administration in regards to issues of war, free speech, obscenity and other arguments specific to the emerging New Left movement. It was the first salvo

VOL. 1 NO. 9 **underground** 20 cents

Copyright 1967 by Thomas De Baggio — Wednesday, January 25, 1967

WEIRDO

BEGINS HERE

S.F. HUMAN BE-IN p. 12

THE LOVE BOOK P. 5

What is really weird about these three stories is that, to my knowledge, none of them received any kind of major publicity through established media.

This is actually not surprising when you consider that even the self-acknowledged leader in the pandering of middle-class illusions and triviality, The New York Times, carries that renowned adage "All The News That's Fit To Print." This sublime expression of perfidious prior censorship is a bold admission on their part that there is some news not fit to print.

At the Times, as well as numerous other stench-filled press parlors across the country, one must accept the judgment of several fat-bottomed editors who cull the news while working the daily crosswords on the sly.

No panacea here; yet it explains a lot about a lot.

It is here, in newsrooms across the country, bellied-up to their private and sacrosanct communion over the delicatessen of news, that the major dailies of the establishment often expediently exhaust and embellish the vulgar trivialities of scare-scene thoughtlessness to the detrement of some of the more meaningful and singular expositions of cultural and societal aberrations that inform the fulminations of so-called kooks and weirdos—sometimes in their own peculiar ways true seers into the cruel anthropophagy of our world.

The reasons for this deceitful antiphlogistic are obvious—or should be. When a man wacks off about three dactylologic letters from the sacred gaggle of his upper extremities in a fit at the dacoities of "public servants" or the general paralysis, you don't ordinarily, if you're a newsman, admit what you've seen as what you've seen. You might get cynically humorous about it, laughing uproariously in your fulvous beer, or you don't tell anyone about it at all and get tight alone, the stretch of your own nerves loud in your ears.

Fortunately, I am in almost daily contact with this graceless spawn of the general ruck that does tell about it, those madmen and joyous denunciators of rigor mortem unum pluribus. I can report quite honestly that they are not half the jackals that most of the simple-minded morons are who believe every propagandistic public lie and sentence awash with the bejasus bumme of official utterance.

These brethern are blessed with the singularity of individuals tortured by their own angry binges at fame and philosophy. They tend to listen with more than

continued on page 4

INFO ON DAMNED SCIENCE page 3

Underground, January 25, 1967. *Courtesy the author.*

that would define the relationships of underground papers and their young readers to their establishment critics for years to come.

Underground met its first challenge on the AU campus with Physical Plant director Don Dedrick, himself a member of the AU class of '52. Melodramatically insulted by the paper, Dedrick confronted Joyce on December 8 in front of the Mary Graydon Center as she hawked copies ("in the tradition of a Fourteenth and H Street 'newsie'") for twenty cents each. "Mrs. De Baggio's intention at lunchtime to sell as many copies as she could of *Underground*, the family's twelve-page, half-size, avant-garde newspaper, had gone awry," reported the December 13, 1966 edition of the *Eagle*. The AU student newspaper described an inner circle of bickering participants and two hundred student onlookers surrounding De Baggio and a determined Dedrick. "Dedrick was using pointed language to denounce the paper, and the expressions on the faces of Mrs. De Baggio's student defenders were fierce and unpleasant."

Dedrick admitted to the gathered students his objection to the paper's subject matter was personal, as it included articles on homosexuals, civil rights, aesthetic realism in art, sex, narcotics and "astral projections."

"I believe [*Underground*] goes beyond the ideals of the university and beyond my own ideals," Dedrick said when he declined to issue a vending permit for the paper. "It goes against my own religious upbringing. The newspaper is just plain filthy."

"You're against free press and free speech!" one student in the crowd yelled.

"Oh, son, don't give me that," Dedrick reportedly replied, claiming he was not telling anybody what he or she could or could not read.

"Much of what is printed in *Underground*...is silly, pseudo-intellectual smut," stated *Eagle* editor Tom Shales. "But among the many words in its pages, there just might be some of wisdom, intelligence and pertinence. Now...Donald Dedrick has decided that whatever its possible virtues, *Underground* is just too filthy to be distributed on this campus."

Student reactions to the faceoff were universally in favor of De Baggio. "I don't care if it's trash, that's not the point," government student Ed Stern told reporter Judy Kaul after paying Joyce five dollars for one hundred copies and selling most of them himself before they were confiscated from him by Physical Plant office aide Ralph Dunn. "I've never read it in my life; I'm selling it on principle."

Assistant English professor Frank Turaj said, "The basis of [Dedrick's] decision is inadmissible, illiberal and stupid. We could probably lead him through the library and clean out half the stacks on the same grounds."

Joyce De Baggio stoically endured the confrontation with Dedrick and the students in seeming good spirits, dressed in a homemade flannel zebra-skin pantsuit and clutching a half-eaten apple in one hand and her two-year-old son, Francesco, in the other. She even fielded some questions by the goggle-eyed students, many of them seemingly fascinated with their first face-to-face encounter with what they thought was a real-life hippie. "Do you believe in free love?" one "virile-looking" student asked her.

"I believe in free anything," she replied. She "then had to talk her way out of a barrage of propositions."

By the end of that particular confrontation, which broke up peacefully around 4:00 p.m., Joyce had sold over one hundred copies, which she said was "good and unexpected."

A week later, Tom De Baggio wrote an open letter to Dedrick in the December 16, 1966 edition of the *Eagle* requesting written permission to distribute the paper there. "I do not feel, as the publisher and editor of *Underground*...that I can allow a lone administrator to single-handedly limit (through accessibility) the reading matter of the thousands of citizens whom he pretends to control at his university campus; nor can I accept verbal intimidation from him to my employees."

De Baggio also pointed out that as a fellow member of the Underground Press Syndicate, the *Eagle* had automatic reprint rights on any articles appearing in *Underground*.

After Christmas break, the *Eagle* published an interview by Ann Beattie with the De Baggios titled "The Man from *Underground*" in an effort to offer a more balanced perspective on the family-run underground newspaper. "De Baggio is thin and soft-spoken," Beattie wrote in the January 10, 1967 story. "A scarf hung around his neck that he never bothered to remove, and his eyes moved constantly around the room, keeping track of inanimate objects."

While Tom and Joyce produced and distributed the paper themselves, Tom reached out to numerous contributors, including his college friend Robert Hurwitt, a "bartender with a master's degree in English," who in 2014 is still the theater critic for the *San Francisco Chronicle*. Artist and University of Virginia alumnus John Carr, who was a contributor to Jack Conroy's 1930s leftist literary magazine the *Anvil*, and artist Dorothy Koppelman also contributed on a regular basis.

"I thought [*Underground*] was courageous," Koppelman said in 2014. "[Tom] really liked all the aesthetic realism material we sent. He saw that the true avant-garde in art and ethics was being overlooked by the mainstream press. I was so happy with his paper, I did everything I could to have people see it."

Tom felt that readers like AU students who did not like *Underground*'s content should be more interested in the free speech principles involved in alternative publishing, admitting that it was an uphill battle. "I almost got into a fight with a guy at AU the other day about the views expressed in *Underground*," he said in the interview. "He said it wasn't fit to show to a twelve-year-old."

"I did get a phone call saying I would be shot if I came back [to American University]," said Joyce in 2014. She elected at the time not to report the incident.

Tom expressed surprise when the term "obscene" was used to describe his paper; he believed the term applied more to "what [President Lyndon] Johnson is doing in Vietnam." He also claimed to see nothing wrong with "yellow" or "advocacy journalism," because he believed that nothing printed could be purely objective—a concept embraced and refined by the underground papers printed after 1967.

Tom and advocacy journalists like him considered the mainstream press a collective failure in covering the unconventional "new community" developing in the United States. They pointed out the straight media's refusals to present antiestablishment points of view on social issues, such as abortion, communal lifestyles, legalizing marijuana and especially the war in Vietnam. They thought the mainstream press obscured their collusion with elitist ruling class ideals behind a façade of "objectivity."

"We really got in trouble when we were accused of exploiting the faces of napalmed [Vietnamese] children on a cover," Joyce said. "It was quite stunning. But Tom knew that people needed to see what we were doing in Vietnam."

Underground experienced few distribution problems. Newsstand and small business sales were generally consistent, and the news service distribution complex left the paper alone since they weren't even sure what it was. From October through December 1966, the De Baggios also had no problems selling papers on Catholic University and on Howard University campuses, but that eventually changed.

"I sold several and ran," Joyce said about her experience at Howard just before Christmas. In January 1967, director of Howard Auxiliary Enterprises George Miller abruptly stopped a young vendor and artist named Jan Houbolt from selling *Underground* on campus. "Presumably, the decision outlawing *Underground* on the Howard campus came from assistant to the president G.L. Washington," said Miller, who indicated the paper was not conducive to the overall educational methods of the university.

"Miller knew as well as I that the paper's black power edition had been the basis of [campus] debates and even became the substance of at least one formal classroom discussion," stated an uncredited article titled "The Fire Next Time" in *Underground* number 9. "He also was aware that several students of the university had done term papers using information from *Underground*, in particular drawing upon Warren Adkins's article on homosexuality that appeared in issue number 5."

Warren Adkins was a pseudonym used by gay rights pioneer John Richard "Jack" Nichols Jr., who co-founded with Frank Kameny the Washington, D.C. chapter of the Mattachine Society in 1961 and led the first gay rights march on the White House in 1965. He appeared full-face as Warren Adkins on the first television documentary about homosexuality called *CBS Reports: The Homosexuals*, hosted by *60 Minutes* reporter Mike Wallace on March 7, 1967. Nichols used the pseudonym after being threatened by his father, FBI agent John Nichols Sr., who was afraid his son's public sexuality would jeopardize his own security clearance. Nichols Jr. died in Florida in 2005.

"We were put with other gay publications on the newsstands because of that," said Joyce. "It was annoying because it wrongly categorized us."

Other than annoying issues with newsstand placement and scattered vendor harassment, Tom and Joyce encountered none of the monster legal challenges that would plague later D.C. papers like the *Washington Free Press* and *Quicksilver Times*. "I remember two guys dressed in black coming to the door once and wanting to see where the paper was published, which was our basement," Joyce recalled, "and Tom wouldn't let them in and they went away. It was obviously FBI."

Underground was not just about controversial news reporting; it also had strong art, literary and poetry sections. One early issue edited by former Walden School student Floyd Davis was devoted solely to poetry and carried two poems by Will Inman, who was AU's poet in residence for the fall 1967 semester.

Another 1967 issue was devoted to the art of Ken Friedman and the Fluxus international experimental multimedia art movement that pursued and championed the ideals of such radical movements as Dada, De Stijl and Bauhaus.

In issue 9, Robert Hurwitt wrote a remarkable firsthand account of the infamous "Gathering of the Tribes for a Human Be-In" in San Francisco's Haight-Ashbury, the formative event called by the *San Francisco Oracle* on January 1, 1967, that officially kicked off America's hippie movement. "At one o'clock the day's festivities began when poet Gary Snyder raised a conch shell to his lips and blew long, loud and clear a summons to the gathering of the tribe. Some 12,000 had arrived and kept pouring in while [Allen] Ginsberg, dressed in white, led most of the poets on stage in mantras... Nearby was a small beribboned booth marked LSD Rescue—an SF State college group set-up to help people on bummers."

Hurwitt's conclusions of the first be-in contradict history's rose-colored memories of that influential event. "There was something wrong with that whole dichotomy of participants and audience...The whole thing never got off the ground if you weren't already off the ground when you got there. And nobody walked off to see the sunset."

"Hippies preach altruism and mysticism, honesty, joy and nonviolence," *Time* magazine wrote in the July 7, 1967 edition, trying to explain the movement after the gathering. "They find an almost childish fascination in beads, blossoms and bells, blinding strobe lights and ear-shattering music, exotic clothing and erotic slogans. Their professed aim is nothing less than the subversion of Western society by 'flower power' and force of example."

Tom De Baggio, however, seemed to have nothing in common with such a gathering. Joyce claimed that despite articles on drug use, Tom was strongly against using drugs. In fact, Tom's father was head and chief legal counsel of the Bureau of Narcotics and helped write many antidrug laws still enforced today.

"Tom was a loner," Joyce said. "I went to all the [antiwar] demonstrations, but Tom didn't go to any of them."

Despite selling their house in early 1967 to continue publishing, a move that netted them about $9,000, Joyce cited a lack of money and just "being tired" of the grind for their decision to stop publishing *Underground*. "I don't remember selling any ads. We were against ads—that's one reason [the paper] didn't last," she recalled with a smile. "The paper was extremely important. We moved into an apartment so he could continue the paper because it wasn't making money."

After *Underground* folded, Tom published a few issues of a Georgetown paper called the *Washington Independent* and worked briefly for the *Northern Virginia Sun* and the *Arlington News* before he and Joyce started selling tomato seedlings in their Ashton Heights neighborhood garden. By 1975, the business had expanded into a home-based plant nursery.

After a diagnosis of early-onset Alzheimer's disease at age fifty-seven, Tom became an outspoken advocate to raise public awareness of the degenerative disease. He wrote two books: *Losing My Mind*, in 2002, and *When It Gets Dark*, in 2003. He appeared on *Oprah*, and National Public Radio reporters Noah Adams and Melissa Block chronicled the progression of his disease in several installments over the last few years of his life, with Block paying a final tribute to him on the February 22, 2011 broadcast.

Thomas De Baggio died in an Annandale nursing home in 2011 at age sixty-nine. As of 2014, Joyce and Francesco still run De Baggio's Herb Farm & Nursery in Chantilly, Virginia.

"We were going to change the world, and everything was going to be beautiful," Joyce said of their 1960s idealism. "It didn't work out that way."

Regardless, the De Baggio Herb Farm still continues to carry the beauty of Tom's original "flower power" message.

WASHINGTON FREE PRESS

1966–68

The Underground Press is "experiential" journalism. We report what we live, see, think and even smell. On occasion the result is trivial in the eyes of many, important only in so far as each individual being's experiences are important. But because we are representatives of a segment of the disaffected, sometimes our mere existence assigns us roles in social change.

—Jenny Diver, April 22, 1968 Washington Free Press *article titled "April 4–8, 1969"*

"Representatives from six area universities have started an inter-university newspaper to be called the *Washington Free Press*," stated an innocuous article by Jim Capra on the front page of the March 17, 1966 edition of Georgetown University's student newspaper, the *Hoya*. "The editors hope to make the newspaper a biweekly publication."

The committee of representatives from the six D.C.-area colleges (American, Georgetown, Howard, George Washington, Catholic and Maryland) stressed that the newspaper was designed as a service only. "Thus, there will be no editorial pages as such."

It was a simple, low-key introduction to a publication that, exactly four years later, would become the most harassed and persecuted newspaper between New York and Atlanta. It would, at great cost, butt heads in epic clashes with the FBI, CIA, D.C. Intelligence and Narcotic squads and various legal systems. It would raise a middle finger to a Maryland grand jury by successfully eviscerating that state's McCarthy-era anti-subversive

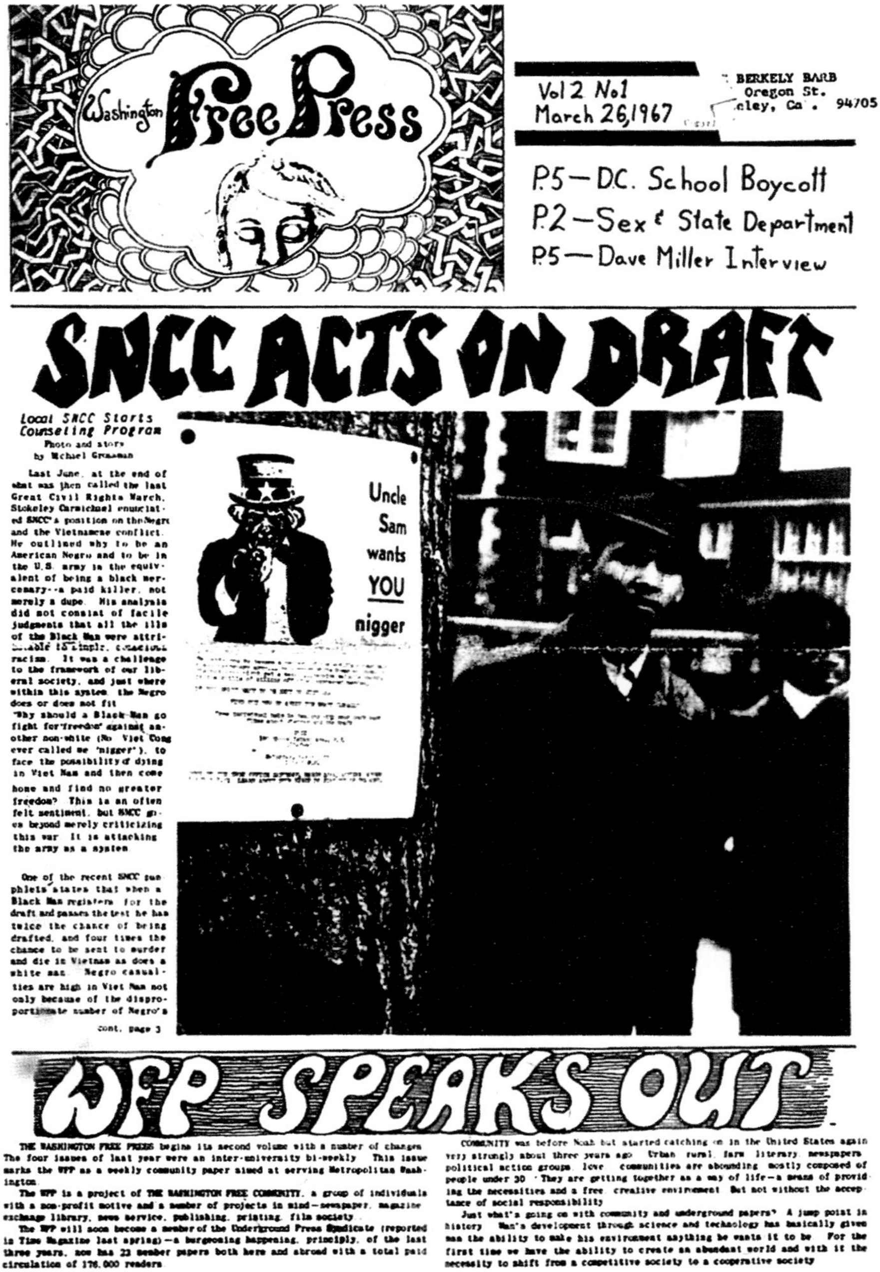

Washington Free Press

Vol 2 No1
March 26, 1967

BERKELY BARB
Oregon St.
...eley, Ca. 94705

P.5—D.C. School Boycott
P.2—Sex & State Department
P.5—Dave Miller Interview

SNCC ACTS ON DRAFT

Local SNCC Starts Counseling Program

Photo and story
by Michael Grossman

Last June, at the end of what was then called the last Great Civil Rights March, Stokeley Carmichael enunciated SNCC's position on the Negro and the Vietnamese conflict. He outlined why to be an American Negro and to be in the U.S. army is the equivalent of being a black mercenary--a paid killer, not merely a dupe. His analysis did not consist of facile judgments that all the ills of the Black Man were attributable to simple, conscious racism. It was a challenge to the framework of our liberal society, and just where within this system the Negro does or does not fit.

"Why should a Black Man go fight for 'freedom' against another non-white (No Viet Cong ever called me 'nigger'), to face the possibility of dying in Viet Nam and then come home and find no greater freedom?" This is an often felt sentiment, but SNCC goes beyond merely criticizing this war. It is attacking the army as a system.

One of the recent SNCC pamphlets states that when a Black Man registers for the draft and passes the test he has twice the chance of being drafted, and four times the chance to be sent to murder and die in Vietnam as does a white man. Negro casualties are high in Viet Nam not only because of the disproportionate number of Negro's

cont. page 3

WFP SPEAKS OUT

THE WASHINGTON FREE PRESS begins its second volume with a number of changes. The four issues of last year were an inter-university bi-weekly. This issue marks the WFP as a weekly community paper aimed at serving Metropolitan Washington.

The WFP is a project of THE WASHINGTON FREE COMMUNITY, a group of individuals with a non-profit motive and a number of projects in mind—newspaper, magazine exchange library, news service, publishing, printing, film society.

The WFP will soon become a member of the Underground Press Syndicate (reported in Time Magazine last spring)—a burgeoning happening, principly, of the last three years, now has 23 member papers both here and abroad with a total paid circulation of 176,000 readers.

COMMUNITY was before Noah but started catching on in the United States again very strongly about three years ago. Urban, rural, farm, literary, newspapers, political action groups, love communities are abounding, mostly composed of people under 30. They are getting together as a way of life—a means of providing the necessities and a free, creative environment. But not without the acceptance of social responsibility.

Just what's going on with community and underground papers? A jump point in history. Man's development through science and technology has basically given man the ability to make his environment anything he wants it to be. For the first time we have the ability to create an abundant world and with it the necessity to shift from a competitive society to a cooperative society.

Washington Free Press, March 26, 1967. *Courtesy Alderman Library microfilm collection, University of Virginia, Charlottesville, Virginia.*

Ober Law as well as almost singlehandedly roll back definitions of obscenity—making its legacy a far cry indeed from that "inter-university" newspaper that enjoyed startup funding by professors from those original six colleges.

Frank Speltz was a white student at predominantly black Howard University when he started the *WFP* with Art Grosman and Suzanne Lebovit to promote civil rights news and report antiwar demonstrations. The original lasted four issues and then ceased publishing over the summer of 1966 due to a lack of funds and little student interest. It resurrected as an "underground" paper in the spring of 1967 when the *Los Angeles Free Press*'s Conrad Averitte stopped in D.C. and rallied Grosman and Speltz with five more members: Ann Speltz, William Blum, Marjorie Stamberg, Rachel Rubenstein and Michael Grossman. Together, they secured a location in a town house at 1737 Q Street Northwest and set up the Washington Free Community with an editorial collective of fifteen members, formed as a "community paper that wanted to deal with Washington as a forgotten city.

Volume 2, number 1 of the reconstituted *WFP* was published on March 26, 1967, to "provide a communication network...by establishing a newspaper, a library, a news service on a nonprofit basis we involve the community around us. The WFC is an attempt to provide alternative ways of life that are educational, relevant, creative and loving." With the exception of Blum, none of the original planners had any publishing or journalistic backgrounds other than a desire for universal peace and justice and shared contempt for the war in Vietnam.

Bridging the uneven road from hippie ideology to militant activism, the appearance of the first non-collegiate eight-page issue of the *WFP* was rough, with handwritten headlines, typed copy and murky illustrations. But it reflected a typical unifying concern of so many 1967 underground papers, espousing peace, love and contempt for the war as well as creating a cohesive radical Washington community whose members desired to separate themselves from the co-optive influence of "straight" institutions.

In his book *Famous Long Ago*, Ray Mungo described the paper as "a biweekly specializing in lurid colors, wretched typography and anguished struggle with the politics of communal living."

"It never quite lost the appearance that it had been laid out on drugs," wrote Bill Blum in his 2002 book *West-Bloc Dissident: A Cold War Memoir*. "I was the only one who cared about the quality of the writing," he said in a 2014 interview as he recalled a sign on a wall in the *WFP* office that read "Grammar Is Bourgeois." "I pushed that, but with modest success."

"Its contributors," wrote Carl Bernstein in the *Washington Post*, "[include] vintage 1967 flower children, impassioned advocates of psychedelic drugs, mystics, neo-Marxists, anarchists, a few middle-aged marchers of the old Left, free style New Leftists, yippies and high school revolutionaries."

Allen Young wrote in a 2014 e-mail that in 1966 he was in South America and was "unaware" of the underground press. Back in the United States, he first worked for three months as a night police beat reporter at the *Washington Post* and then became a member of Liberation News Service for several years. "I got involved with the *WFP* because it was visible to me in D.C. at a time when I was reevaluating my life. I met the LNS people at that time and calculated that my skills would be better utilized in an organization directed nationally rather than local."

Contents of that issue included a page-one story by co-founder Michael Grossman titled "SNCC Acts on Draft" about the position SNCC president Stokely Carmichael took of the inequities of black men and the draft. "When a black man registers for the draft and passes the test he has twice the chance of being drafted, and four times the chance to be sent to murder and die in Vietnam as does a white man," Grossman quoted from an SNCC brochure. "Why should a black man go fight for 'freedom' against another non-white, to face the possibility of dying in Vietnam and then come home and find no greater freedom?"

Bill Blum made the leap to the *WFP* from his job as a computer programmer at the State Department. Mungo wrote that Blum was "the very picture of a mild-mannered reporter for a great metropolitan freak sheet—horn-rimmed glasses, crumpled sport shirt open at the throat and neatly-pressed slacks."

"Working for a sensitive government agency can be a lot of fun...if you're willing to sell your soul for a pay check and/or the Cold War," Blum wrote in the first issue of his experiences at the State Department, describing a two-hour interrogation about his sex life when it was discovered he had been corresponding with pen pals in Yugoslavia and the Soviet Union.

"I was one of the leading antiwar protestors while I was employed at the state [department], and for some reason, my employers thought there was some sort of contradiction there," Blum recalled of his transition from the "bourgeois" working world. "I was called in by security, and they suggested I would probably be happier in the private sector."

One fascinating early story that reflected the newness, almost naiveté of the 1967 hallucinogenic pharmaceutical scene was a short (and possibly tongue-in-cheek piece) by John Vieira, with the title "Banana Peels Forever," a reference not just to Strawberry Fields but also to what became the great banana hoax of 1967.

Spurred by the rumor that the 1966 Donovan hit song "Mellow Yellow" was about smoking banana peels, in April 1967, both *Time* and *Newsweek* magazines reported that the craze "touched off a banana-buying boom from the Haight-Ashbury to the Harvard Square."

The band Country Joe and the Fish admitted that smoking peels really made them high before a show in Vancouver, Canada—apparently forgetting that prior to smoking bananas they also drank water with LSD tabs dissolved in it. Directions for a "banana high" handed out at the New York City Easter Sunday Be-In on March 26 instructed users to "scrape the inside of a peel, bake two hours inside a two-hundred-degree oven, smoke it…and kiss your head goodbye."

Even *Mad* magazine's Don Martin acknowledged the bogus craze with a cartoon called "A San Francisco Trip," showing a hippie cooking peel scrapings on the stove and then unsuccessfully trying to smoke them in a pipe. Giving up, the hippie tosses the pipe, angrily takes a step and slips on the discarded peel. He falls and smacks his head on the stove (with typical "Swit-Klang!!" sound effects), and the final frame shows him finally enjoying his psychedelic banana peel "trip."

Donovan eventually confessed that the song "Mellow Yellow" was inspired by an ad for a yellow personal vibrator he had seen in the back of a magazine.

After the second issue of the *WFP*, a squad of D.C. policemen descended on the free community house, ostensibly looking for a runaway. The *WFP* had a strict policy, however, of keeping drugs out of the house as they knew they were under police surveillance. The police left empty handed.

While a core staff of about a dozen people lived in the commune and produced the paper, many contributors simply walked in off the street with poetry or stories in hand. Production and artwork were sometimes done by whoever happened to be in that day; thus, the paper retained a somewhat inconsistent, piecemeal look.

"[The underground press] has carried out the notion that if good writing, clean design and layout and fastidious editing are qualities of the establishment press, then [they] must be just the opposite—incomprehensibly rhetorical, anarchic, dirty and virtually unedited," wrote Jon Stewart in the April 1971 issue of *Aquarian Age* magazine. "[Most] papers offer hard-nosed coverage and analysis, but the writing is so shrouded in revolutionary rhetoric that it's difficult to take them seriously."

Frank Speltz wrote a column titled "Free Press Blues" in volume 2, number 3, describing the eclectic mix of runaways and visitors received at their house on an almost continuous basis, creating an unanticipated obstacle inherent to a true collectively run organization: no one person was in charge, and everyone had the same say in the workings of the organization. Since runaway teenagers arrived almost daily, declaring themselves staff members, it was difficult to determine exactly who could vote and who could not. Since nobody was authorized to deny their status, meetings could sometimes run for "ten or twelve shouting hours."

Mungo pointed out the intrinsic complications of a free community in *Famous Long Ago* when he said that the Washington Free Community operated on a "dead-wrong assumption…the whole point is that a free community does not have meetings, and your attendance is never required in a free community…nothing is expected of you, nothing is delivered."

"Of the eight who started the *Free Press*, seven lived in the same house," said Blum. "I lived alone because I was the only one who had any money—I was just coming off working in the bourgeois world for several years, and I had some savings, so I lived in an apartment by myself."

"We did, at the time, reject electoral politics to a great extent, especially the Democratic Party," said Allen Young, reiterating that it wasn't just the ruling Republicans but a rejection of all mainstream politics that triggered the free community form of governing.

It was probably from witnessing the pitfalls of this excessive form of democratic participation that Mungo and his partner Marshall Bloom had free rein to make decisions about the structure of Liberation News Service, which, for a while, operated in the same three-story house as the *WFP* at 3 Thomas Circle Northwest in a house known as the "Liberated Zone."

Liberation News Service was formed as a coast-to-coast connecting device for the growing number of underground papers appearing around the country. For a small fee, LNS would reprint and distribute in bulk mailing packets of the best stories of the underground as well as generate original material that could be reprinted by member papers. "It was the AP and UPI of the madcap underground," wrote Harvey Wasserman in Ken Wachsberger's book *Insider Histories of the Vietnam-Era Underground Press, Part I.*

"I stumbled over the LNS office (a storefront at that time called Student Communications Network) and began volunteering," wrote Katya (Nina) Sabaroff Taylor in a 2013 e-mail. She went to work at LNS in April 1968. "Journalism was in my blood; I had been editor of my high school paper and was a devoted writer, and once I got involved, I realized that 'radical journalism' was what was calling me much more than becoming a high school English teacher."

Because of bizarre zoning codes, the *WFP* could only publish on the first floor of this house that it shared not just with LNS but periodically with such groups as the National Welfare Rights Organization, a local SDS chapter, the Washington Area Mobilization to End the War, a high school underground paper and, briefly, a Dick Gregory for President campaign headquarters. An almost continuous stream of young people stopped by looking for a place to crash.

Traditional distribution was a Catch-22. Newspaper distributors would not touch the *WFP*, and newsstands would not stack the paper since it was not distributed by a news agency. Some copies were sold, however, at D.C.-area head shops and other outlets sympathetic to the cause of the struggling paper.

Street vendors became the solution. Young people could sell the paper for twenty cents and pocket ten cents for themselves—a fairly lucrative proposition for someone who could live on five dollars a week. On a busy sunny day in Georgetown, a vendor could sell two hundred papers. And it wasn't just read by hippies: Ray Mungo said a public relations official for the Office of Economic Opportunity told him that "all the boys at OEO" and at the Peace Corps bought and read the *WFP* to "see what you kids are thinking."

Local police, however, did not appreciate the street sellers. On July 28, 1967, Rehoboth Beach, Delaware police fired the first warning shot in what was to become a relentless campaign of vendor harassment by arresting two teenage sellers on the boardwalk, Vincent Smith and John Whipple, and charging them with selling obscene literature. They spent two days in jail before the *WFP* posted $1,000 bond.

On September 28, 1968, the *Washington Post* reported that "long-haired reporter" Christopher Webber was arrested for trespassing at Walt Whitman High School in Bethesda, Maryland. Principal Darryl Shaw reportedly asked Webber to leave the school building when he would not stop smoking a cigarette. Webber told his attorney, John Karr, that Principal Shaw poked him in the chest and called him a "kook." Webber was fined $250 and given a five-day suspended jail sentence.

On February 8, 1969, Montgomery County, Maryland councilwoman Rose Kramer's son David Kramer was arrested outside Northwood High School in Silver Spring for violating a county ordinance against peddling within five hundred feet of the school building. Kramer was told he had to stop selling the paper, so—taking the officer's word literally—he began giving the papers away for free. Not appreciating Kramer's sarcasm,

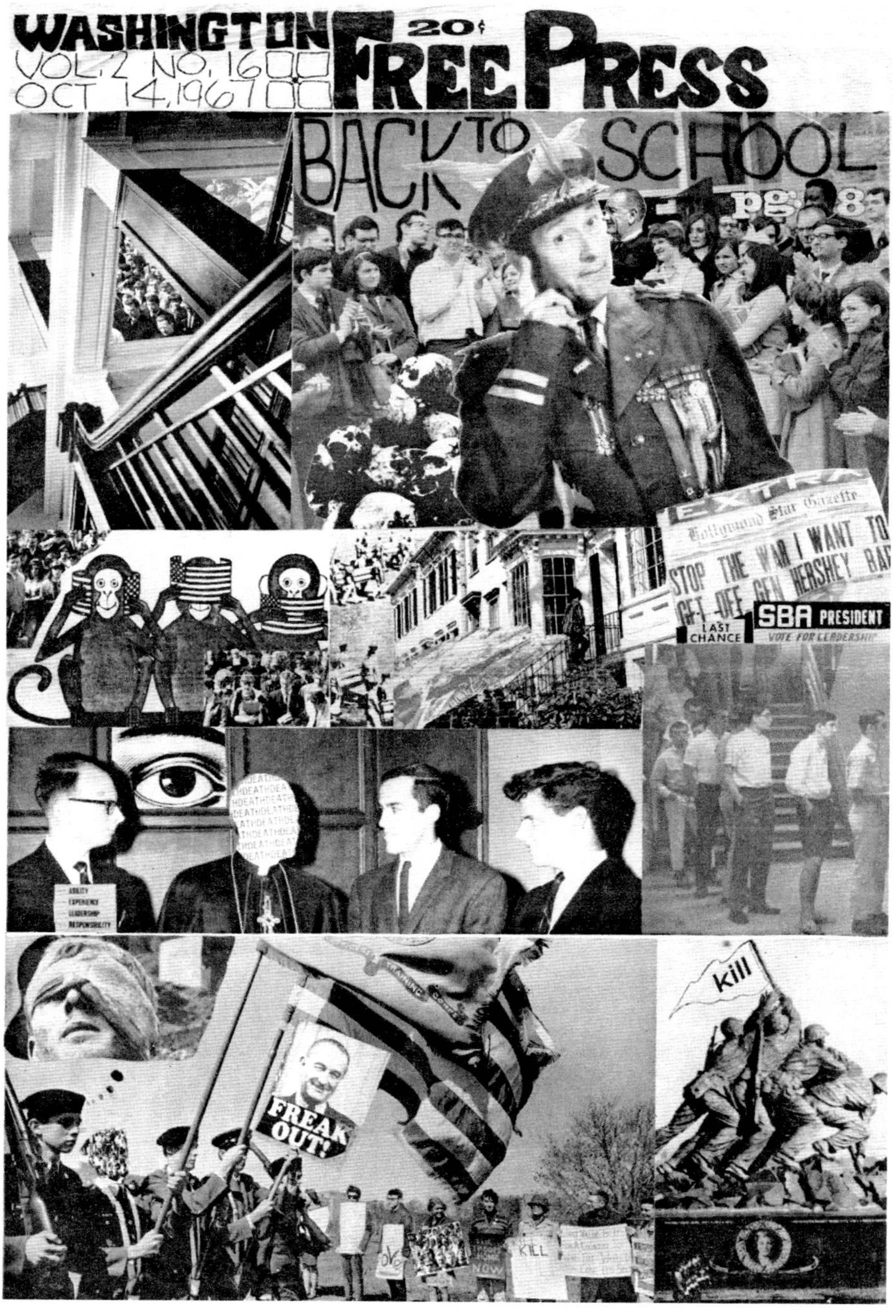

Washington Free Press, October 14, 1967. *Courtesy Sean Stewart,* Babylon Falling.

Corporal Don Black jerked the papers out of his hands, cuffed him and hauled him downtown. Kramer's father posted the $52.50 bail. Charges were later dismissed when a judge ruled that the permit requirement was aimed primarily at food trucks and ice cream vendors.

Because the radical political goals of the typical underground paper were often more important than making a profit or even paying their bills, publishing was a risky financial proposition. When the UPS polled seventy-nine of its member papers about their fiscal stability, only 28 percent said they were on stable financial footing; the others were breaking even or losing money. Many papers like the *WFP* also put ethics before profit by turning down full-page record company advertisements, saying that they refused to aid an industry that was "making a profit by co-opting our music."

There was another reason why record companies stopped advertising not just in the *WFP* but also in other papers around the country. In January 1969, the FBI's San Francisco field office wrote in a memo to headquarters that by advertising in the underground press, music powerhouse Columbia Records "appears to be giving aid and comfort to enemies of the United States." Agreeing with the memo, FBI headquarters then utilized its contacts nationwide to persuade Columbia to pull its ads in all underground papers. The February 1969 issue was the last *WFP* with any lucrative full-page record ads. Columbia never acknowledged any strong-arming by the FBI, claiming instead the underground press was no longer a "viable" advertising vehicle.

This financial inconsistency triggered a nearly continuous turnover in ideological goals, publishing objectives and staff members, who seemed to come and go with the issue of the day. Opposition to the Vietnam War, however, was the single unifying element of the paper's staff. The *WFP* ran a biweekly column called "Dear General Marsbars—Advice to the Draft Resister," a serious feature written by Frank Speltz that offered a thumb in the eye of Lieutenant General Lewis Hershey, director of selective service, who was a frequent target of many underground papers.

Finding and keeping a reliable printer was another challenge. In September 1967, the Montgomery County Press refused to publish any more editions of the *WFP*, with a spokesman stating that the *WFP*'s use of "four letter words offends the sense of good taste of the Montgomery Press staff."

Cognizant of the turnovers and tensions associated with communal underground paper production across the country, LNS founders Marshall Bloom and Ray Mungo called the first national meeting of the underground press, held at Washington, D.C.'s Logan Circle on October 20, 1967—the day before a huge anti–Vietnam War rally at the Pentagon—to address these issues.

The meeting reportedly degenerated into a "circus of movement politics." Bloom either opened or concluded the meeting (accounts vary) by burning his draft card in a Beatles-style Sergeant Pepper jacket. *East Village Other* editor Walter Bowart was accused of embezzlement as he tried to extol the virtues of Underground Press Syndicate membership. Independent filmmaker Kenneth Anger insulted attendees and (according to the *WFP*) "acted like an ass" before he was asked to leave.

"Chaos reigned," wrote Michael Grossman in the November 23, 1967 issue of the *WFP*. "The community of papers we hoped would develop did not."

Chaos also reigned the next day when the attendees, along with either 100,000 or 50,000 other demonstrators (depending on which media outlet one wants to believe), went to an antiwar rally with the intent of circling the Pentagon, joining hands and "levitating" the massive symbol of war. According to Native American tradition, the pentagon was a symbol of evil, but forming a circle around it drives out the evil. "Skeptics about the efficacy of the Indian magic will be free to use more conventional methods, such as blocking the Pentagon's doors," wrote Bill Blum in the *WFP*.

Organized by the National Mobilization Committee to End the War in Vietnam, MOBE was a coalition of almost 150 groups, all united by the common aim of ending America's involvement in Vietnam. As the protestors surrounded the Pentagon, instead of levitating the building, they got battered with billy clubs, fists and rifle butts wielded by military police and later by Eighty-second Airborne Division paratroopers.

It was a universal consensus among the movement participants that media coverage of this demonstration was biased and factually incorrect, playing up the bad behavior of a few troublemakers and ignoring the peaceful actions of the majority. Novelist and *Village Voice* co-founder Norman Mailer wrote that the media "created a forest of inaccuracy which would blind the best efforts of an historian."

Some of the 700 arrested at the rally included Mailer (fined fifty dollars and given a thirty-day suspended sentence), Women Strike for Peace founder Dagmar Wilson and march organizer David Dellinger. Three members of the American Nazi Party were arrested for disturbing the peace for displaying a flag that said "Gas the VC" and then were brutally beaten by almost 150 peace marchers. An iconic photo of a young man inserting a flower into a soldier's rifle barrel was taken at this rally.

Liberation News Service got the stories of a few soldiers sympathetic to the protestors. One anonymous GI told an LNS reporter that he personally witnessed a sergeant grab a protestor who was just standing still and beat

Washington Free Press
EXTRA!
20¢ Vol2 No.18 25¢ Out of town
1703 R Street NW Washington D.C. 20009

PENTAGON SPECIAL

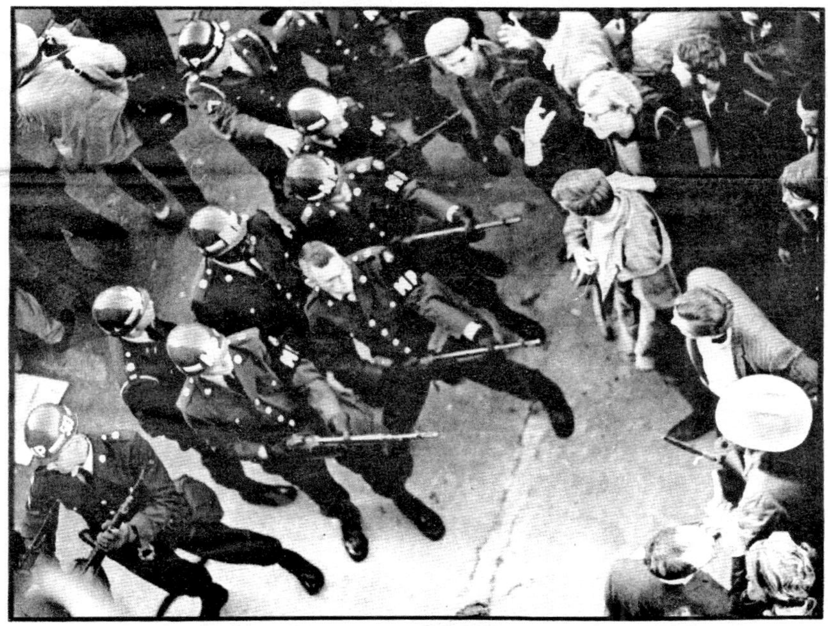

THE WAR-PEACE GAME

From the last gasps of the shuffling, confused Movement was born at the Pentagon the American Resistance. Accounts of the battle fronts are still coming in, the wounded and the arrested are still being counted and treated, mopping up of the graffiti and the bon-fires is in process. Out of this confusion, the FREE PRESS attempts to piece together the jig-saw of the various fronts. All facts stated here are as true as we can ascertain, all accusations are backed up with written eye-witness accounts, affidavits, and personal statements.

THE FIRST ASSAULT

While the mass of the mobilization marched in various contingents along the roads of the main parade group, two groups, the Revolutionary Contingent, consisting of the Committee to Aid the [illegible] National Liberation Front, [illegible] Black Mask, and other anti-imperialist groups, and the Students for a Democratic Society, split off from the parade at the Memorial Bridge. Going across the woods, they entered the Pentagon by slashing a fence off the North Parking Lot and pushing their way through the American Legion on the outside of the fence and the first contingent of military [illegible] police on the inside. Walter Teague, of the Committee to Aid the NLF was arrested at this point, but most of the two groups managed to force Jacques Bonnard through. This took place at approximately 4:30 P.M.

STORMING THE PLAZA

SDS and the Revolutionary Contingent came through the North Parking Lot and stormed the pier at the west side of the main entrance to the Pentagon. They rushed to the top of the plaza into the illegal zone of confrontation. The permit regulations had specified the top steps of the

continued on page 3

Washington Free Press, Pentagon Issue. No date. *Courtesy Sean Stewart,* Babylon Falling.

him senseless. "[He] jerked him back behind the line and the next thing I know…this sergeant was beating him." Later, the GI asked the sergeant why he had gone against orders and beat the protestor, and the sergeant reportedly replied, "Oh, I just didn't like his looks."

The *WFP* devoted an entire issue to the Pentagon riot, with George De Vincent providing numerous photos and staff writers Margie Stamberg, Roger Boyd, Austin *Rag* editor Thorne Dreyer and others recording compelling first-person accounts. Cathy Wilkerson wrote an article entitled "Victory or Defeat?" in which she questioned if either side actually won the confrontation.

A member of the Weather Underground—a paramilitary offshoot of SDS that formed in October 1969 and advocated violent overthrow of establishment power—Wilkerson and Kathy Boudin later narrowly escaped being killed in an accidental homemade nail bomb blast in the basement of her parents' Greenwich Village town house on March 6, 1970, that killed fellow WU activists Terry Robbins, Diana Oughton and Theodore Gold. The blast was devastating to the movement, furthering the schism between those who advocated peaceful solutions and those who did not. After the explosion, Wilkerson went underground, not emerging until 1980.

Throughout 1967 into 1968, the *WFP* plugged along with sections labeled "Letters"; "News"; "Culture"; at least one drug column ("The dope scene in Washington of late leaves a lot to be desired," stated the September 1969 issue); an events calendar; underground comics by big names such as Rick Griffin, Gilbert Shelton, R. Crumb and others; and, of course, General Marsbars's draft tips. Syndicated LNS and SDS stories rounded out the typical sixteen- to twenty-page issue.

Even the culture section featured unflinching honesty. In reviewing the brand-new Beatles album *Sgt. Pepper's Lonely Hearts Club Band*, Joeffrey Bartman seemed less than thrilled: "For the first time, I have found that the Beatles have given us an album of new recording production techniques rather than new musical innovations in the compositions themselves."

Although the paper's staff seemed to be galvanized by the Pentagon and the Martin Luther King riots, in May 1968, the first of several upheavals rocked the *WFP*, leading to the resignation of Bill Blum. "I was dissatisfied with where the paper was going," Blum recalls. "It was becoming much less political in the substantive sense that I wanted. The yippie types were taking over with more emphasis of doing crazy things to blow people's minds and less emphasis on the analysis of society."

The coup became known as the battle between the "feelies," the poetic adventurous types, and the "wheelies," the go-to-hell revolutionaries gunning for shocking the paper's straight readers. The paper's content during that year focused more on that radical rhetoric aimed at high school and college students, urging them to drop out, seize school buildings and subvert authority of all kinds.

"For a short while after that, each faction put out [alternating] issues," said Blum. "That didn't last too long."

Following the Martin Luther King riots that surrounded the Thomas Circle house of LNS and *WFP* during the first week of April 1968, LNS—then with over 280 member subscribers and branch offices in Berkeley, California, and London—moved to New York City.

Unfortunately, the move and disagreements over structure and leadership fractured the staff, and after a few tense weeks (and a reputed forty-eight-hour staff meeting in the Harlem basement), LNS brutally split, with half the staff—led by Marshall Bloom and Ray Mungo—spiriting away equipment in the middle of the night to a farm in Montague, Massachusetts, that had been at least partially paid for by a benefit showing of the Beatles film *Magical Mystery Tour*.

"I always felt it was a shame how the split happened," said Katya Sabaroff Taylor. "Rather than an amicable separation, it was done in an undercover and shameful (to my sensibilities) way, not respecting our general alliance as movement people who shouldn't have acted like those we criticized in capitalist society."

Soon afterward, the Montague group elected to get out of the news service business and focus on agrarian farming. "The dichotomy between farm life and the news service life had become more than apparent," said commune member Steve Diamond in his 1971 book *What the Trees Said: Life on a New Age Farm*. "Each was choking off the other. The schizophrenia was setting in." The New York office, however, flourished and, according to Abe Peck, by 1969 boasted 500 member subscribers and a readership of almost 4.5 million.

The *WFP* lost some major talent due to the LNS move, including Allen Young and longtime staffer Sheila Ryan, who had just been released from the Washington Women's House of Detention, where she had served six months for her role in a Selma, North Carolina civil rights crisis.

Another reason why LNS left D.C. was because the riots following the assassination of Dr. Martin Luther King Jr. had decimated the inner city. President Nixon had dispatched over 13,500 federal troops, machine gun nests were set up on the Capitol steps and the White House was surrounded by Third Infantry troops.

"I remember when King was shot," said former Lanier Place commune member Bill Shaefer in a 2014 interview. "There were tanks and troops in the streets. We drove up Fourteenth Street that afternoon, and it was a war zone. Sometimes you could see civilians running with guns. It was serious."

"I was selling Waring blenders in a grocery store in lower Maryland," said Joyce De Baggio, whose husband, Tom, founded *Underground*. "The [King assassination] announcement came over the speakers, and people actually applauded. I got out of there very fast. It was very upsetting."

By Sunday, April 8, twelve people had been killed and over six thousand arrested in D.C. Nearly one thousand buildings had been burned, and damage was estimated at $27 million. It took the city decades to recover.

The year 1969 proved to be a formidable one for the *WFP*, with intense law enforcement harassment and persecution worsening. The paper started the year strong with articles on the "counter-inauguration" and by outing several undercover policemen, including a particularly persistent one named Larry Elliot.

The paper was also contrite if it made a mistake, such as in the April 16, 1969 issue. "It is really life and death that we expose undercover pigs but it is also life and death if we finger the wrong guy" after a misidentification in a Fairfax bust. "It was our mistake. Sorry!"

Just before the Nixon inauguration and the accompanying Student Mobilization Committee counter-inauguration in January 1969, the FBI and the 166th Military Intelligence Detachment broke into and ransacked the *WFP* offices with no search warrant, supposedly looking for evidence of "overseas communist influence." Former Intelligence sergeant John Wagner said in the May 31, 1973 edition of the *New York Times* that they "went in a second-story window at night. I knew it was illegal. The break-in was part of the security operation in advance of the President's inauguration."

While the burglars found no evidence of foreign ties to the *WFP*, they stole about five hundred addressed postcards that were to be filled out and mailed by Washington residents willing to house out-of-town counter-inaugural demonstrators. The FBI agents filled out the cards with fake names and addresses and mailed them in, resulting in arriving demonstrators searching all over town trying to find nonexistent addresses.

At least ten thousand showed up in the streets of D.C. for the counter-inauguration. "The barrage that greeted the Nixon motorcade and the street battle that followed revealed surprising determination and strength," said writer Wolfe Lowenthal in a *WFP* article titled "Rome Wasn't Destroyed in a Day." "A lot of the credit for the quality of the counter-inauguration goes to the Washington Free Community whose spirit, that of her folk and communes, provided not only a base for many demonstrators, but a living workshop."

Despite the movement optimism projected by Lowenthal, the legal harassment was taking a toll. "Free Press Co-op needs help desperately," stated a classified ad in the January 15, 1969 issue. "We need tables, chairs, silverware, dishes, lamps and money."

A benefit dance for the *WFP* held at the Collier Room at American University on February 11 further soured the university's unsteady relationship with the paper. According to the *Eagle*, by the end of the dance, "the Collier Room was on fire, a door was torn off its hinges on Mary Graydon Center's third floor…and of course, the aroma of pot permeated the entire building."

By late February, the *WFP* found itself in the crosshairs of a grand jury investigation into seditious activity under the Montgomery County, Maryland judicial system and Circuit Court judge James H. Pugh. In instructing the grand jury, Pugh cited the Maryland Ober Law, an anti-subversion statute, to investigate and ascertain if the *WFP* had feloniously committed "any act intended to overthrow, destroy or alter, or to assist in the overthrow, destruction or alteration of a political subdivision of the state by revolution, force or violence." According to the *Washington Post*, Pugh advised the jury they should "indict the staff, publishers and printers of the paper" if found guilty of violating that law.

Pugh handed jury foreman Don Andrews two copies of the February 1–14, 1969 issue of the *WFP*, which contained an article titled "Revolution in the High School" that said, in part, "We must proceed with the destruction of the state which is attempting to defeat us by regaining control of the drug supply, which can then be used in support of the established order." The article resulted in three students at Gaithersburg High School being suspended for distributing the paper, and fifty copies were confiscated from student lockers.

The result of this negative publicity was unsurprising. A spokesman for Rockville printer Comprint Incorporated told the *Washington Post* it would no longer print the *WFP* "because of the highly controversial nature of their editorial policies and our strong disagreement with them," leaving the paper scrambling to find yet another printer. A printer was found five hundred miles away on New York's Long Island, causing several issues to be printed late.

Not to be held down, however, the *WFP* moved to Connecticut Avenue Northwest and published, in the March 15, 1969 issue, a seven-page response to Pugh's subversion probe titled "A Pornobiography," with a cartoon portraying a naked judge masturbating in front of a dais bedecked with instruments of torture, such as a whip, flagrum and a hypodermic syringe, among other items. The oddly misspelled phrase "He'Comm D'Judje"

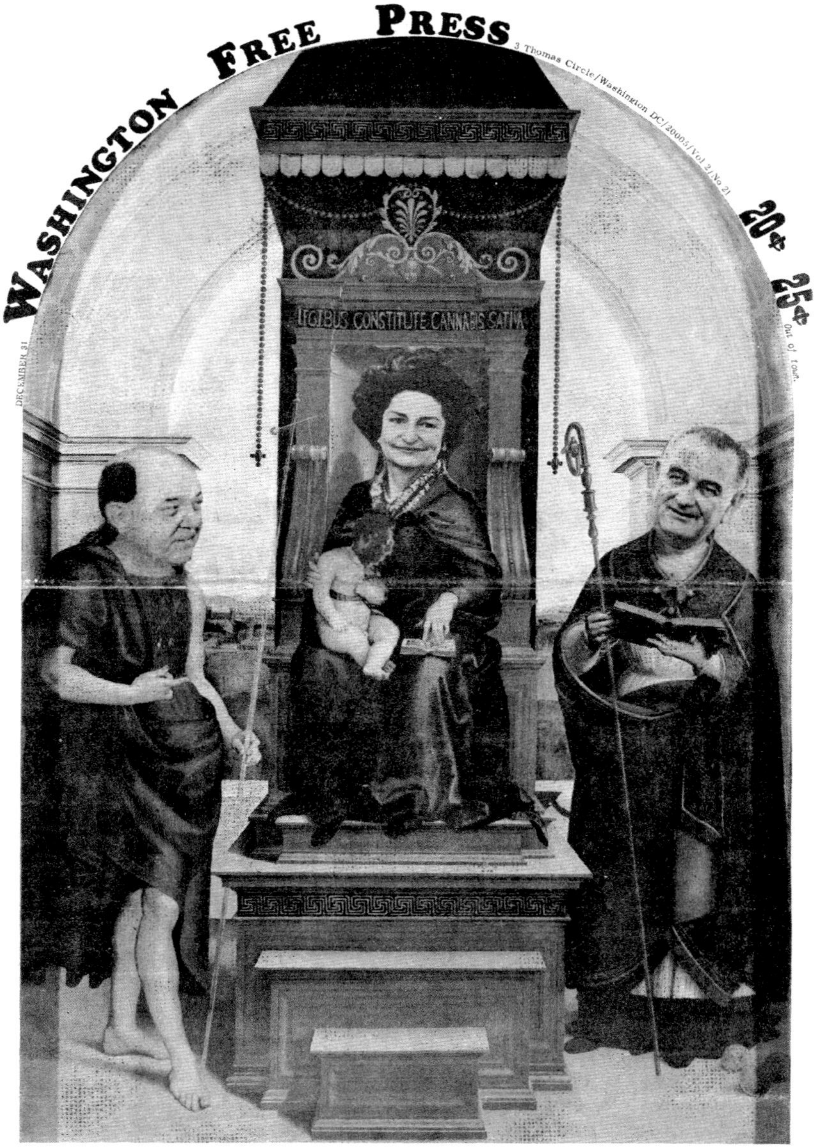

Washington Free Press, December 1967. *Courtesy Sean Stewart,* Babylon Falling.

adorned the top of the drawing. One of the articles in the section printed Pugh's unlisted phone number and advised readers to feel free to call or visit him at his Chevy Chase address.

On March 21, police retaliated by confiscating over one hundred copies at the Empire Records store on Old Georgetown Road, charging the owner with selling obscene material. Later that day, J. Brinton "Brint" Dillingham—a former Montgomery County probation officer, activist and executive director of a Bethesda, Maryland social action organization called Compeers—heard of the incident at Empire Records. He grabbed a bundle of papers somewhere and started hawking them outside the Bethesda police station. When he and his seventeen-year-old companion sold a copy to a policeman, they were promptly arrested and charged with possession of obscene literature.

It became open season on the *Washington Free Press*. On April 4, attorney Joseph Forer filed suit in federal court to overturn the sections of the Ober Law cited by Judge Pugh.

The Montgomery County Bar Association issued a resolution condemning the *WFP*, writing that they were "outraged at the vilification of a member of our bench."

"They talk about flouting the Constitution," Forer responded. "My opinion is that the constitutional rights of those who publish and distributed the *Free Press* have been grossly flouted."

On April 7, Brint Dillingham was prosecuted by Montgomery County state's attorney William Linthicum in a courtroom packed with Dillingham supporters, including one young man in a nun's habit with a sign on his back that said "Custer died for our sins." During the trial, Forer pointed out the hypocrisy of the case by showing that a Walden Book Store managed by Linthicum's wife openly sold Phillip Roth's sexually explicit novel *Portnoy's Complaint*.

Washington Evening Star art critic Frank Getlein testified about the cartoon that "the judge depicted sublimates sex into his judgments…[he] gets sexual gratification from judicial sadism." Unfazed by this testimony and the double standard presented, People's Court judge J. Willard Nalls Jr. convicted Dillingham of distributing obscene material and sentenced him to six months in the county jail.

The sentence provoked a storm of protest inside the packed courtroom, leading to two contempt-of-court citations. Dillingham's bond was set at $5,000, prompting outrage from Forer, who, after promising an appeal, pointed out that was higher than some murder cases.

In light of the conviction, police stepped up the harassment. On April 8, a *WFP* vendor was arrested at Sixteenth and K Streets after being stopped by police. He reportedly told the officer, "Arrest me if you want, I'm tired of this shit." A Kensington, Maryland man was arrested and charged with possession of obscene literature when police stopped him for a traffic violation and found two copies of the *WFP* in his car.

D.C. city government launched an investigation into the *WFP* for operating without a corporation franchise license, and shortly thereafter, the district court ordered yet another fruitless search of the paper's offices. They claimed this time that the paper's publication of certain document excerpts allegedly had been obtained during an SDS takeover of the Sino-Soviet studies offices at nearby George Washington University.

Then, the April 16 edition of the *WFP* responded to the grand jury investigation with a punk-slap to the Maryland legal system by republishing the explosive cartoon of the masturbating Judge Pugh as a "connect the dots" on the front cover, stating at the bottom, "Hey gang! Connect the number dots and display your artwork at the institution of your choice. (Evaporated milk and a sponge will do the job.) The name of the game is 'Subversion-Perversion.'"

On June 9, Brint Dillingham's appeal opened to a packed Montgomery County courtroom. Forer argued that the charge was "an attempt to pervert the law by using the obscenity statute to punish someone for his political views."

State's attorney William Linthicum presented three expert witnesses who, he contended, showed the attack on the judge violated the three Supreme Court tests for obscenity: that it was utterly without any redeeming social value, that its dominant theme was a prurient interest in sex and that it exceeded the customary community limits of sexual candor.

He called publisher Leo Paulin, who testified the cartoon of the masturbating judge was "lewd, vulgar and exhibitionistic." St. Mary's Catholic Church priest Reverend Ernest Gatta said the cartoon was an "aberration." In cross-examination, Forer maintained that Father Gatta was setting his own moral standards and was in fact not familiar with community standards, as the movie *I Am Curious—Yellow* and *Portnoy's Complaint* were both available in his county.

Kensington pychologist Ralph Oropollo testified that the cartoon's theme contained a "shameful and morbid interest in sex, nudity and excretion." On cross-examination, however, Oropollo admitted that the dominant theme of the drawing was instead "criticism of an individual."

On July 3, 1969, Dillingham was again found guilty and sentenced to six months in jail. "I know that you are not a dangerous person in the county, and I am not sentencing you with the idea that I'll rehabilitate you, change your thinking or change your way of life," Judge O'Donnell said in the sentencing. "I am considering the deterrent effect on others in the community who might have the same idea in mind. No obscene matter is worth anything if it is undistributed." Dillingham was released on $5,000 bond while Forer petitioned the Maryland Court of Special Appeals to consider the case.

While the fate of Brint Dillingham hung in limbo, the *WFP* found its troubles mounting, first in northern Virginia and D.C. and then in Prince George County, Maryland, where state's attorney Arthur Marshall called for an injunction against the paper's distribution to anyone under age eighteen. Police seizures became more common, and sometimes, entire bundles were carted away. The Montgomery County Council passed a resolution to prohibit *WFP* distribution in the high schools. One *WFP* staff member told the *Washington Post* that their biggest subscriber was the Montgomery County police department.

A Salisbury, Maryland *WFP* vendor was then arrested on April 26, and another D.C. vendor was arrested on May 12. On June 20, two Fairfax police officers walked into Discount Variety store, bought two copies and then arrested owner Billy Morrow, charging him with distributing obscene literature. Later that day, a detective bought two copies at Second and Pennsylvania Avenue and then arrested vendor Brian Neville on the identical charge.

On June 23, two policemen entered a College Park store called Joint Possession, bought a back copy of the June 1, 1968 issue and then seized almost three hundred current copies and arrested the minor who sold it to them. A comic by underground icon R. Crumb got store owner Marshall Woodruff arrested for possession of obscene material with the intent to sell it. Apparently on the verge of panic, on June 24, the City of Alexandria, Virginia, ordered police to arrest all *WFP* distributors.

During all this suppression, the paper managed to crank out issues, but the publishing frequencies and copy became more and more erratic. Oddly enough, there were always new street vendors to replace the arrested ones. Washington, D.C., by this time, had become a Mecca for teenage runaways who were willing to risk arrest to make a few easy bucks.

"A kid from Maine comes to D.C. not to Boston," John Buono of the D.C. Metro Police youth division told the *Washington Post*, obviously trying to downplay the appeal of the D.C. area and reroute the runaways farther north. "I don't completely understand the reasons—if a kid is really hip, there's not that much here for him. There's much more in the arts for young people in, say, Boston."

A fifteen-year-old runaway from Silver Spring, Maryland, named "Kitten" told reporter Carl Bernstein of her life in a D.C. commune: "I get my meals and a place to sleep free, and if I need a couple of bucks, I can always sell the *Free Press* or *Quicksilver*."

One more demonstration rocked Washington before the close of the decade—the antiwar rally on November 15, 1969, described by *Post* commentator von Hoffman somewhat prematurely as "the best, the biggest, and the last of the antiwar demonstrations."

"There is nothing more they can do to win the minds and hearts of the men who run the American government," he wrote in the November 16, 1969 edition of the *Post* of the thousands who clogged the D.C. streets. "Either these men understand the shame and reproach of having tens of thousands of people implore them for life and clemency on the streets, or the youth will turn to other ways of stopping the killing."

Commentators and pundits mostly praised the good behavior of the demonstrators before and during the massive rally on the Mall. Afterward, a large throng of people carrying Vietcong flags and a papier-mâché mask of Attorney General John Mitchell marched to the Justice Department, shouting, "Stop the trial!" in protest of the conspiracy trials of the Chicago 7, who were seven men (Jerry Rubin, David Dellinger, Abbie Hoffman, Tom Hayden, Rennie Davis, John Froines and Lee Weiner) accused of conspiracy in planning a riot at the Democratic Presidential Convention in Chicago the previous year.

Facing a police line at Constitution Avenue, march organizers persistently held back a small group of radicals itching for a confrontation. When someone threw a string of firecrackers, followed by a bottle, police unleashed volleys of tear gas that started a three-hour mêlée and forced crowds (including middle-age and older couples and children who were simply trying to get back to their buses), police, federal troops, civil defense and national guard soldiers through the shopping district, smashing windows and wreaking havoc among exploding gas grenades.

"It was my first and last awful experience with tear gas," said Katya Sabaroff Taylor. "We ran, holding desperately to our 'buddy's' hand, and when we got to the fringe an older couple was handing out handkerchiefs soaked with vinegar to help us breathe. One of our photographers came back with a huge bandage on his head from being hit by a canister. It was truly frightening."

The Woodruff obscenity trial convened on January 28, 1970. Prince George County Circuit Court judge Roscoe Parker called the *WFP* "a piece of trash" and ruled the two-page R. Crumb cartoon "hard-core pornography."

Witness and *Washington Post* art critic Paul Richard disagreed, testifying that Crumb was "an artist of stature" and that the cartoons had been displayed and offered for sale at the Corcoran gallery. Walter Hopps, acting director of the Corcoran, also testified that Crumb's work compared favorably with that of Toulouse Latrec, Matisse and Picasso and that the very cartoon in question hung on the wall at the museum. Judge Parker was also told that copies of the *WFP* were available at county libraries, but he refused to let a librarian testify, sustaining an objection from the prosecution that she did not qualify as an expert witness.

"To say that this is art is ridiculous," the judge blustered in delivering his verdict. "It's truly obnoxious, and it's repulsive to even suggest they are art. I disbelieve the evidence of both the professional witnesses because it is so farfetched it isn't even worthy of belief. That's what I think of your professional witnesses."

"What's the maximum penalty for this offense?" he asked rhetorically, releasing Woodruff on a $500 bond so a pre-sentence investigation could be completed. The maximum penalty, by the way, was one year in jail and a $1,000 fine.

What no one in the Maryland legal system realized at the time of the trial, however, was that the *Washington Free Press* had quietly gone out of business. While an official announcement was not forthcoming until March 1970, the last issue appeared in mid-December 1969 (with an all-time high press run of twenty-five thousand copies). Publishing the *WFP* had become a nightmare: advertisers were fleeing, businesses would not carry the paper out of fear of arrest and the Long Island printing and transportation was prohibitively expensive.

The staff tried to put together another issue around the December 6, 1969 murder of Black Panther Fred Hampton by Chicago police—a direct result of the FBI's COINTELPRO program, whose Chicago field office had sown lies and discord among rival black groups. The lies led to a police raid on Panther headquarters and the murder of a drugged Hampton while he slept beside his pregnant fiancée. "We couldn't get any office space," staff member Judy Freeman told Carl Bernstein in the March 9, 1970 *Washington Post*. "Finding a printer who would touch us was always a big hassle."

"The lack of money was always a factor," said Blum. "We would start production in the early evening and finish sometime in the middle of the night, then someone after being up all night would drive the flats all the way to Long Island to get it printed. That was an ordeal."

Adding insult to injury, the *WFP* office on Connecticut Avenue was again broken into on January 2, 1970, by someone who punched holes through the wall of an adjacent men's room. Files on undercover and narcotic squad police officers were stolen, but typewriters, production equipment and personal items were left alone. Of course, no arrests were made. Shortly after that, the paper lost its lease.

Despite being run out of business, the *WFP*'s name and reputation continued to be vindicated in the court system well into 1970. The paper enjoyed a post-mortem win and a devastating rebuke to Judge James Pugh on February 7, when Pugh's grand jury returned no anti-subversive indictments. A three-judge panel then officially declared most of the provisions of Maryland's McCarthy-era anti-subversive Ober Law unconstitutional and even admonished Judge Pugh for ordering the *WFP* investigated under the statute.

The Ober Law was now as dead as the *WFP* and the investigations against it.

Then, on July 15, 1970—Brint Dillingham's twenty-seventh birthday—the Maryland Court of Special Appeals surprised everyone by throwing out his conviction for distributing obscene literature. The majority ruled that the cartoon of the masturbating judge failed to meet any of the Supreme Court's standards for obscenity and failed to prove that it exceeded contemporary community standards in the depiction of sex. In a majority opinion, Judge Charles Thompson noted that the Supreme Court gave publications wide latitude in discussing the conduct of public officials: "Although Freudian concepts of sexual motivation for human conduct, as expressed by the cartoon, have come under fire recently," the judge wrote, "they are not so discredited that the Court could say those ideas are utterly without social worth."

Despite finding the cartoon a "vile and malicious attack [on Judge Pugh]," Judge Charles Orth Jr. chastised the U.S. Supreme Court, writing that "I am constrained to conclude that it is practically impossible for the state to meet the burden of proof required of it to show that material is obscene."

"It appears that this newspaper was not disseminated in such a way as to cater to members of society who would have an interest in buying a picture of a man masturbating," stated the court transcript of *Joseph Brinton Dillingham v. State of Maryland*. "Instead it appears that the periodical intended to attract subscribers who shared its iconoclastic attitude towards society."

"The *Free Press* is now extinct," Blum told Carl Bernstein in 1970, adding that it succeeded as a catalyst toward a new community that consisted of a free clinic, two homes for runaways, several communal houses, a food buying co-op as well as people continuing to rally in the streets.

Of course, another legacy of the *WFP* was the creation and stability of *Quicksilver Times*, which published biweekly until August 1972.

Brint Dillingham's conviction reversal emboldened him. In November 1969, he ran for Montgomery County "people's sheriff" in the County Democratic Primary under the slogan "Get off it." Not winning but continuing his activism, he died on March 23, 1990.

The final victory for the much-maligned *WFP* occurred in August 1971, when Federal District Court judge Howard Corcoran ruled that a National Park Service regulation frequently cited to arrest *WFP* street vendors was unconstitutional. While the paper was not around to enjoy the ruling, the *Quicksilver Times* vendors reported that police harassment came to an end—one of many final and lasting legacies of the battered *Washington Free Press*.

QUICKSILVER TIMES

1969–72

The underground press has its force and impact because it began with the supposition that the government is corrupt and writes from there.
—Realist *founder and editor Paul Krassner*

I represent [redacted] *in their advertising and PR. I was told that you had stopped in and suggested they advertise in your paper. I've read through a copy of* Quicksilver…*and to be as blunt as your publication, I wouldn't use it to wipe my ass.*
—*Letter to the Editor,* Quicksilver Times, *July 10–20, 1969*

The last split at the *Washington Free Press* forced a group of dissenters back into the streets to regroup and figure out how they would continue to fight the good fight without the voice of their tabloid paper. The obvious answer to prematurely balding insurance salesman and *WFP* advertising manager Steven Guss and former Newhouse Press Service reporter Terry Becker Jr. was to start all over. So with artist John Hagerhorst, they secured an office at 1932 Seventeenth Street Northwest in Washington and set to work on what would become *Quicksilver Times*, D.C.'s second underground newspaper. The

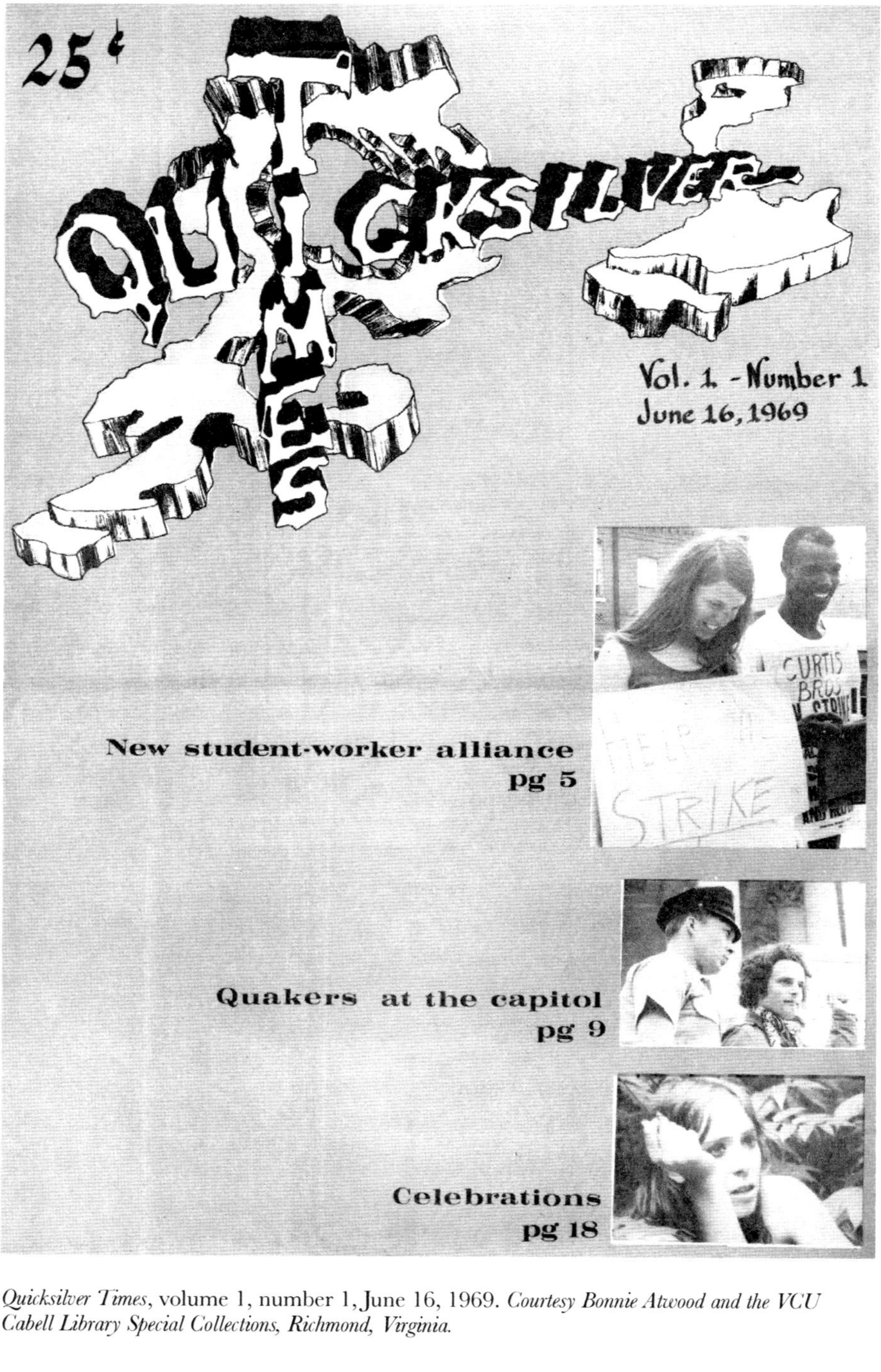

Quicksilver Times, volume 1, number 1, June 16, 1969. *Courtesy Bonnie Atwood and the VCU Cabell Library Special Collections, Richmond, Virginia.*

fifth member, Bill Blum, reluctantly backed out of any leadership roles when anticipated seed money never materialized.

The group had become disenfranchised with the *WFP* anyway. "The *Free Press* had been taken over by a whole new crowd," Blum wrote in *West-Bloc Dissident*, describing the embattled paper as "a ragamuffin bunch of hippies and dopesters, putting out a drugs-as-panacea, sabotaging-schools, mystical, bombmaking, lotsadirtywordsandsex sheet…it was embarrassing to see my adolescent son reverting to infancy."

A lawyer, insurance broker and drug teetotaler, Guss claimed to have no definable political ideology. "I'm not a Marxist-Leninist," he told *Washington Post* reporter Philip Carter. "I think I'm anti–corporate capitalism." His plans for *Quicksilver* were to make this "radical newspaper" as relevant to the D.C. area as the *Village Voice* was to New York City without it becoming an ultraliberal wing of the Democratic Party. He also discovered quickly that radicalism was a saleable product that could earn him 25 percent commission.

From almost the first day, the *QT* was befriended by someone who turned out to be an unwanted guest. Salvatore John "Sal" Ferrera was a Chicago native with Beatles-style hair, a nervous demeanor and a master's degree from Loyola University (his thesis was on Marxism). He supposedly moved to Washington, D.C., to pursue a PhD in political science at George Washington University.

"In 1969, I received a phone call from Sal," reported Blum. "He had heard that I was planning another underground newspaper in Washington, in which he expressed an interest to take part."

Blum took Ferrera up to the *QT* house to meet Becker, who was building light tables in preparation for the first issue. They shook hands, and Ferrera became a full-time member.

Blum and Ferrera went to political events, shared meals and hung out together. They even carpooled when substitute teaching at Western High School in Georgetown. "He was my closest friend for a year and a half," Blum said.

No one had any idea Ferrera was an undercover CIA operative.

Undercover infiltration of New Left organizations was tops on the FBI, Secret Service and CIA to-do lists. A $30 million Consolidated Law Enforcement Training Center in Beltsville, Maryland, offered training in undercover investigation, searches and raids and development of informants. One course, called "Appraisal of Crowds and Mobs," offered a "terminal objective" of identifying a crowd by size and type and determining "what, if any corrective, neutralizing, offensive or defensive action" would be required to calm it.

As a result, infiltration of the New Left became pervasive; of the forty substantive witnesses for the prosecution of the Chicago 7 (accused of trying to start a riot at the 1968 Democratic convention in Chicago), thirty-four were undercover agents. Writer Kirk Sales, in his 1973 book *SDS*, reported that, in 1969, there were two thousand full-time agents working undercover in the New Left. And according to police authorities quoted in the December 1970 issue of *Ramparts* magazine, 90 percent of all intelligence gathered on the New Left movement was the work of infiltrators and informants.

Much of Ferrera's espionage work still remains classified, but it is known through declassified FBI documents and books by Angus Mackenzie and Philip Agee that he also spied on former Republican Karl Hess (who headed that party's platform committee in 1960 and 1964 for Barry Goldwater) and Youth International Party (yippie) leaders Jerry Rubin and Abbie Hoffman. Ferrera made friends with the Chicago 7 defendants and interviewed their lawyers, William Kunstler and Leonard Wingless, providing the CIA with critical intelligence about their trial tactics. Ferrera's "hip" looks, demeanor and cover as a reporter admitted him inside many antiwar strategy planning sessions.

Some *QT* collective members harbored suspicions of Sal's lifestyle—he had the latest camera equipment and more money than he should have, but no one pegged him as a plant. "I remember Sal well," said former member Bob Sumner in 2014. "He was around at least since the move to the new 17th and R collective house."

"He credited his having the very latest in expensive camera equipment to a trust fund," said former collective member Stan Flouride in 2014.

"I knew Sal Ferrera, but I don't know which faces in the office were the FBI," wrote Susan Tichy, who was not a collective member but just hung out. "In the pre-paranoid days, anyone who happened to be there when a meeting happened was invited to take part, so I do remember sitting in a circle on the floor upstairs listening to the rest of them talk."

Former friend Patti Heck told columnist Jack Anderson in 1975 that Ferrera held a fascination with electronic equipment. In fact, Blum reported that Ferrera actually brought a "bugging detector" to their house and swept the walls and phones for listening devices.

About seven thousand copies of the first issue of *Quicksilver Times*, published by "the Sixth Column" (later changed to the Washington Independent Publishing Company), hit the streets on June 16, 1969. The lead story was on the DC-9, seven men and two women who "destroyed the D.C. office of the Dow Chemical Co." on March 22.

Terry Becker wrote a piece titled "Bridging the Gap" about the current state of the SDS across America. Sal Ferrera co-wrote a news story with Lenore Patterson titled "Peru v USA," about the Peruvian government seizing American Standard oil wells in that country and charging Standard with corruption. Ferrera had a second byline on page twelve, where he reviewed the book *Coup D'etat* by Edward Luttwak. While he contributed to over twenty-five issues, it was the last time his real name appeared, choosing to write under the name Sal Torey from then on.

Like all underground papers that eschewed traditional objectivity, the *QT* developed "participation journalism." "Most of us participate in events [that we cover]," Sumner told a *Washington Post* reporter. "We're either supporting it or trashing it."

While the vitals box claimed the paper was to be published weekly, it was actually published every ten days to two weeks. It was supported by ads and single-issue sales; an issue sold for $0.25, and a fifty-two-issue subscription was $8.00. Becker told writer Dale McFeatters at Scripps-Howard News Service in June 1970 that a twenty-thousand-copy edition cost about $1,200.00 in printing expenses, office supplies, utilities and rent.

While papers were sold at several local businesses, it was more likely for D.C. residents to see street vendors earning up to eighty dollars a week hawking the *QT* in various neighborhoods (they paid ten cents each for papers to sell at twenty-five cents). In 2014, former Lanier Place collective member Bill Shaefer reported spending "many a Friday evening on the corner of Wisconsin Avenue, my son Chris on my shoulder, selling, selling, selling" the *QT*.

Street selling was not without its challenges. "Jesus freaks preach us off our corners," stated an editorial in a later issue. "Sexist dogs pinch and proposition women vendors while they harass and pick fights with our long-haired brothers."

Staff members were given four hundred free copies to sell. The $100 proceeds were the only monetary benefits of working there. There were local laws they had to follow; for example, it was illegal for vendors to call out the name of the paper after 8:00 p.m. or to hawk them in the street.

"I would go to the *Quicksilver* office on Saturday mornings in time for the papers to arrive from the printer, then head to Georgetown, where my most successful spot was the northwest corner of Wisconsin and M [Streets]," said Tichy. "I had to get there early to secure that spot, then wait for customers to show up."

"If I had poems in the issue, I got one hundred free copies; otherwise [I paid] ten cents apiece. I didn't often sell the whole hundred, but if a friend came with me we generally did unload the whole pile. Twenty-five dollars was a lot then."

"Some are spiritually excited by the spirit of the outdoors and dread the business suit boredom of a desk job," stated a story about *QT* hawkers in the AU student paper the *Eagle*. "Others enjoy making their own hours. Still others merely like to rap with people."

Vendors reported that the most frequent buyers of *QT* were businessmen "trying to find out what their kids are doing" and "teenyboppers." "They come to Georgetown in their freshly pressed dungarees and coolly tuck a copy under their arm," said a September 25, 1970 article in the *Eagle*, pointing out also that "the freaks" generally didn't buy the paper because they "[don't] have much bread and besides he knows what's happening."

The *Quicksilver* collective was one of forty across D.C. at the time. Typically, there was a core group of steady residents, but constant turnover of fringe members sometimes made for a rather uncomfortable existence. "Nothing came easy," Bill Shaefer recalls of his time living at Lanier Place. "One of the responsibilities at the house was that both men and women had to cook." According to Shaefer, one resident was known as "the cereal man" because when it was his turn to do dinner, he would line up like sixteen boxes of cereal and milk. "So that is what we had for dinner that night."

"[Lanier] was set up so it would be a community-action commune," Shaefer continued. "We were working in the neighborhood, dealing with landlords against lead-based paint and community organizing. When the war heated up, more people moved in, and it became a real center for movement activities."

Inside the *QT* collective, Stan Flouride recalled "the endless meetings and debates, supposedly over the fine points of Marxist revolution but in actuality just dick measuring contests."

The FBI Washington field office took notice of the influx of people into collectives and communes and reported their activities in blizzards of memos. One stated that in the neighborhood of 1779 Lanier Place Northwest, "members of 'Hippies' are constantly seen to enter and leave at all hours of night and day."

In July 1969, Ferrera approached Blum with a unique *QT* story idea that he claimed had been suggested to him by Karl Hess: stake out the CIA headquarters in Langley, Virginia, and record as many license plates entering the property as possible; match them up with names and addresses available in the Virginia, D.C. and Maryland divisions of motor vehicles; and publish them. The point, according to Blum, was to "throw a monkey wrench into the covert circuitry of the CIA," an organization so shrouded in secrecy that even their building was unlabeled, sitting on an exit marked "Bureau of Public Roads."

Blum and Ferrera parked a Volkswagen out front of the building entrance on the morning of August 4. Blum pretended to repair a flat tire while Ferrera read off plate numbers into a recorder hidden under his shirt. They were even questioned by two security guards but left alone.

Virginia SSOC liaison Bruce Smith helped match up the Virginia plates and addresses at the Richmond DMV. "They had a book and you could look up ten at a time," he said.

On August 26, the *QT* published a four-page list of 215 CIA employees, titled "Know Thy Neighbor." The story was laid out simply so as not to arouse the printer's suspicions. A preface stated (somewhat ironically, considering Ferrera's true identity) that "these names were provided the *Quicksilver Times* by a person closely associated with the CIA…the list is a combination of employees, spouses of employees and persons doing associate and consulting work for the CIA."

The list garnered a respectable amount of attention. People on the list contacted by the *Washington Daily News* either hung up, denied being employed at the CIA or declined to comment.

In Blum's CIA file, acquired through freedom of information, he found out the agency referred to the published listing as an "attempted exposure of CIA connected persons as a means of harassment and sensationalism calculated to 'sell papers' and to establish the paper's own image."

While the CIA complained of being harassed by two *QT* reporters, harassment and infiltration at the paper by FBI, CIA and D.C. police was a more persistent problem, and the collective had no real strategy to stop it. "Everybody knew, if you had eighteen people living in a house, probably six of them were plants," said Shaefer, relating a personal experience with a "mousy little girl" that he had an "odd feeling about" who asked him to take her to the old post office so she could drop off some cassette tapes. "I knew the building had an area of what I had been told were FBI offices," he recollected. "Of course there are no labels on the doors, and she walks in and tells someone, 'This is for so and so.' On the way out I realized Oh shit! She's an informer! And she was so secure of how dumb I was. Shortly after that, things got bad, and she left."

The steady stream of hippies, addicts, informers and runaways flooding the *QT* house eventually led to a fracturing internal dispute on April 18, 1970, that shut down production for almost three weeks. A struggle for control erupted between the ten original members and a Weathermen faction of SDS over the true purpose of an underground newspaper. The decision to suspend publication was made after an eleven-hour staff meeting in which the paper's founders were called "racist, petit bourgeois, white chauvinists" and then ordered out of the house.

The Weathermen, who advocated violence to accomplish certain goals, felt that an underground newspaper should stress internationalism, focusing more on the struggles of groups such as the National Liberation Front, the Palestine Liberation Front, the Pathet Lao and Latin American guerrillas. The original *QT* faction maintained that in such a paper, "the intense rhetorical analysis and berating of people new to the movement who don't match up to a revolutionary ideal…would in the end turn off readers and hence, potential fighters."

It wasn't the first time an underground paper split—a Weathermen splinter group had also taken over the *Guardian* in New York and replaced it with the *Liberated Guardian*. When the SDS split in 1969, the Weathermen and Progressive labor groups fought over control of *New Left Notes*, changing the name to *New Left Notes: The Fire Next Time* and then to *Fire!*

After leaving, Becker issued a statement that read in part:

> The Quicksilver Times *newspaper is suspending publication. Evil, blue meanie, antilife forces bent on a bloody revolution utilizing indiscriminate violence swarmed through the newspaper office and forced a confrontation… staff members fleeing the blue-gloved onslaught predicted the eventual victory of the Washington community over any violent, rhetorically shouting, lifeless newspaper offshoots that may be spawned in graying Quicksilverland.*

"We weren't mindless robotrons parroting the party line; we were all pretty emotional about the revolution," former *QT* collective member Robert Whalen said in 2014 of the stress many of them felt at the time. "I think we took the suffering of the Vietnamese as our personal responsibility to end."

On April 30, during the three-week suspension, President Nixon ordered an invasion of Cambodia ostensibly to block supply routes to the Vietcong. Then, on May 4, Ohio National Guardsmen opened fire on unarmed protesting students and bystanders on the campus of Kent State University in Kent, Ohio, killing four students and bystanders and wounding nine. The Kent State tragedy was a movement turning point and sharpened opposition

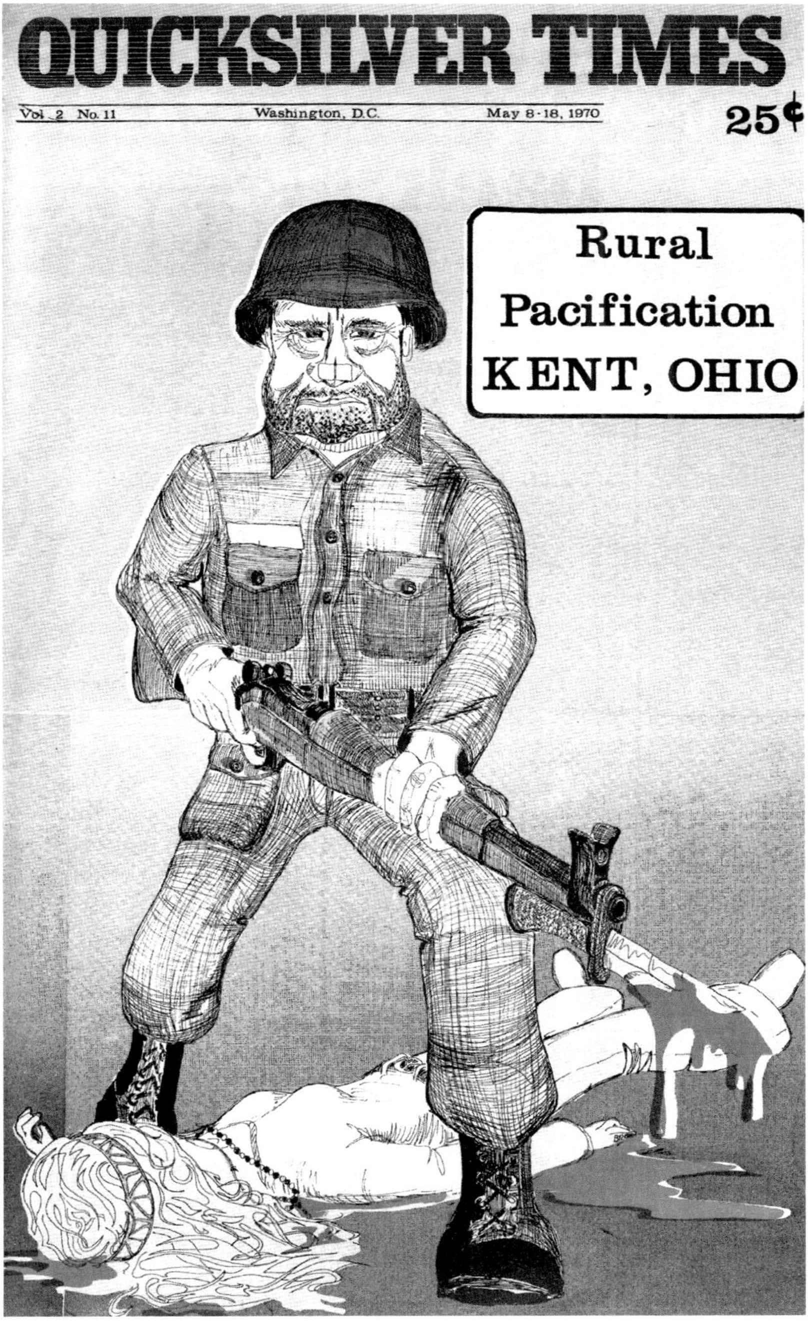

Quicksilver Times, May 8–18, 1970. *Courtesy Paul Collinge.*

between Vietnam protestors and law enforcement. *Quicksilver*'s internal tempest unfortunately robbed itself of the ability to report two of the most scandalous events of the Southeast Asian war and its violent aftermath.

On May 9, the day of a massive antiwar rally in D.C. that drew almost 100,000 protestors, *Quicksilver Times* reappeared on the streets in a twenty-four-page issue dated May 8–18, 1970. The original ten ousted founders had restarted production in a newly opened office at 1736 R Street Northwest, and the press run of twenty-five thousand copies capitalized on the huge crowds. The cover was an illustration of a sadistic national guardsman holding a bloody rifle over a bloody, prone student with the headline "Rural Pacification, Kent, Ohio." The *QT* staff wrote that the newly reconstituted paper was "an organizing tool, focusing primarily on community events and then linking these local news items to greater national and international struggles."

Meanwhile, the dissident faction still occupying *QT*'s former location published its own underground paper, *Voice from the Mother Country*. While a *Voice* spokesman refused to comment on the dispute between them and *Quicksilver*, Becker claimed he held no animosity toward the *Voice* staff.

During its short lifespan, *Voice* experienced its own share of police hassles. "A Black Liberation Rally was scheduled for Thursday afternoon, but *Voice from the Mother Country*, an underground paper which was helping to coordinate the rally, was raided by the police and the FBI," reported *QT* in May 1970. "About 200 GWU students and other people arriving for Saturday's demonstration were joined by black high school students and black people of the surrounding community in an attempt to block a potential 'police riot.'"

The FBI raided *Voice* again that same month, looking for Weather Underground fugitive Cathy Wilkerson. After three issues, *Voice* changed its name to *Red Earth* before announcing in June 1970, "This is the last issue of *Red Earth*. Now we move to action."

Also that June, shortly after the *QT* dispute, President Richard Nixon called a meeting with FBI director J. Edgar Hoover, CIA director Richard Helms and army and navy intelligence to put together a plan of action against what he called "revolutionary activism." The result was the redefining of an existing, technically illegal and heavily covered-up federal initiative called Operation CHAOS (also known as MHCHAOS), which was the centerpiece of a major CIA effort begun in 1967 in response to White House pressure for intelligence about foreign influence on American dissent. The CHAOS mission was to gather and evaluate all available information about foreign links to racial, antiwar and other New Left activity in the United States.

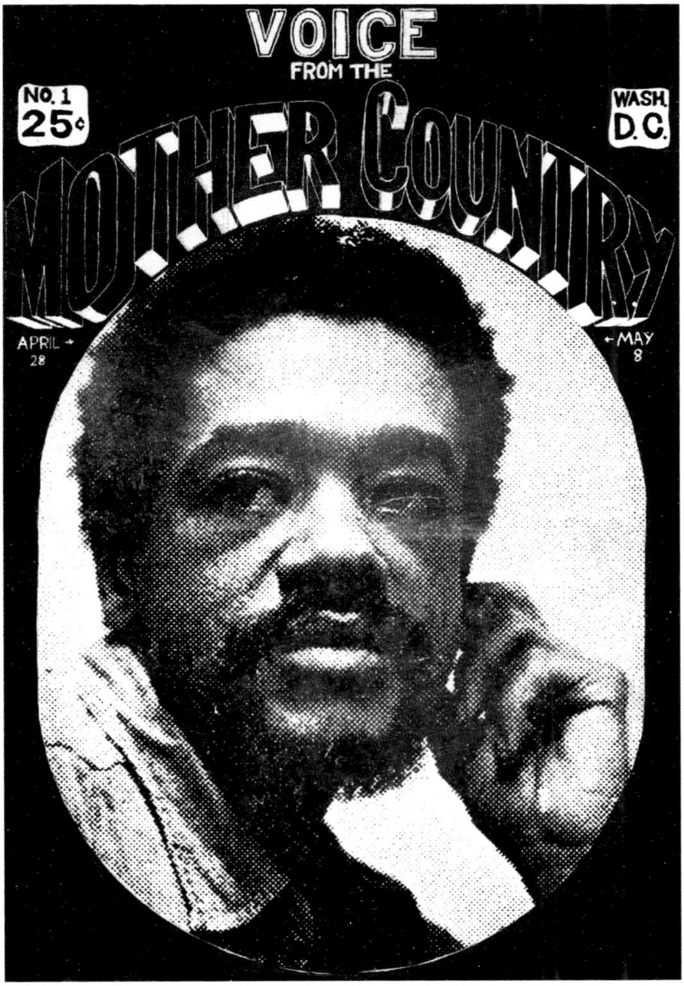

Voice from the Mother Country, April 28–May 8, 1970. *Courtesy Sean Stewart,* Babylon Falling.

Career CIA operative Richard Ober was placed in charge of the super-secret initiative. Ober served as deputy under CIA counter-intelligence chief James Angleton, and according to author Angus Mackenzie in *Secrets: The CIA's War at Home*, he was a senior figure in a special operations branch (its "dirty tricks" department) that "carried out wiretaps, break-ins, and burglaries as authorized by their superiors." Ober had also led the government charge of multiple agencies against *Ramparts* magazine in 1967 and '68.

Unbelievably, Ober had also been charged by the CIA to spy on the Nixon White House as he worked closely with the president and his aides H.R. Haldeman and John Ehrlichman on CHAOS.

Operation CHAOS failed to find any significant foreign influence in the New Left movement. "Foreign funding, training, propaganda, and other support does not now play a major role in the U.S. New Left," stated a declassified findings summary dated January 5, 1971. "At present the U.S. New Left is basically self-sufficient and moves under its own impetus."

Despite evidence that the *QT* (and all New Left movement organizations) were not receiving foreign financial help, a skeptical Nixon was determined to keep the program alive, so Ober, at the behest of the president, kept investigating the *QT*. CHAOS was supposedly terminated in 1974.

By summer, the mainstream press speculated that perhaps the underground press was digging its own grave with its constant fracturing and establishment pot-stirring. "Even the most casual sidewalk paper-buyer in Washington must be vaguely aware of the chaotic publishing history of the local underground press," remarked Michael Kernan in a *Washington Post* commentary published on July 6, 1970.

"The shock value has waned," he continued. "Papers come and go, change their names and their mastheads, but the casual reader finds they all look alike and sound alike."

Underground Press Syndicate founder Tom Forcade disagreed, stating that the syndicate started in 1966 with five papers and fifty thousand readers but, by 1970, boasted two hundred member papers and, by his estimate, six million readers. "The phenomenon is booming not drying up," he told Kernan.

A random July 1971 survey of movement groups in the D.C. area by a *Post* reporter regarded the *QT* as much titillation for tourists as serious proponent of social change. Acutely conscious too of the sexism that frequently ran rampant throughout the early underground press, the *QT*, in early 1971, stopped accepting any advertising that used women's bodies to sell products. Classifieds that advertised straight-only or gay-only roommates were also refused, as were thinly veiled sex ads that the *QT* thought reinforced notions of sexism. Still, Reggie Haynes of Washington Gay Liberation said, "[*Quicksilver*] relates more to the white community. It's a sexist paper, male chauvinistic."

Aware that the continuous incursion of troublemaking volunteers had led to the coup d'état at the former *QT* location and suspecting, too, that either the FBI or CIA or both was behind the disruption, Terry Becker instituted stiff rules for house members, barring and locking the doors and windows

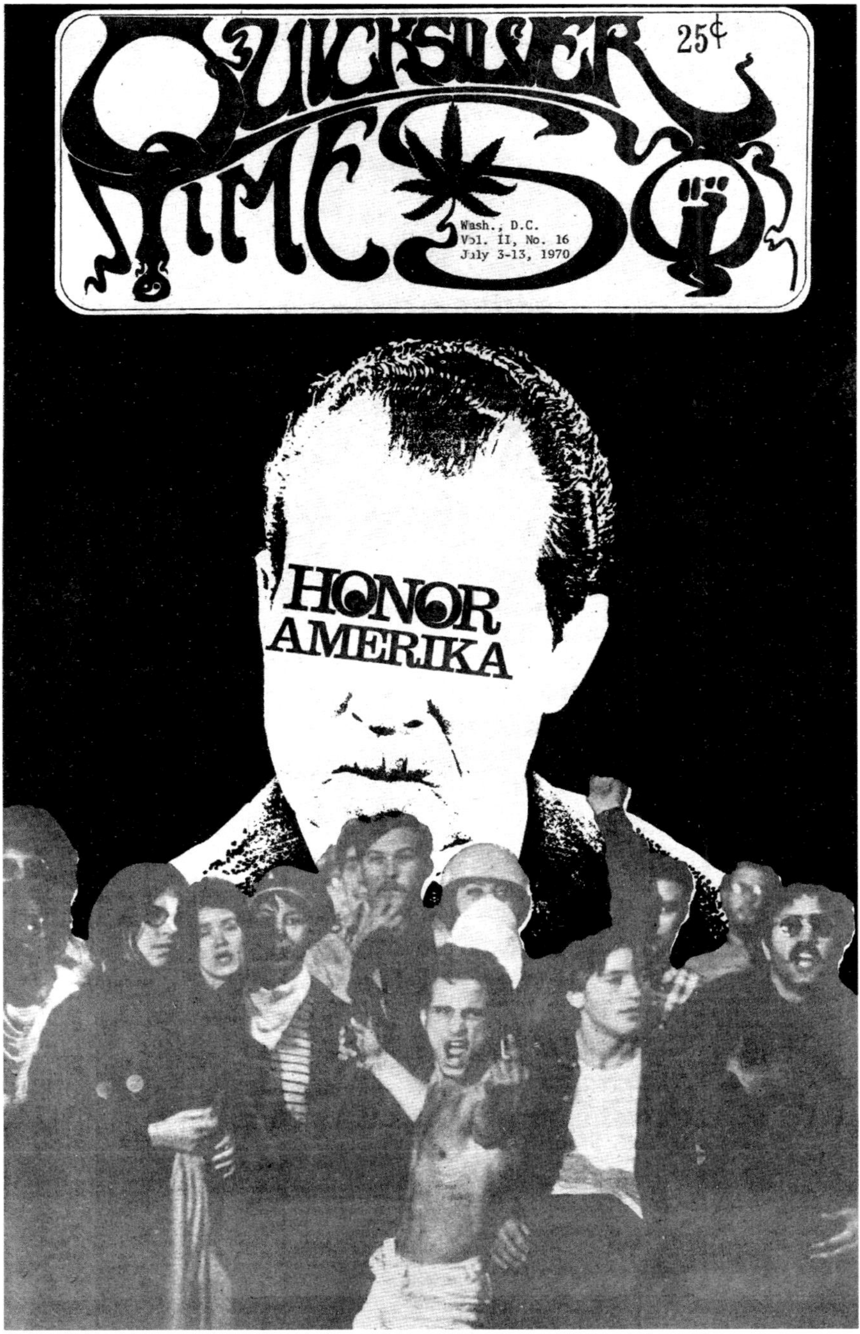

Quicksilver Times, July 3–13, 1970. *Courtesy Paul Coltinge.*

to keep out not only police, rednecks and zealous right-wingers but also potential overthrowers. "We collectivized at that point," Becker told Angus Mackenzie. "If you worked on the paper, you had to live in the house. No outside income. If you had outside income, you pooled it. No outside jobs. The paper paid everybody's bills. We were criticized for being too closed, but it was the only way to avoid a repetition of what had happened."

In October 1970, Sal Ferrera reported the mode of operation for *QT* operation: "The day following each issue going to the printers, a staff meeting of all workers, lasting all day and all night, goes into every phase of operations…to decide articles for the next issue."

By the winter of 1970, the chaos, infiltration and increasing fear of police harassment took a toll, and the *QT* found itself $3,000 in debt, with its printer refusing to accept another issue until the bill was caught up. The paper was still selling, but the advertising was drying up; small businesses could no longer afford ads, and larger advertisers were slashing budgets or moving on to safer venues.

Worse, collective members believed government agents were harassing and threatening potential contributors and advertisers. The reporters also complained of harassment at demonstrations and police refusing to honor press passes.

Somehow, though, money came in, and the paper was able to maintain a publishing schedule, with stories about D.C.'s new "no knock" law (in which police could enter a private residence on the scantest suspicion of wrongdoing), the Revolutionary People's Constitutional Convention in Philadelphia, drug laws, Vietnam and the Mayday riots of 1971.

After infiltrating some papers in Chicago, Ferrera returned to the *QT* collective just as planning started for the ten-day Mayday antiwar demonstrations from April 28 to May 8, 1971. Mayday was going to be a joint effort between the National Peace Action Coalition (NPAC), the People's Coalition of Peace and Justice (PCPJ), the Student Mobilization Committee (SMC) and numerous splinter groups, including a national women's contingent. It was all spearheaded by the Militant Mayday Movement, headed by former Chicago 7 defendant Rennie Davis, who was provided food and shelter while in D.C. by the *Quicksilver Times* at 1736 Lanier Place.

The ever-vigilant Ferrera infiltrated the Mayday organizing committee and reported back to his boss Ober that the *QT* would be a rich source of information related to the demonstrations. With Ferrera's help, the information relayed to the CIA and then to the White House was very accurate, although Ferrera told Ober in a memo that "Mayday is the most disorganized demonstration I [have] ever seen."

As predicted, the April 14–27 *Quicksilver* published a two-page spread titled "Mayday Tactics and Targets" that outlined the strategies, communications and tactical approaches that were going to be used. "The Mayday strategy for stopping the government is to halt the inanimate machinery that makes it work by using the tactics of non-violent creative disruption," stated the introduction. "This will take the form of masses of people moving to and blocking strategic locations along major traffic arteries used by government employees."

On the day of the demonstration, almost twenty-five thousand radicals calling themselves the Mayday Tribe tried to establish roadblocks and other tactics to bring the government to a standstill. "I dropped a load of sand from a dump truck at the Key Bridge at 7:00 am Monday morning," wrote Richmond resident Bill Beville. "We backed up traffic for miles and miles that morning."

Approximately 14,000 D.C. and national guardsmen, however, read the *QT* and their planning manuals and, before many were even in position, arrested between 7,000 and 13,000 (*QT* reported 12,000), including 150 Quakers in a silent vigil for peace in front of the White House.

On Monday, an estimated 2,400 people were placed inside a fenced athletic field rigged as a makeshift detention camp. For several hours, they had no food, no water and two holes in the ground for toilets. By that evening, police responded to public outrage over the presence of a third-world detention camp in the middle of the nation's capital by moving the prisoners to various places around the city.

About two hundred Federal Bureau of Narcotics agents were sent into the crowds incognito on orders from President Nixon in a plan dubbed "Operation Bent Penny." Its purpose was to spot drug use to revoke special use permits. The name came from the instructions that the agents were to carry no gun or identification—only a bent Lincoln penny to prove their ID to other agents.

Later, an estimated 90 percent of the cases of those arrested were thrown out by the courts, which found numerous improprieties by the police in their rush to clear the streets and a lack of "adequate evidence" to link defendants with the charges against them.

The protest was widely considered a failure. Mary McGrory wrote in the *Boston Globe* that "it was the worst planned, worst executed, most slovenly, strident and obnoxious peace action ever committed." Even planner Rennie Davis told the *Washington Post*, "We failed."

Maybe not entirely—the sheer volume of protestors and arrests apparently left the Nixon administration "shaken," according to White House aide Jeb Magruder. CIA director Richard Helms called Mayday "a very damaging kind of event" and said that it "increased pressure on the administration to find a way out of Vietnam."

The *QT* May 15 issue published seventy remarkable photographs of the multiday protest, along with some of the lessons learned from it: mass sit-downs are ineffective; disruption is best accomplished by small groups of hit-and-run guerrillas; and huge numbers of demonstrators lead to open suspension of constitutional arrest procedures and detention camps, with the threat that such procedures could become institutionalized.

Despite the paranoia and the financial stress, the *QT* did allow *Washington Post* reporter Liza Bercovici into the house to write a profile for the August 11, 1971 edition. Many of the house members took advantage of Bercovici's perceived naiveté to trick her, as she reported that "business, breakfast and self-criticism sessions are conducted in the nude 'because [house members] are less defensive that way.'"

"I think we should tell the truth about the nude breakfast," Robert Whalen admitted in 2014. "We thought we'd have fun with the straight reporter. The *Post* reporter wasn't really amused, as I recall, and declined to join in the nudity."

"[*Quicksilver*] has undergone a heady political evolution," the fully clothed Bercovici wrote, "from a free-swinging, politically hip community newspaper with plenty of underground pornography to a heavy-ideological 'communist' organ of the revolution."

"I think that language is pretty charged, and I don't think the tone really matches the *QT* reality," said Whalen of the description. "I liked to debate ideology with Terry [Becker], but no one else was very interested in that."

"We're communists because we advocate the overthrow of capitalism and replacement with a communist structure," Sumner told Bercovici, pointing out he does not mean "state capitalism" as found in the Soviet Union but the kind found in North Vietnam, China and Cuba.

At this time, Sal Ferrera discreetly exited from the "too tense to tolerate" collective, without Becker, Blum or anyone else ever discovering he was a CIA agent.

The paper was still able to rouse attention through its "participation journalism." A story by Richard Williamson titled "Committee to Defend the Assassination of President Nixon" raised many free speech discussions in the mainstream press. "Assassination as a means to an end in politics is a reliable recourse against even a more obstinate bureaucracy," stated the article in part.

A shocked Michigan commentator named Ralph deToledano wrote, "The New Leftists speak about our 'violent society' but they talk to each other with a self-fulfilling bloodthirstiness of incalculable horror.

"At what point must speech cease to be protected by Constitutional privileges?"

Undaunted by the outrage, *Quicksilver Times* plugged along, but the money and staffing problems were getting worse. Also, its relationship with Washington, D.C., had dramatically changed in the two years since the first issue appeared in the summer of 1969, when staff member Peggy O'Callaghan told the *Washington Post*, "Some of us are worried that, in a small way, we imitate exactly what we're fighting." It was a conundrum faced by every underground paper across America—by making money to continue publishing, they risked becoming the very capitalist enterprise they disparaged.

While image-conscious D.C. urbanites interpreted the presence of an "underground paper" as proof that D.C. had come of age as a legitimate metropolitan area, an ideological opaqueness remained. No one really knew where exactly the New Left stood by this point, and by late 1971 and early 1972, issues of *Quicksilver* started reflecting several competing principles.

"There was this constant struggle to define the direction we were moving, either away from violence or into violence," said Bill Shaefer. "The temptation to just tear shit down was just so much easier…and at the end of the day, that is what we did."

Local stories dwindled. More and more copy came from Liberation News Service, with a particular emphasis on drugs, food additives, profiles of Castro and Mao Tse-tung and instructions on how to rip off the phone company.

One story in the January 14, 1972 edition titled "Rip Your Skool [*sic*] Apart" was reprinted from a pamphlet called "School Stoppers Textbook" and featured ways for high school students to start trash can fires, short out electricity and plug toilets. The article was less about being a revolutionary and more about pointless vandalism, leading to speculation (by this author) that the pamphlet was an FBI-produced plant.

"*Quicksilver* Fights to Survive" read a headline in the March 3 issue. Money had gotten so bad that instead of selling papers for only two to three days per issue, the staff resorted to selling ten days per issue. "*QT* still could use office supplies," read a house classified ad in the March 23 issue. "IBM Selectric carbon ribbons, 8x5 file cards, pens, paper…in other words, anything you can get your hands on."

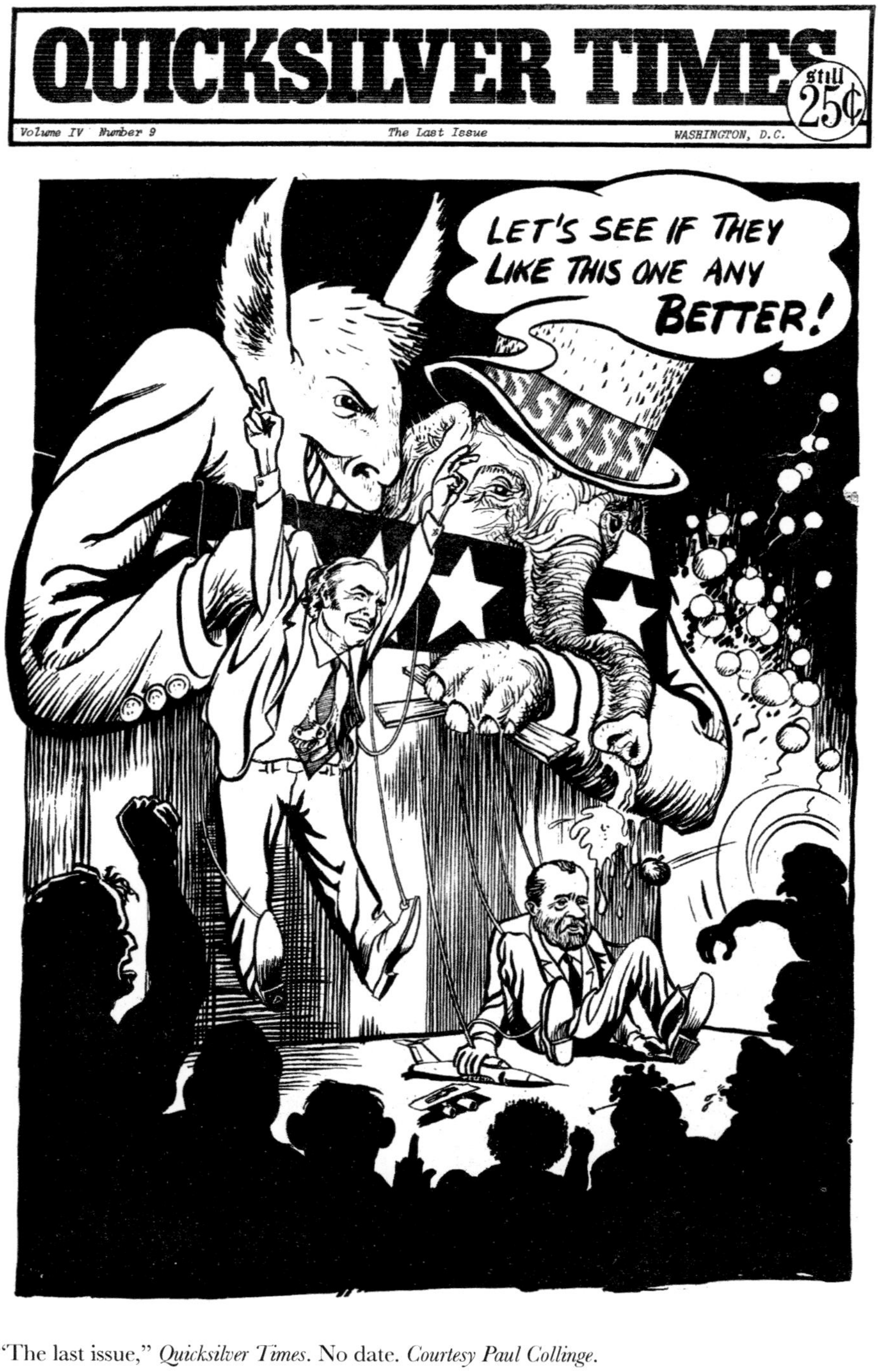
QUICKSILVER TIMES still 25¢

Volume IV Number 9 The Last Issue WASHINGTON, D.C.

"The last issue," *Quicksilver Times*. No date. *Courtesy Paul Collinge.*

It was apparent to some that strength and focus of the antiwar movement was ebbing. One story was as tired and uninspired as the demonstration it described: "On Monday, May 22, PCPJ (People's Coalition for Peace and Justice) had called for two actions at the Pentagon—a Mayday-like traffic blockade and a march from the Lincoln Memorial for a civil disobedience rally. PCPJ's planning was abysmal, so the traffic blockade simply never happened…they heard the usual speeches till about noon, when they were asked to decide what sort of civil disobedience to do."

Finally, around the end of July 1972, ten thousand copies of an undated twelve-page *QT* appeared, stating it was the "Last Issue."

While the working staff had diminished (at the end, only four were living in the commune, down from ten), it was ultimately all about the money. Larger advertisers were fleeing to more benign venues like *Rolling Stone* magazine. Two national advertising agencies closed, owing *QT* money. While many ads ("probably too many") were turned away by the paper because of sexism, many who did run ads never paid for them. Two lawsuits filed against *QT* by James Vito Plumbing and Pearl Printing Company sucked a precious $1,500 from their coffers. At least once, the staff spent hours addressing and bundling 1,100 subscriptions only to discover there was no money to mail them. Street selling made hundreds of dollars per edition, but vendors had to put in grueling hours, for up to ten straight days, and it still wasn't enough. Two benefits netted $12.

Prior to the *QT* folding, collective member Richard Harrington left to start with Mike Schreibman a D.C.-based music, arts and culture paper called *Woodwind*, which published from early 1972 until January 1973. Harrington later edited *Unicorn Times* before becoming a music writer for the *Washington Post* in 1980.

Its revolutionary fervor going down swinging, the last issue of *QT* featured a very long explanation of its demise, hinting that some staffers might return and start a new underground paper in the fall. "There are no definite plans yet," an anonymous staff member told *Post* reporter Jeannette Smyth. "It's not the end, for sure."

The vitality of the underground press was directly proportional to the health of the New Left movement in general. *Quicksilver Times*, like so many papers around the country, arose from the tumult of the times, and the abatement of that fervor undercut its strength. As the draft ended, opposition to the war waned, and the largest unifying reason for radical mobilization splintered.

After leaving *QT* the second time, CIA informant Sal Ferrera asked Chip Berlet at the College News Service if he needed a Paris correspondent.

When his *Quicksilver* reference checked out, Berlet offered him twenty-one dollars per month for one or two dispatches from his Paris apartment, which became the news service's foreign news bureau.

In Paris, Ferrera met a mysterious woman named Leslie Donegan. Together, they befriended former CIA agent Philip Agee, who was also in Paris—out of reach of his former employer's secrecy contract—writing a tell-all book about his tenure at the intelligence agency. Gaining Agee's trust, Ferrera and Donegan offered to trade their newer typewriter for his old one. Later, Agee discovered that the new portable Royal and its case was filled with microphones and transmitters, which pinpointed his location straight to the CIA. A photograph of the bugged typewriter appears on the cover of Agee's 1975 book *Inside the Company: CIA Diary*.

Ferrera then fled to Chicago, changed his name to Allen Vincent Carter and then reportedly moved to Costa Mesa, California.

Bill Blum was introspective on his former friend in *West-Bloc Dissident*: "I probably never will know [the forces] that were pulling [on Sal] unless he and I sit down someday and have a long heartfelt talk."

"When I saw the Agee book, I cried," Patti Heck told Jack Anderson of Ferrera. "I didn't want to believe it. I really liked him."

OFF OUR BACKS

1970–2008

Although we do not want to become an "internal organ" of Women's Liberation in the structural sense of the organization, we see ourselves responsible to and active in creating a strong women's movement.
—"On Our Feet," by Marlene Wicks, Off Our Backs, *April 25, 1970*

One of the more distasteful phrases of the late '60s protest movements was "chicks up front," meaning that in a demonstration, women were sent to the head of the line under the assumption police would be less likely to club a woman, especially if TV cameras were rolling. While it is unknown how effectively this tactic worked against the police, it infuriated the women. They had gone into a movement expecting to be treated as equals only to be used as human shields.

January 23, 1970
Washington, D.C.

off our backs
A WOMEN'S NEWS-JOURNAL

Off Our Backs, a bi-weekly women's newspaper, will begin publication in February, 1970. It is a paper written by women to be shared with other women who are also struggling for liberation.

Male supremacy pervades this society, preventing direct and honest communication between women. Nowhere, in either the underground or Establishment press, are our issues adequately analyzed or discussed. Several of us, after working on local underground and/or "movement" papers, have become convinced that we can no longer work where we see repeated failure to print articles of importance to our sisters and ourselves, and where degrading sex ads and nudie photos are the accepted norm of "political" coverage.

Our political and economic analysis, necessary for building the revolution, is regarded as inconsequential by even the most "radical" of publications. We have been denied print space to develop our analytic and poetic abilities. We feel the needs of the growing women's movement can no longer be served by an occasional article or special supplement. We need to create and support our own media.

Many journals, magazines and mimeoed papers are now emerging. Although they provide a forum to share our thoughts and experiences, they do not serve the vital function of critically reporting the news on a regular basis. We feel we need an inexpensive paper that can be sold on streets, at newstands and by subscription.

Off Our Backs will cover news events and stories relevant to women's struggles for liberation and include continuing articles on medical-survival issues and women's history, media reviews, poetry, activities of women's groups, personal reports on the condition of women at school, on the job,etc., and on-going analysis reflecting the thinking of a growing movement.

To make this paper work we need your help. We need articles about what you are thinking and doing. We need you to share the paper with sisters you know. And especially we need your ideas!

Off Our Backs, 2318 Ashmead Place, N.W., Washington, D.C. 20009.

Please enter my subscription for one year (24 issues) at $6.00.

NAME: ______________________

ADDRESS: ______________________

ZIP: ________

I will distribute the paper in my local area and want bulk copies. Yes__ No__

Press release announcing *Off Our Backs: A Women's News-Journal*, January 23, 1970. *Courtesy Bonnie Atwood and the VCU Cabell Library Special Collections, Richmond, Virginia.*

One of the original leaders of the women's liberation movement, Marilyn Webb, still bristles at the phrase. "One of the reasons the women's movement appeared was because of stuff like that," she said in 2014.

Off Our Backs (*OOB*) appeared on February 27, 1970, at a time when the founders—Marilyn Webb, Francis Chapman, Onka Dekkers, Nancy Ferro and several others—despised the concept behind "chicks up front." More importantly, they saw that existing media—mainstream and alternative—did not pursue issues pertinent to women. "I considered [*OOB*] the voice of women," said Webb. "It was before *Ms.* [magazine] came out. We wanted our own newspaper for women with issues women were concerned about."

The first edition's introduction pointed out that women working in the establishment news media endured ongoing discrimination. Competent female journalists, they said, could expect to remain research assistants or be assigned trivial assignments that, because of their gender, appeared only on back pages. Even the supposed enlightened underground press acknowledged that women's stories sold papers but revealed their true consciousness with their dependence on sex ads and sexist and misogynistic cartoons by established underground cartoonists.

Subtitled *A Women's News-Journal*, the name *Off Our Backs* was chosen to suggest that men should "get off our backs" and that women should "get off *their* backs" and work for their liberation. Coincidentally, *OOB* appeared three weeks after the female staff of a New York underground paper, *The Rat Subterranean News*, took over and published their first all-women's issue on February 9, 1970, which included a groundbreaking feminist article by Robin Morgan entitled "Goodbye to All That."

Although *OOB* first started organizing in January 1970, Webb says at the time, they had no inkling of the women's takeover at the *Rat*. "We were just doing our own thing," she said. "But it probably was not so coincidental considering where the movement was going. The time was right."

As a graduate student in 1966, Webb was a co-founder of Chicago's first women's Consciousness Raising group and co-organized a similar group in Washington, D.C., in 1967. She also worked in the Washington bureau of the New York paper the *Guardian*.

While feminism as a social movement was largely overlooked during the first few years of the underground press, a women's liberation movement was gaining strength. Betty Friedan founded the National Organization of Women (NOW) in 1966, and from 1968 through 1969, feminist groups organized in at least forty American cities. Former activist Bonnie Atwood recalled taking

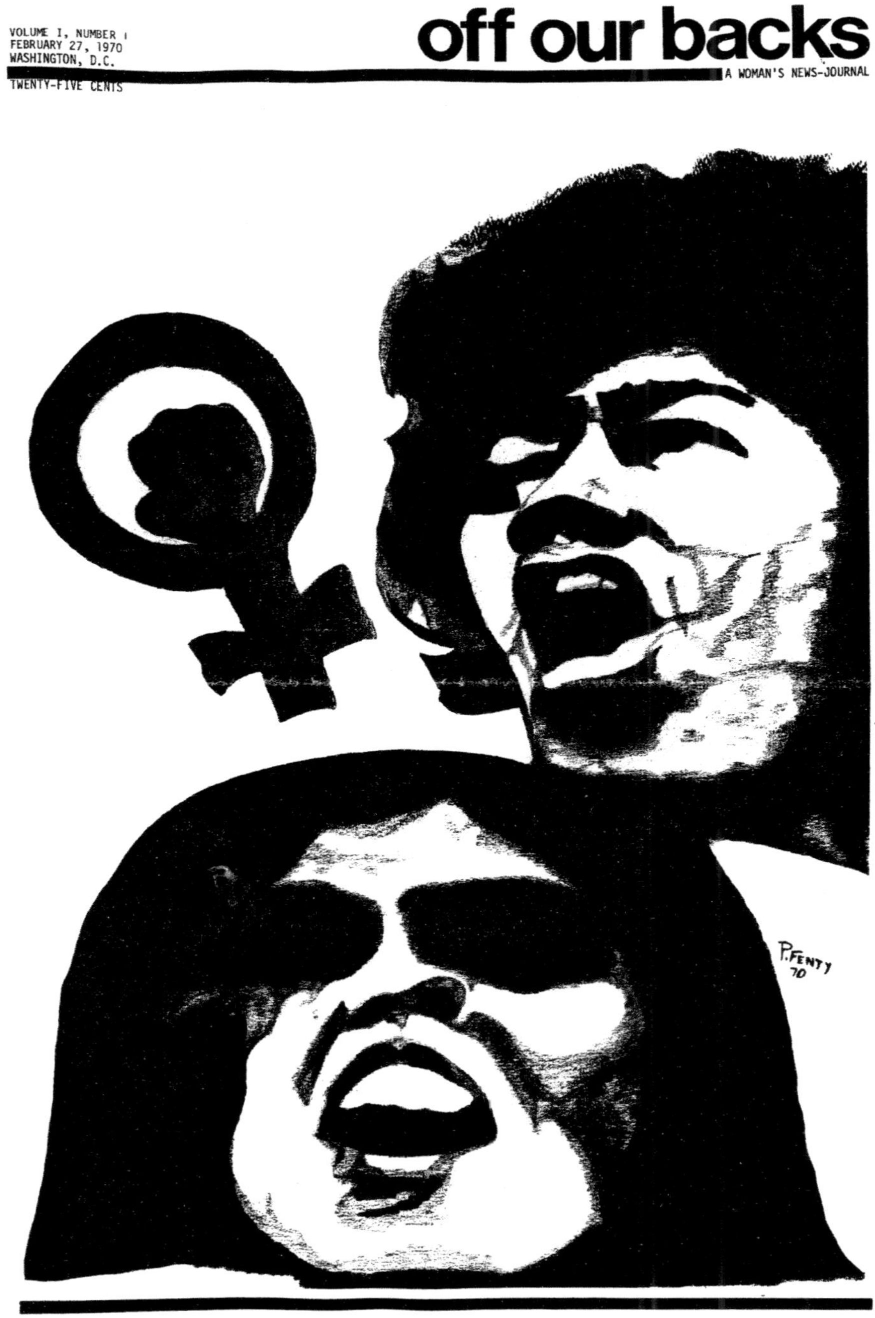

Off Our Backs, volume 1, number 1, February 27, 1970. *Courtesy Bonnie Atwood and the VCU Cabell Library Special Collections, Richmond, Virginia.*

a class in women's liberation at D.C.'s Institute for Policy Studies in late 1967 to early 1968. Later that year, five feminist publications—including the first national newsletter, *The Voice of the Women's Liberation Movement*—were founded by a coalition of women's groups in Chicago.

The earliest visible event of the women's liberation movement occurred at the September 1968 Miss America contest in Atlanta, Georgia, when protestors, many of them members of a radical feminist organization called WITCH (Women's International Terrorist Conspiracy from Hell), engaged in an all-day demonstration on the boardwalk chanting, hexing and performing guerrilla theater that, at one point, crowned a live sheep Miss America. When only a few burned their bras in protest of the pageant, they created a stigmatizing trademark that stayed attached to the movement for years.

"When the paper started, I was one of the key founders of the women's movement in Washington, and we wanted, in 1968, to create a mass movement immediately, and we had a problem of how we were going to coordinate that movement," Webb recalled. The answer was a collectively run coordinating body called "Magic Quilt." Magic Quilt synchronized the quilt "pieces," composed of all the women's organizations' ventures: equal pay, abortion counseling and antiwar organizing. "The leadership in each group changed so that the content of the quilt always changed too," said Webb.

Webb recalled that during the January 1969 Nixon counter-inaugural in D.C., the women's movement split from the larger New Left movement.

> *I* [along with pioneer activist Shulamith Firestone] *was one of the speakers* [for] *women's liberation, speaking on behalf of women. Chaos broke out during our speeches; people screamed, "Take her off the stage!" People started punching each other, it was pandemonium, so over the top. After that the women's movement decided to be separate.*

In July 1969, the women's movement produced the *Washington Women's Liberation Newsletter*. "We must examine our relationship to SDS, the Panthers and other radical groups, to NWRO and other women's groups, and must examine Women's Liberation and how it relates to U.S. racism and imperialism," said the introduction in the August 25, 1969 issue.

But Magic Quilt was not without its difficulties, and Webb soon found herself forced out. "I was considered the leader of this [collective], and at some point—and this happened repeatedly—I was asked to not lead and to get out." It was then that Webb and some close friends decided to start a women's paper.

NEWSLETTER

Washington Women's Liberation

Issue #2 -- August 25, 1969

A major portion of this newsletter is devoted to the relationship between Women's Liberation and the ~~radical~~ movement in this country.

The future direction of the women's movement will undoubtably be affected by pressures from within and without. We must examine our relationship to SDS, the Panthers and other radical groups, to NWRO and other women's groups, and must examine Women's Liberation and how it relates to U.S. racism and imperialism. (See articles on North Vietnamese women and on United Fruit).

We have divided the Newsletter into three parts:

Part L concerns Washington Women's Liberation activities, Part II women's Liberation and the Movement, and Part III, a variety of articles on subjects important to women's liberation.

This issue was compiled and reproduced by:
Linda Carcione
Johanne Klodzen
Sue Orrin
Judy Spelman
Pat Williams

TABLE OF CONTENTS

PART I
On the State of Washington Women's Liberation
with responses by Anne Brann
three women, new to WWL ---------- pp.2,3,4
Women's Liberation Course - WAFU ---------- p. 4
The Children's Community -- articles by
Jan Fenty
Susie Buckley
Lynda Clover ---------- pp. 5&6
Orientation Sessions ---------- p. 7
St. Stephen's Project ---------- p. 7

PART II
Lilith Manifesto ---------- p. 8
On the 3rd Birthday of NWRO ---------- pp. 9,10
also comments by Judy Spelman
Linda Carcione
SDS -- Proposed Unity Principle on Women's Liberation ----- p. 11
Response from Mary Mattson ---------- p. 11
excerpts from PL Statement on Women's Liberation ---- pp.13&14
We Come in Peace and for Independence
on a meeting with NLF and North Vietnamese women
by Sue Orrin ---------pp.15&16
excerpts from Bananas and Rifles, Sugar and Death
A Saga of the United Fruit Company
by Heidi Steffans ---------- pp.17&18
excerpts from Eldridge Cleaver to Erica Huggins ----------p. 19

PART III
Notices ---------- -pp. 20
excerpts from Abortion by Marilyn Webb ---------- pp.21&22
On meeting with Roxanne Dunbar by Marilyn Webb ------ p.23
On meeting with Bev Jones by Pat Williams ------ p.23
On Programmatic Direction by Marilyn Webb ------ p.24
What Does it Mean to be a High School Girl by Cynthia Elston -- p.25
<u>Turning on</u>: A Review by Johanna Abrahamson ------ p.25

Washington Women's Liberation Newsletter, August 25, 1969. *Courtesy Bonnie Atwood and the VCU Cabell Library Special Collections, Richmond, Virginia.*

Off Our Backs was established with money Webb and Marjorie Stamberg raised to open an antiwar GI coffeehouse in D.C. "We ended up making $400, and we decided it was a dumb idea to start a coffeehouse," Webb recalled. "Marjorie moved to California, and I stayed in Washington. I asked Marjorie if I [could use] the money to start *OOB*, and she said fine." The paper started with two full-time workers, a basement office on Ashmead Place Northwest in Washington, D.C., and equipment "begged, borrowed and improvised."

"*Off Our Backs* will cover news events and stories relevant to women's struggles for liberation and include continuing articles on medical-survival issues and women's history, media reviews, poetry…and ongoing analysis reflecting the thinking of a growing movement," stated the January 1970 press release.

Like most startup publications, production was a shoestring operation: type galleys were produced on typewriters and word processors and manually pasted up. Headlines were produced with rub-on press-type. With the exception of some original photographs, graphics were mostly clip art or "borrowed" from other movement publications. Page layouts were done in a marathon "layout weekend," an important time for socializing and involving more women—inside the collective and out—in the publication of the paper.

"Up against the wall hip revolutionaries! We're onto you now," stated an editorial by Webb titled "Seize the Press, Sisters," in the April 25, 1970 issue of *OOB*. "For women, working on an underground paper is like working for the *New York Times*—only worse, since we naïvely believe there is hope for change. There is no hope since sexism runs in the blood of male freaks."

A lone exception to this tokenism among the underground press was the *Richmond Chronicle*, a Richmond, Virginia paper that, in August 1969, boasted a female editor, Nina Sabaroff (now Katya Sabaroff Taylor). Originally a 1968 member of Liberation News Service, Sabaroff Taylor served as *Chronicle* editor for six months before returning to LNS, where women's liberation was taking hold in February 1970.

"Women's liberation hit big at LNS," Taylor said in 2013. "We were not allowing any more men to join the collective until there were an equal number of women." Because of that rule, her boyfriend could not join.

OOB hit the streets just when the "traditional" underground press began fracturing from internal ideological conflicts, financial problems, local law enforcement harassment and FBI COINTELPRO persecution. *OOB* and other feminist publications like it rapidly emerged in part from student rights, civil rights and the antiwar movement but more so from reforms advocated by the suffrage movements of the previous century. When *OOB* launched in 1970, up to the introduction of *Ms.* magazine in 1972, almost five hundred feminist and women's liberation newsletters, magazines and journals appeared nationwide. Obviously, the time was right.

Defined by news coverage and opinions that were tough and unflinching, many stories in the early issues of *OOB* were accounts of women's activism, both in D.C. and in cities around the country. Rachel Scott reported in the first issue the planned picketing of the Gridiron Club dinner, a prestigious male-only event for Washington's journalists. "Who needs them anyway?" quoted a reporter for the *Washington Star*. "They're so deadly boring."

OOB reported that on February 13 in Boston, thirty women from a women's liberation organization called Bread and Roses stormed the offices of radio station WBCN, demanding and receiving one hour of primetime programming on March 8, International Women's Day, to present a women's liberation program.

Contraception and abortion were critical topics to *OOB* and women's liberation in pre–*Roe v. Wade* 1970, especially toward "the pill," which they saw as a barely tested government-sponsored scourge foisted on an unsuspecting female populace. An anti-pill story by Ann Hutchinson in the March 1 issue reported that WITCH descended on a government- and corporation-sponsored panel on population control on February 27. During a speech by Texas senator Ralph Yarborough, women suddenly rose from the stunned audience chanting, "We are witches. We have come to yell. You population experts can all go to hell. You think you can cure all the world's ills by forcing poor people to take your unhealthy pills."

It wasn't WITCH's first appearance—they had "attacked and hexed" (according to the *Washington Women's Liberation Newsletter*) the D.C. office of the United Fruit Company in April 1969, chanting, "United Fruit makes lots of loot by robbing the poor who pick its fruit. Bananas and rifles, sugar and death, war for profit, tarantula's breath. United Fruit makes lot of loot. The CIA is in its boot. Workers unite; dictators fall. United Fruit perish; freedom for all!"

In "Politics of the Pill," Regina Stigal reported that on March 7, the D.C. Women's Liberation was holding a national women's hearing to present previously suppressed information on oral contraceptives and to expose the sexist-racist-imperialist reasons behind that suppression. *OOB* reported that even though the FDA approved and released the pill in 1960, it had only been tested on 132 American women for less than two years and that the FDA suppressed information on five pill-related deaths in the original Puerto

Rican study of 850 women. "It is clear women will never be informed of the dangers of the pill unless we hold our own hearings with testimony from our own sisters," the story concluded.

"The right to control our reproduction has been robbed from us," stated a centerspread story by Webb and Norma Allen Lesser in that first issue about the upcoming International Women's Day. "Misinformation surrounds birth control. Male supremacist laws and prohibitive costs make safe abortions the last resort of only the rich. Many of us, especially black and brown women, are forced into tube-tying operations at city hospitals."

An interview with Sue Baker in the February 27, 1970 issue described her time in Cuba with the "Venceremos Brigade," a group of Americans who, along with representatives from other countries, went to Cuba for six weeks to help Cuban workers cut sugar cane. The goal of Venceremos was to help Cuba export at least ten million tons of sugar, since Russia promised to buy it at a higher price than the world market, stimulating the Cuban economy to mechanize cane cutting and freeing people to pursue more productive economic pursuits. "The Brigade was 300 people. 216 of us were North Americans," Baker said of the multinational effort. "I cut beside a Cuban as my cutting partner. The Vietnamese cut with us for about four days."

OOB also taught women practical tips, from changing a tire to fixing a leaky water faucet. "Changing a tire is a simple and gratifying task which has generally been left to men for cultural, not physical reasons," said the illustrated procedure on page twelve. "It requires about the same energy output as shoveling snow and only a little more knowledge."

Page two of every issue was the advertising and classifieds page, listing movies, media, publications and services, all costing a flat rate of ten dollars, payable in advance. There was no display advertising in *OOB*—the staff believed that American advertising was vulgar and "anti-human." "It profanes women's bodies to push products which violate one's essence," wrote Marlene Wicks in the April 25, 1970 issue. "It depends and grows on the fears and weaknesses of us, it's [*sic*] 'prospects'…by using jingles, graphics and sensory-appealing gimmicks."

"We didn't want to get into that mess of deciding which ad exploited women and which ad didn't," said Webb.

The April 11, 1970 issue listed eleven other North American women's liberation publications available for subscription, including Berkeley's *It Ain't Me Babe*; *The Pedestal* from Vancouver, British Columbia; and New York's *Up From Under*. A listing for New York's *Rat Subterranean News* stated that "women are in control and they are doing a great job!"—a reference to the women's takeover there.

Other early D.C.-area line advertisers included the Biograph Theater, WETA-channel 26, Mark Weiss Camera Center and Empire Music, which had survived a *Washington Free Press* obscenity bust a year earlier.

Despite Webb's admission that "we weren't exactly good businesspeople," the bulk of *OOB*'s revenues were made by subscriptions and selling the paper for twenty-five cents in such local D.C. businesses as Toast & Strawberries, Sunflower Seed, Soul Shak, Joint Possession (also the victim of a *Washington Free Press* bust in June 1968) and a few small bookstores in the DuPont Circle area.

OOB was never a contents hodge-podge or put together with whatever articles came in that month; issue themes were planned almost a year in advance. For example, in issue two a schedule showed the themes for the next twenty issues of 1970, including "Muckraking on Mother's Day" on May 11, "Liberated Sex" on June 8, "Women in Politics" on October 5 and "Women and Drugs" on December 14. The story idea list for the April 17, 1970 "Feminist" issue contained over thirty tentative articles, planned or in progress, including "female separatism," interviews of Vietnamese women at George Mason University and "shit jobs I have had."

In the summer of 1970, the women's movement was capped by an equal rights rally at D.C.'s Farragut Square. *OOB* staff members were willing to talk about women's issues to the mainstream press at a rally such as this but did not give their names to reporters, saying that from its beginnings, the movement fought against formal structure, downplaying elitist leadership roles (as attested by Marilyn Webb's dismissals) and stressing individual growth.

By the fall of 1971, the women's movement either experienced growing pains or began fragmenting (depending on who was asked) due to political differences, money and, ultimately, lesbianism—a dispute that resulted especially from a confrontation between straight and homosexual women at a retreat in northern Virginia. The riff had actually first started in the summer of 1969 when *Village Voice* critic Jill Johnston interrupted a speech by NOW founder and author of *The Feminine Mystique* Betty Friedan by jumping into a swimming pool topless, calling attention to lesbians within the movement whom Johnston believed were being ignored.

"It all erupted when the gay women took the stand that not to be gay was not to be political," an anonymous attendee told the *Washington Post* of the confrontation in Virginia. "They felt that gayness was the highest form of feminism."

That attitude apparently put the heterosexual women in a dilemma, as many felt that lesbianism would stereotype movement members as man haters and diminish the cause. "If you relate to men it could be said that you're not really for your sisters," the attendee continued. "Straight women got very uptight when accused of relating to men who were oppressing lesbians."

The dispute shattered the cohesiveness of the D.C. women's movement. Soon after, even *OOB* forced out the open lesbians, and many of those women, in the spring of 1971, formed a separatist collective called the Furies, and published their own paper, *The Furies: A Lesbian/Feminist Monthly*.

In September, the women's center on Biltmore Street shut down, a casualty of the differences, leaving a lone hotline to dispense information about all the smaller groups that began appearing. "We're pretty fragmented right now," an evening phone volunteer told the *Washington Post*. "There are so many smaller groups that you need someone to act as a referral service."

The split was so pervasive it even affected the newsletter published by the Washington Area Women's Center at 1736 R Street Northwest. "As usual, an astonishing lack of interest and commitment on the part of the eight hundred women that regularly receive this essential communication resulted in a workforce of two disgusted feminists," stated the opening paragraph of the January 1972 issue.

The hotline was supplemented by proceeds from women's literature sold at two D.C. bookstores, the Community Bookstore, managed by Paul Collinge, and the Red House, managed by John Seeley, that opened in the fall of 1971.

What no one in the women's movement, nor anyone else, knew at the time was that the Red House was a "phony" bookstore, a front set up at 1247 Twentieth Street Northwest near DuPont Circle by the D.C. metro police. Manager John Seeley was actually John Rees, a police and FBI informant who covertly gathered data for a private intelligence newsletter called *Information Digest* that he in turn circulated to local police, the FBI, CIA and Congress. Through *Information Digest*, the names of thousands of persons associated with the antiwar movement went into police files.

Rees was known among activists also as John O'Connor and, sometimes when he posed as a priest, Father John. After the May 1971 Mayday antiwar demonstration, Rees suggested to D.C. police that if they rented an office and installed listening devices, he could monitor leftists drawn to the business. Using the alias, he and his wife, Louise ("Sheila"), opened the Red House and ran it for almost nine months to attract New Left dissidents and provide cover for himself. Located one floor below the headquarters of the Vietnam

Veterans Against the War, the Red House was rented and paid for by the intelligence division of the Washington, D.C. police department.

Rees and the Red House's cover was so authentic the FBI at one point allegedly wiretapped the place not knowing it was a creation of the D.C. police. Columnist Jack Anderson reported in 1972 that at the instigation of FBI agent William Tucker, an informant named Earl Robert Merritt Jr.—who, as "Butch," committed numerous burglaries for the police and

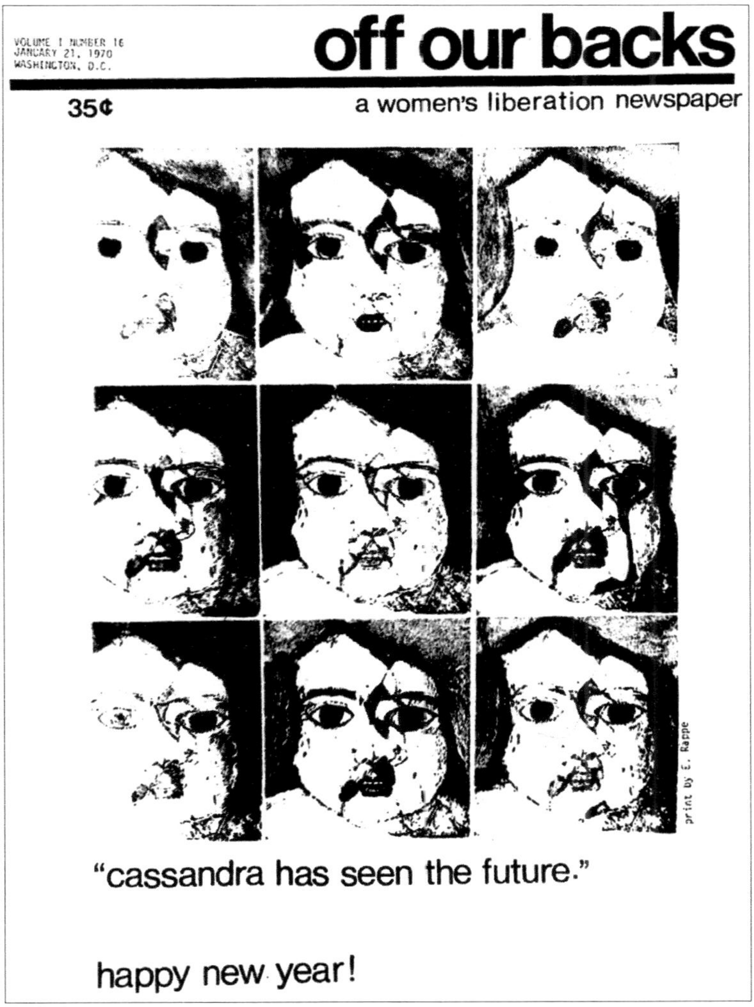

VOLUME I NUMBER 16
JANUARY 21, 1970
WASHINGTON, D.C.

off our backs

35¢

a women's liberation newspaper

print by E. Rappe

"cassandra has seen the future."

happy new year!

Off Our Backs, January 21, 1970. *Courtesy Alderman Library microfilm collection, University of Virginia, Charlottesville, Virginia.*

FBI—entered the Red House and stole their mail, which he turned over to the FBI.

In 1975, Rees was one of several figures investigated by the U.S. attorney's office under allegations of illegal surveillance tactics by the intelligence division of the D.C. police department during the late 1960s. The investigation ended inconclusively with no action recommended against any suspects.

That same year, Paul Collinge left the Community Bookstore to open Heartwood Used and Rare Books in Charlottesville, Virginia. In 2014, he insisted with a sly smile that neither Heartwood nor Community Bookstores was a front.

In 1971, after trading messages with some members of the Weather Underground, the *OOB* office was broken into. Cabinets and papers were shuffled, but nothing seemed to be taken. The staff assumed (probably correctly) that it had been an FBI job, as Webb has suspected since then that the FBI might also have been behind her being forced out of the collective around that same time. "We didn't have any rules, so whoever showed up at the meetings was in the collective," she said. "Then a group of people showed up who I always had suspicions about." When Webb was portrayed again as a leader and a spokesperson by this group—titles forbidden in this collective—she was kicked out.

Webb did not know any of those people or where they came from. "I was suspicious because that exact same scenario was repeated in almost every single women's organization at the time." Those people who came in to disrupt then left as abruptly as they appeared—leading Webb to believe they were possibly D.C. law enforcement or with a coordinated FBI initiative.

"So you're talking to a person who was kicked out twice for leadership issues!" she said with a laugh.

Despite the early difficulties, *Off Our Backs* lasted an amazing thirty-eight years, finally folding for good in 2008. "It hit a nerve," Webb said, "a voice waiting to be heard, and I am very proud of it.

"I think we got pretty far, but there is still a long way to go."

THE FURIES

1971–73

Lesbianism is not a matter of sexual preference, but rather one of political choice which every woman must make if she is to become woman-identified and thereby end male supremacy.
—Ginny Berson, The Furies, *January 1972*

The split of the lesbian feminists from the women's liberation movement in the spring of 1971 led twelve women—including Rita Mae Brown, Charlotte Bunch, Joan E. Biren and Sharon Deevey—to create a separatist collective called the Furies, which, between early 1971 and late 1973, was located at three locations on California Street Northwest and then later in southeast Washington, D.C.

"A handful of women are involved in the overall, male-dominated gay subculture here," wrote Robert Mott in an April 24, 1973 *Washington Post* series, "but a greater number have formed their own groups, an isolation apparently created partly by their double sense of oppression—as women and as gays."

The Furies—first called "Those Women," composed solely of lesbian women wholly separated from the influence of men and heterosexuals—were influenced by a New York collective called the "Radicalesbians," which had been co-founded by Brown in 1970. Its statement, "the woman-identified woman," said that lesbian feminists best embodied the ideals of their struggle, with "women creating a new consciousness of and with each other, which is at the heart of women's liberation."

Radical lesbian feminist separatist collectives believed that only those "woman-identified" women could experience absolute liberation. "We have separated from the women's liberation movement which lacked a comprehensive analysis of sexism," wrote Lee Schwing and Deborah George of the reason for the break with women's liberation. "[Women's liberation] failed to…identify heterosexuality as one of the keys to male supremacy."

The Furies ideology maintained that any woman could be a lesbian regardless of her natural inclinations and a failure to be sexually attracted to other women indicated a submission to male political domination. The promotion of this strict dogma enjoyed a few quick successes. By 1971, lesbianism had become a more mainstream feminist concern, and the national meeting of NOW passed a resolution including lesbian rights as part of its national agenda.

It also brought detractors. Activist Alice Wolfson reportedly "experienced discomfort" with many of the collective's beliefs, including the insistence that having male children prevented pure women's liberation. Others, like *Off Our Backs*' Fran Chapman, stated that demanding women "become lesbians" for strictly political purposes seemed "inhuman" and was antithetical to women's liberation's original canon of allowing a woman to explore and accept her own sexuality, whatever it happened to be.

While the Furies was not the first or only lesbian feminist separatist collective (an earlier D.C.-area collective known as Amazing Grace, including three future Furies members, lasted only one week), it was by far the most influential and the most innovative for creating its own media vehicle to mobilize supporters and start their revolution. After publishing a special edition of a United Methodist publication called *Motive*, the Furies created its own newspaper, aptly named *The Furies: A Lesbian/Feminist Monthly*. "We call our paper *The Furies* because we are also angry," stated Berson's lead story on the cover of the debut issue, dated January 1972. "We have been fucked over all our lives by a system which is based on the domination of men over women, which defines male as good and female as only as good as the man you are with."

"*The Furies* newspaper was one way we defined and spread our ideology as radical lesbian feminist separatists determined to create revolutionary change," wrote former collective member and filmmaker Joan E. Biren in 2014. "We lived and worked in a way that challenged class privilege."

Many Furies members had been active in civil rights, women's liberation (including the women's liberation newspaper *Off Our Backs*) and the antiwar movement, and some helped organize Washington's first antiwar women's collective house in the Adams-Morgan neighborhood. At least two had even been married prior to coming out as lesbians. "We are rural and urban," Berson's story continued of the demographic makeup of the collective. "Our ages range from 18 to 28. We are high school dropouts and Ph.D. candidates. We are white. Some of us have been Lesbians for twelve years, others for ten months."

Biren reported that the collective sent some of its members to printing school, but everyone cooperated to produce the paper. "The basement of one of our collective homes at 219 Eleventh Street Southeast was the office where we did our own layouts and packed *The Furies* for distribution."

The layouts then had to be driven to Atlanta, Georgia, for printing by the female-owned Sojourner Truth Press "because local printers rejected our content and refused to print the paper," according to Biren. Selling

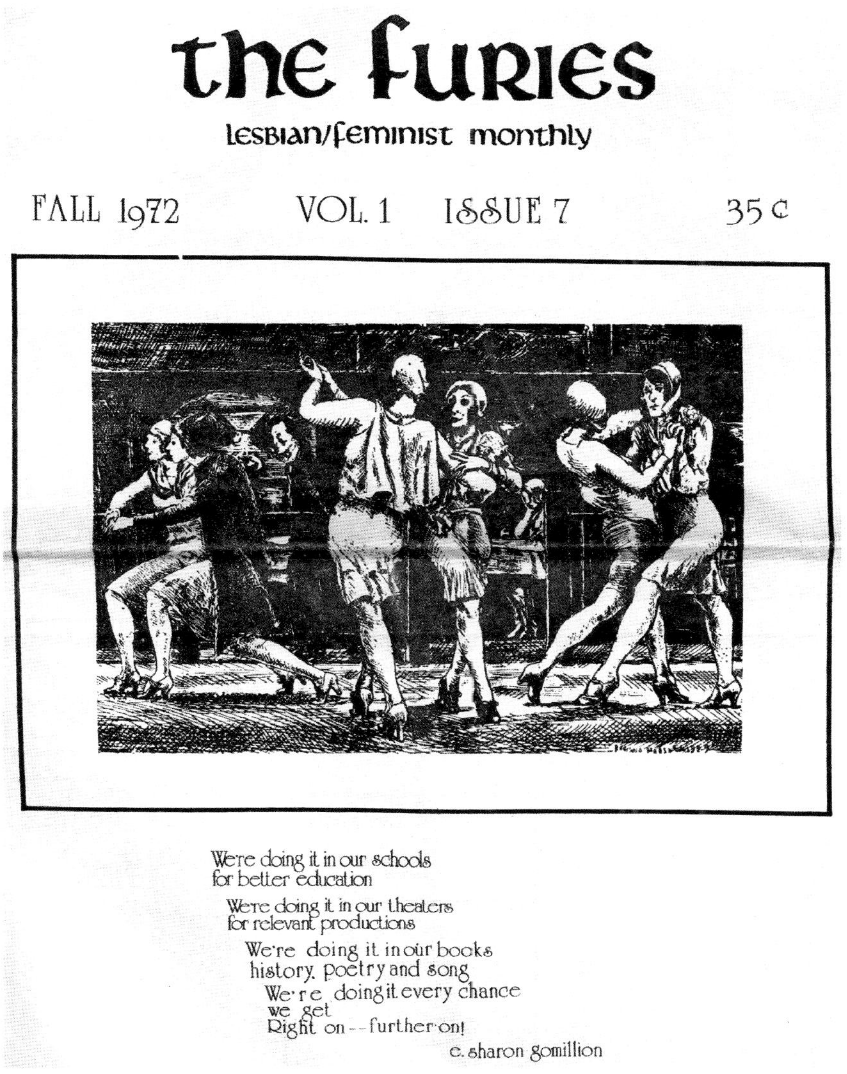

the furies

lesbian/feminist monthly

FALL 1972 VOL. 1 ISSUE 7 35¢

We're doing it in our schools
for better education
We're doing it in our theaters
for relevant productions
We're doing it in our books
history, poetry and song
We're doing it every chance
we get
Right on--further on!
e. sharon gomillion

The Furies, fall 1972. *Courtesy Bonnie Atwood and the VCU Cabell Library Special Collections, Richmond, Virginia.*

for fifty cents, the ten issues featured many commentaries on the lesbian-feminist movement, news shorts and lots of literary works. Advertisements on the back page were all from female-operated businesses, including Roselake Graphics, Everywoman Bookstore in Los Angeles and Lammas Handcrafted Silver Jewelry in southeast D.C. Other ads were for women's liberation publications, including *Off Our Backs*, *Ain't I a Woman* (from Iowa City, Iowa) and *Rat: A Woman's Paper by Third World and White Women*.

The Furies tried to dispel the stereotype that radical lesbian feminism had no sense of humor; in fact, it maintained that humor and the enjoyment of life was an antidote to the challenges of living under male and heterosexual authority. Charlotte Bunch wrote that the movement must have fun so its members do not "go mad in male supremacist, heterosexual Amerika [*sic*]."

In addition to serious articles on the movement and the occasional humor, *The Furies* featured a lot of lyrical, free-verse poetry, much of it erotic. The book of poems *Edward the Dyke* by Judy Grahn, with illustrations by Wendy Cadden, Brenda Crider and Gail Hodgins, was very popular in lesbian feminist communities. Coletta Reid wrote in *The Furies* that "Judy Grahn…is one of the few lesbian poets to celebrate the strength and survival capacity of women. No self-pity or whining here."

Volume 1, number 2 featured a two-page spread of poetry by member Rita Mae Brown from her book *The Hand that Cradles the Rock*.

The Furies did not shy from national political topics, including Vietnam. The May 1972 issue featured an article by Susan Hathaway titled "The Power and the Glory," accusing President Richard Nixon of keeping the war in Vietnam going for his own self-aggrandizement. "By now almost the whole world thinks the U.S. should get out of Vietnam," the article concludes. "But Nixon doesn't think so. He still thinks the U.S. should win—for the power and glory of Nixon."

In the spring of 1972, the original Furies collective began purging members and then in April disbanded entirely due to conflicting ideologies, members working full-time jobs and attending school and the realization that the day-to-day activities of the collective made it too difficult to accomplish their larger goals.

"The first people purged from this barrel of laughs were Sharon Deevey and Joan Biren," Brown wrote in her 1997 book *Rita Will: Memoir of a Literary Rabble-Rouser*. "They spent more time with each other than with us…They must have been as bored and antsy as I was. Out they went."

"I was next," she continued. "I was a leader in a leaderless group. I'd gotten ideas above my station. Out with me."

Even after the living collective dissolved, the newspaper continued publishing with a shoestring staff of women trying to expand the ideology of the original members. "Combining the reality of working to survive, our political work, plus the need to deal with our present ideology on a larger level…not one of these directions can reach all women," wrote Schwing and Harris. The collective's dissolution was not announced, however, until the July 1972 issue.

The paper drew both accolades and criticism. "As for the article on man-hating," wrote Rosina Richter, a member of a similar collective in Minneapolis, Minnesota, called Radical Feminists 28, "why should we be spending our time trying to figure out what men we can work with when we haven't even created a strong revolutionary feminist movement of women?"

"Rosina's letter is totally correct," responded Schwing. "What is the best way to build a strong women's movement and ideology; then be a powerful enough movement to deal with men?"

The Furies reflected much anger about suffocating patriarchy but also expressed optimism for the future. While the women of *The Furies* saw themselves in the center of creating a new society, their ideology did not attract new members. Consequently, the final twelve-page issue appeared in May 1973 after the staff dwindled to only two—Harris and Schwing.

"These changes have occurred mainly because of changing priorities," said a published goodbye. "The paper cannot continue with only two members, therefore we have decided to make this the last issue."

The Furies collective was pivotal in presenting lesbian presence to the women's movement and legitimizing lesbian feminism as a political issue. Feminist groups in such places as Durham, North Carolina, and Dayton, Ohio, credited the work of the Furies in their understanding lesbianism as a political force and not just a biological determination.

After disbanding the collective and the newspaper, the original Furies members embarked on other pursuits. Charlotte Bunch started *Quest: A Feminist Quarterly*; Ginny Berson and Jennifer Woodhul founded Olivia Records; Coletta Reid and Helaine Harris started Women in Distribution; Joan E. Biren founded Moonforce Media; and Rita Mae Brown became a successful novelist.

Biren wrote, "It was simultaneously exhausting and exhilarating to be part of The Furies collective."

THE GAY BLADE

1969–

We the members of the Mattachine Society in full awareness of our social obligation as members of the human community hold it necessary that a highly ethical homosexual culture be integrated in society.
—Preamble, the Mattachine Society original constitution, April 1953

In February 1950, ninety-one federal government workers identified as homosexuals were forced out of their jobs under the pretense that homosexuals were susceptible to blackmail and thus were national security risks. The surveillance, entrapment and interrogation techniques used by the D.C. vice squad had a crushing impact on D.C.'s already wary gay community.

In the face of the purge, a small group of gay men organized a discussion group one month later in Los Angeles, leading to the creation of the Mattachine Foundation, which was incorporated in California in April 1953—the same time President Dwight Eisenhower's Executive Order 10450 barred individuals found to be involved with "any criminal, infamous, dishonest, immoral, or notoriously disgraceful conduct, habitual use of intoxicants to excess, drug addiction, or sexual perversion" from the federal workforce.

The blatant prejudice faced by gays inside the federal government at that time can be summarized in a 1962 memo written by John Steele, who was chief of the Civil Service Commission's program systems: "[We] set homosexuality apart from other forms of immoral conduct and take a much more severe attitude toward it. Our tendency to 'lean over backwards' to rule against a homosexual is simply a manifestation of the revulsion which homosexuality inspires in the normal person."

The Los Angeles Mattachine Foundation also started a monthly publication, *One: The Homosexual Magazine*, to publish articles, fiction and poetry pertinent to the homosexual man.

Despite law enforcement, FBI and even post office persecution, the organization persisted, and in 1961, a chapter was finally formed in Washington, D.C. One of the D.C. chapter founders, Jack Nichols Jr., frequently used the name Warren Adkins since he was the son of an FBI agent. The other, Frank Kameny, had been fired from his job as an army civilian astronomer. In light of some positive developments during the '60s, including a court decision (*Norton v. Macy*) that determined homosexuality was not, alone, cause for firing, and the Mattachines' shift from government

page one

We are gay people and we are poor. We are refugges from straight America-women and men of many nationalities and races.

We live in the gay community which surrounds Dupont Circle. We are here be-the dying American empire has no place for us. We are constantly unemployed or made to work at shitty jobs for shitty wages. We are often forced into living off the streets-begging, stealing, selling our bodies and dealing dope in order to survive.

We are all outlaws. We have no regard for the "law of the land"-except to escape its clutches. We have no careers and no security. The system is our biggest enemy. Our only hope for the future lies in rev-revolution.

We must understand our own oppression in order to unite because it is our oppres-ion which keeps us apart. Our racism,sexism, and self-hatred can only be overcome by uniting as a class and fighting together.

These problems may seem impossible to overcome but the answers can be seen. We have begun to unite and we must continue; the revolution has begun and we must carry it forward.

"Page One" from *Bread Box: A Revolutionary Gay Newspaper*, volume 1, number 1. *Courtesy Bonnie Atwood and the VCU Cabell Library Special Collections, Richmond, Virginia.*

to a community focus, Nichols and Kameny created a mimeographed newsletter called *The Gay Blade*, "an independent publication serving the gay community," with volume 1, number 1 appearing on October 5, 1969.

The *Blade* appeared less than four months after a police raid on Greenwich Village's Stonewall Inn on June 28, 1969, galvanized a burgeoning gay rights movement. Such raids were an everyday risk of the '60s gay lifestyle, but this

The Gay Blade

August 1971 Vol. 2, No. 11

An Independent Publication Serving the Gay Community

BLACKMAILER CAUGHT, STILL UP TO OLD TRICKS.

The "DuPont Circle Blackmailer", of ill fame, was arrested in mid-July, but is now free on bond, and is apparently back to fleecing unsuspecting men of their $$.

Marshall Lee Farmer, a 48-year-old Landover man, was arrested by DC police after he picked up 3 envelopes containing $1,000 that had been left for him at a downtown hotel by a plainclothesman.

Farmer's past technique, and the pattern he is still using, is to sit in DuPont Circle and copy the license plate numbers of cars he sees cruising the area. He calls the owners, identifies himself as a policeman (which he is not) and threatens arrest if he is not paid off.

He has been charged with blackmail. Maximum sentence is 5 years, not more than $1,000, or both.

Our congratulations to the police dept. They've been working on this case for many years.

All gays who know anyone who frequents the DuPont Circle area, as cruiser or as cruisee, warn them that their troubles aren't over yet--the guy is still operating. And just one successful attempt will net him the money for his fine.

Please be wary.

The gay musical Hey Kid! has ended its run at Trinity Theater, but will re-open during August at another location. Watch for their ads.

Washington was represented at the Christopher Street parade on June 27 by upwards of 200 people. Total number participating is estimated to have been between six and eight thousand. A good time was had by all...

SHA and GAA are co-sponsoring a dance at Cambridge Dining Hall at the north end of the Univ. of Md. campus on Sat., Aug. 7. 8PM on. Call Larry at 927-0207 for more info, directions.

PUBLIC NOTICE

The Mattachine Society of Washington has for many years successfully served the gay community in a variety of ways. Our telephone is indispensible for this. We have, for this reason, rented a telephone answering and message recording device, but it is badly straining our budget. Send donations in any amount to Box 1032, DC 20013 or call 363-3881. Help us continue to help you.

MCC will have a special solemn eucharist on August 15 to celebrate the feast of the Assumption. Pastor Breton, an Episcopal deacon, and a Methodist minister will jointly celebrate.

GAA sponsors a picnic, Rock Creek Park Area 1, on Aug. 15. 528-6642 for information. GAA will have a beer-and-soda dance Aug. 21 at Temple Sinai, 3100 Military Rd. $1 adm.

Two cases arising from arrests in Georgetown have had good conclusions. In one, the prosecutor didn't come forward, in the other the policeman involved himself dropped the case.

UP IN BALTIMORE...

A group of lesbian women are meeting every week in Baltimore "in the hopes of starting a lesbian movement" in that city. The "informal, free and open" rap sessions begin every Tuesday night between 7 and 8 at the Women's Center, 3028 Greenmount Ave. For more information, call 301-366-6475.

Plainclothes District trolls continue to haunt the Black Forest (below P St. Beach).

The Gay Blade has obtained descriptions and the license plate numbers of unmarked police department cars which are working this "perversion detail".

One car is a dark green, custom Ford 4-door sedan, with DC plates 779-328. The driver wears shirt-&-tie to foster the closet queen image.

A second car is a white late model sedan, possibly a Ford, plate number 777-911.

Several people have said, that if MPD really wanted to stop sex in the area, it would station a uniformed patrolman in the vicinity. Special details of men and cars smacks of statistic-getting, and wastes your taxes and mine.

Gay women's open house every Wednesday night, 7:30 to 10:30. Just come and rap--there's no organization to join. Call 671-3762 for more information and the address.

The Metropolitan Community Church holds a weekly service Sunday afternoons at 2PM at 705 7th St. SE.

Each Tues. at 8PM there is a group discussion at the church with couples either already married or interested in "tying the knot". On Wed. at 8PM there is a training course for preparation to be MCC missionaries. Thurs. at 8PM is an informal "rap with the Pastor". All are welcome.

Among the Church's other activities are preparation of a hymnal and a prayerbook, training of a campus minister for the U. of Md. and a trip by Pastor Paul Breton and a lay delegate to the denominational meeting in Los Angeles in September.

Blade editors: Art, 270-2018; Nancy, 522-2404. Call them for ads and roommate referral service.

The Gay Blade, August 1971. *Courtesy Bonnie Atwood and the VCU Cabell Library Special Collections, Richmond, Virginia.*

time, five hundred patrons and sympathizers of the inn resisted, touching off four nights of demonstrations and a sustained burst of political activity aimed at making sexual orientation not a crime but a socially acceptable condition.

Published first in D.C., then in Arlington and then back in D.C., longtime lesbian activist Nancy Tucker was the *Blade*'s first and only editor and writer. Bart Wenger (using the pseudonym Art Stone) did distribution, mostly at gay-oriented establishments, such as Johnnie's, Georgetown Grill, the Golden Calf and the Front Porch. The first issue was typed on a single sheet in three columns and printed in an edition of five hundred copies. Stories included news of a blood drive at the Red Cross building at E Street and Twentieth Northwest and that the newly formed Gay Liberation Front in New York City had successfully forced the *Village Voice* to allow the word "gay" in its personal ad policy.

"Warning to DuPont Circle people" read a notice in the *Blade*. "Cars seen too frequently in the Circle area are having their license numbers taken down; their owners later are being harassed and blackmailed."

The August 1971 issue claimed that the "DuPont Circle Blackmailer" had been caught—he was a forty-eight-year-old Landover, Maryland man posing as a policeman but had been freed on bond. "Please be wary."

Issue number 2 briefly described how the National Institute of Mental Health's "Final Report of the Task Force on Homosexuality" might help increase awareness toward gays and change current employment practices by recasting statutes involving sexual acts "in such a way as to remove legal penalties against acts in private among consenting adults."

"Advertise in *Gay Blade*," read a house ad. "Cash donations seized with unimaginable avarice."

Taking a cue from the civil rights movement (even adapting its "gay is good" slogan after "black is beautiful"), more outspoken homosexuals sought to open communication to their cause using a variety of public means, some more radical than others. Militant homosexual Leo Laurence allied the West Coast movement with the Black Panthers, while on the East Coast, Nichols (who led a picketing of the White House in 1965 and that year appeared on a *60 Minutes* show about homosexuality) suggested more peaceful methods, such as subway kiss-ins and dance-ins to integrate straight nightclubs.

Still, the acceptance of a gay scene in Washington was slow compared to the larger metropolitan areas. The 1969 International Guild Guide (a D.C.-based directory of gay-friendly establishments around the country) listed twenty bars, clubs and restaurants that openly welcomed homosexuals, compared to over one hundred in San Francisco. Located mostly along

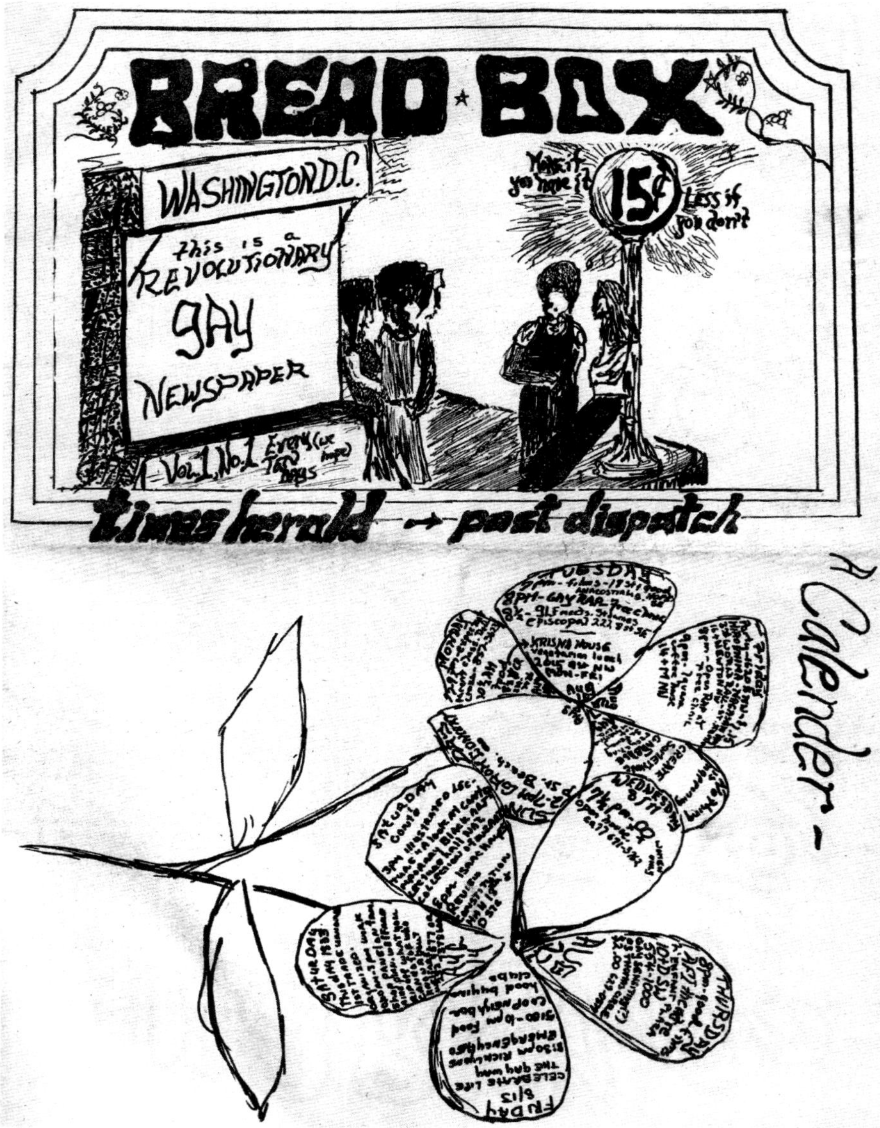

Bread Box: A Revolutionary Gay Newspaper, volume 1, number 1. *Courtesy Bonnie Atwood and the VCU Cabell Library Special Collections, Richmond, Virginia.*

Fourteenth Street, they were coded so visitors knew what to expect: military, hustlers, lesbians, leather jackets, blacks, drag queens and even AYOR ("at your own risk").

FREE! **The Gay Blade**

mid-June 1972 Vol. 3, No. 9

An Independent Publication Serving Washington's Gay Community

The Foresight Saga

Some seven years of planning came to a successful conclusion on May 24 when the DC sodomy statute was declared invalid.

This means that any sexual acts done in private in DC by any number of consenting persons 16 years of age or older (whether or not DC residents) are now fully legal.

Credit for the success goes first to Dr. Franklin Kameny (who else?), who conceived a strategy for it back in '65, and got four volunteers in '70 to carry it out.

Warren Colison, Chuck Hall, Terry Leigh, and Dick Schaefers volunteered to be plaintiffs. They told the court that they were homosexuals who wished to engage in acts of sodomy, at the time (in '71) prohibited by law. This created a "chilling effect" on their social lives by making them fear arrest and having the knowledge they were criminals in the eyes of the law.

Credit for the success of the case also goes to the ACLU, whose lawyers filed it in September of last year.

Sodomy Legalized!

GAA plans to try to have a meeting with Hizzoner the Mayor during the week of June 19 to discuss an executive order banning discrimination against all gays employed by the DC government, and an order enlarging the Human Rights Commission to 16 members, creating a space for an open gay person.

A benefit dance for the National Coalition of Gay Organizations will be held on Saturday night, June 17 in the third floor ballroom, Marvin Center, 21st & H Sts. NW. Admission is just $2 and includes a free bar (all the beer, wine, and soda you can guzzle). Time is 9PM-1AM.

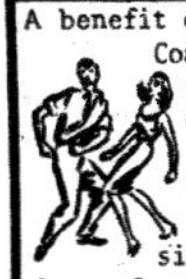

The Gay People's Alliance will sponsor a series of four weekly dances on the theme "Gay Lib in Summer Heat" starting July 8. The dances will begin at 9:30, and will be held in the 3rd floor ballroom of the Marvin Center, 21st & H Sts. NW on July 8, 15, 22, and 29.

The Life Raft is now sailing under a new management. Gary 'n Chuck, and Don are aboard most nights. Sheri Southern's "Viva la Boys" is presented at the bar at midnight and 2:30AM on Fridays and Saturdays, and at 6 and 10PM on Sunday. Small cover charge.

God Squad

The ministers of the Chapel of St. Francis and St. John of the Orthodox Catholic Communion of the Syro-Chaldean United Episcopal Church, dedicated the Chapel's new oratory on Sunday, June 4. Celebration was made with new vestments, flowing wine, and music from Godspell.

Beginning in July, the 3PM mass on the first and third Sundays will be celebrated in Latin.

Also starting in July will be a First Friday Devotional Mass, to include a Sacrament Watch and Benediction. 7PM.

Regular services are held at the Chapel, 1620 S St. NW, every Sunday at 3 and 5PM and on Holy Days at 7PM.

As if DC's gay men hadn't gotten enough this past month with the legalization of sodomy, dear old DC Superior Court Judge Halleck has struck down the District's solicitation law as being unconstitutional, among other things.

Halleck's "magnificent" 15-page decision relies in part upon the legalization of sodomy, partly on vagueness, and partly on the principle of violation of constitutional rights.

What the decision means is that verbal proposals made to persons 16 years of age or older, no matter how explicit, for private, consensual, sexual acts, are now legal in DC unless "the speaker persist to the annoyance, disturbance, or offense of the unwilling stranger," according to the judge.

HOWEVER!!! Don't get too carried away. Since the judge is one of 35 co-equal judges on the DC Superior Court, technically this decision applies only to cases heard before him. But while the decision is being appealed, the police will abide by the judge's written opinion.

San Francisco's claim to being gay Mecca may soon fall...

GAA will sponsor a city-wide drag show in July, to be directed by Mae West. Open auditions will be held at the GAA Center on Sunday June 18 at 4PM. •The Lost and Found will host a "Star-Spangled Salute" and the Miss Liberty Contest on June 28. •Henry Street will hold tryouts for "Son of Showstoppers" on Monday June 19 and Thursday June 22 (8PM sharp at the Warehouse, behind the L&F) and a final tryout on Thursday June 29 at the GAA Center (again 8PM).

On May 23 the DC School Board passed a fair employment resolution covering all school employees. The decision prohibits discrimination in hiring, employment, retirement, and/or job classification practices regardless of sex or sexual orientation. Thus, gay school teachers in DC now have genuine job security! Congrats to GAA for this triumph.

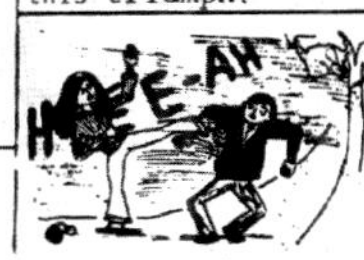

The Women's Crisis Center is now providing medical, legal, and personal counseling for women who have been raped. Also self-defense classes. [!] Call 333-RAPE any time of the day or night.

Here we go again, folks! This time—clearances.

Benning Wentworth, a declared gay who worked on defense contracts in New Jersey, has had his revoked DOD Secret clearance restored by Federal Judge Pratt.

The decision recognizes and grants Wentworth's contention that the revocation was in fact based on a class discrimination of all homosexuals, not on him in particular.

Says Frank Kameny: "This may be the long-awaited BIG breakthrough on GAY security clearances, especially concerning the Defense Department and the Military."

GAA continues its weekly dances, every Saturday night at the Gay Community Center.

The Editor of The Gay Blade is Nancy Tucker (yes! a woman!) at 522-2404. Phone her or Art at 270-2018 (evenings or weekends) to place ads, for news service, and whatever.

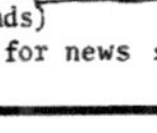

The Gay Blade, June 1972. *Courtesy Bonnie Atwood and the VCU Cabell Library Special Collections, Richmond, Virginia.*

The July 1970 issue of the *Blade* reported that the D.C. Gay Liberation Front was finally established at Grace Church on Wisconsin Avenue. Some of the approximately fifteen attendees "agreed to participate in the marijuana smoke-in July 4 at the Washington Monument as a means of 'zapping' the liberals into accepting gays." The following year saw the establishment of the Gay Liberation Front newsletter (*GLF*), the Gay Activists Alliance and another paper titled *Bread Box*, "a revolutionary gay newspaper," which lasted only one or two issues.

A calendar of events also appeared in the *Blade* that sometimes showcased a self-deprecating sense of humor. "Aug. 2: *Gay Blade* published. Call to join staff or turn mimeograph handle."

"Advertise in the *Gay Blade*," said a house ad in issue number 3. "We're no meat sheet (sell your body in the [*Washington*] *Free Press*...)"

Legal successes for gays were championed in the pages of the *Blade*. The June 1972 edition announced the legal invalidity of the D.C. sodomy statute. The same issue also announced that a Department of Defense employee and open gay man named Benning Wentworth had his revoked DOD security clearance reinstated by a federal judge. "This may be the long awaited BIG breakthrough on gay security clearances, especially concerning the Defense Department and the Military," said Frank Kameny.

When Nancy Tucker left the *Blade* in 1973 to return to graduate school, Pat Price (under the pseudonym Pat Kolar) took over for almost two years. During Kolar's editorship, the *Blade* grew to more than four thousand monthly copies distributed at thirty-five locations. In July 1974, the paper made the leap to newsprint tabloid. Then, in November 1975, Joseph Crislip (a pseudonym for Chris Deforrest) incorporated the *Gay Blade* as a nonprofit corporation under Blade Communications. Under this name, then after 1980 as a for-profit under the name the *Washington Blade*, the organization has published either as a paper or a website for a remarkable forty-five years.

"What is more important than the changes themselves is the attitude toward them, both on the part of homosexuals and the world at large," wrote Nancy Ross in an October 25, 1969 *Washington Post* article titled "Homosexual Revolution." "Therein lies the revolution, of which the new militancy and openness are merely the methods."

THE RATIONAL OBSERVER

1969

Remember you will be faced with joining society upon completion of your academic training. Don't do anything in haste today which could cause you embarrassment tomorrow.

—Anonymous blurb in the Rational Observer, *issue 2, December 1969*

On December 1, 1966, Washington, D.C.'s American University student newspaper the *Eagle* proudly became the first U.S. college student paper to join a national coalition of underground and alternative papers called the Underground Press Syndicate (UPS). The UPS was founded earlier that year by New York City *East Village Other* editors Don and Allan Katzman with John Wilcock and other underground publishers and editors. Initially, the founding papers agreed to exchange one-time reprint story rights, create a central advertising agency and divide any profits. The following year, the members agreed on a free exchange of materials and shared subscriptions for all member papers, with advertising representation and access to a wire service.

Eagle editor Tom Shales announced in the December 16, 1966 edition that the student-run paper had become "one of the pioneer members of the alliance which is still in its formative stages" and that "reprints from other member papers would begin appearing immediately."

Not that the *Eagle* necessarily needed outside journalistic help; one of its writers during this period was Ann Beattie, who went on to become a successful novelist and contributor to the *New Yorker*. Another *Eagle* writer, Gary Nordlinger, today is a business consultant in Washington, D.C.

Despite the relative conservatism of the *Eagle*, militant student activity forming on the AU campus drew the attention of the FBI. Something had to be done.

In May 1968, as the New Left movement reached an apex in the United States and throughout Washington, D.C., FBI director J. Edgar Hoover approved and implemented a secret counterintelligence program called "COINTELPRO—disruption of the New Left," an insidious and constitutionally unlawful campaign designed not just to harass individuals but also to disrupt and infiltrate college organizations and newspapers, collectives and underground papers he considered subversive.

"Our nation is undergoing an era of disruption and violence caused by various individuals generally connected with the New Left," stated a memo dated May 9, 1968, to Domestic Intelligence director William C. Sullivan from his deputy Charles D. Brennan, proposing the COINTELPRO program. "The New Left has on many occasions viciously and scurrilously attacked the Director and the Bureau in an attempt to hamper our investigation of it and to drive us off the college campuses."

"The purpose of this program is to expose, disrupt and otherwise neutralize the activities of this group and persons connected with it. It is hoped that with this new program their violent and illegal activities may be reduced if not curtailed."

FBI director Hoover started, with no legislative or executive authority, the first incarnation of COINTELPRO in 1956 to "infiltrate, penetrate, disorganize and disrupt" the U.S. Communist Party following the fall of McCarthyism. With Supreme Court decisions limiting the Justice Department's ability to prosecute American communists, bureau officials believed that existing laws could not control the activities of certain dissident groups. COINTELPRO's operations utilized antagonistic strategies to "contain and disrupt" radical activists they perceived as threats to the American way of life, such as the Socialist Workers Party, the Puerto Rican independence movement and Black Nationalist groups.

COINTELPRO was most antagonistic toward the black nationalists, especially the Black Panther party. On March 4, 1968, one month prior to the assassination of Dr. Martin Luther King Jr., Hoover escalated the counterintelligence activities against the Panthers into a brutal new phase, outlining five goals that he wished to attain: the prevention of a coalition of black groups, the prevention of a rise of a "black messiah," the prevention of violence from the black nationalist movement, the prevention of black nationalist groups from gaining respectability and the prevention of long-range growth of those organizations. Hoover said in a memo that he feared either Dr. King, Stokely Carmichael or Elijah Muhammed might be that dreaded "black messiah."

"King could be a very real contender for this position should he abandon his supposed 'obedience' to 'white liberal doctrines' (nonviolence) and embrace black nationalism," Hoover wrote.

The FBI also started looking hard at the SDS. Founded originally in 1960, the organization experienced a huge jump in membership after the first antiwar march on Washington in 1965, when thirty-five local chapters increased to over one hundred in less than six months. In 1966, the SDS made draft resistance its top priority and, at its 1967 national convention in Ann Arbor, Michigan, issued its call for a "new working class."

Hoover spoke on record against the SDS in February 1966 when he boldly proclaimed without a shred of proof that "communists are actively promoting and participating in the activities of this organization," so it was no surprise that the New Left movement and especially the SDS found themselves in Hoover's crosshairs following the Columbia University uprising, when Mark Rudd emerged as an important student leader.

American University had an active SDS chapter in early 1967 and even fielded an unsuccessful candidate for the office of student association president. "The purpose of SDS's campaign," wrote an unnamed member quoted in the April 26, 1967 *Washington Free Press*, "is a radical one, taken in the context of the complacency of American University…The [AU] administration has consistently refused to consider fresh ideas."

With SDS activity and anti–Vietnam War sentiment increasing, Hoover personally selected which leftist individuals or groups were deemed national security threats and gave final approval to what would become the final phases of "COINTELPRO—disruption of the New Left," a program linked to questionable CIA domestic surveillance programs like Project RESISTANCE, Project MERRIMAC and Operation CHAOS, all of which circulated intelligence watch lists on radical and antiwar activists, draft resisters, "New Leftists" and others. The lack of any formal FBI definition of "New Left" was not accidental; it gave the bureau leeway to target *every* antiwar group, including even those engaged in legitimate, nonviolent activities.

The bureau's COINTELPRO–White Hate Groups operation had full political support against the Ku Klux Klan after the murder of three Mississippi civil rights workers in 1964, so Hoover utilized that model as a template for New Left. This autonomy was secure as long as the bureau's activities remained secretive and beyond any governmental oversight. Unbelievably, the FBI's primary consideration for the appropriateness of COINTELPRO activities was not the question of whether they were unconstitutional, dangerous or even patently illegal but only whether they could potentially expose or embarrass the bureau. Almost every HQ approval for field office proposals ended with a similarly worded admonition that "you should take all necessary steps to assure that the Bureau cannot be identified as the source."

While the micro-managing Hoover was believed to be directly involved in all aspects of the COINTELPRO program and insisted that no field office could proceed with any disruptive activities without prior approval because of the fear of exposure, he did assign directorship responsibility to several headquarters underlings to approve many of the COINTELPRO initiatives proposed by the field offices. Thus, memos signed to or by the "Director" were not always necessarily from Hoover himself.

And the bureau may have started feeling exposed and embarrassed about what was happening right under their own noses at American University; therefore, the Washington field office wasted no time gathering information on New Left activities on that campus and proposing methods to disrupt it.

American University first started arousing the attention of the pre-COINTELPRO FBI in December 1966 when General Lewis Hershey, director of the U.S. Selective Service System, was picketed by antiwar protestors during a campus speech. Then, in October 1967, sixty-two students and faculty members who objected to America's role in Vietnam walked out on a bestowment of an honorary degree to Ambassador Henry Cabot Lodge at the Seventy-fifth Anniversary Convocation.

Two weeks later, two editors of the *Eagle* were stripped of their positions by the AU Student Publications Board, whose chairman explained there was a "conspiracy of left-wing elements to take over" the student paper. The ousters were prompted by a complaint lodged by the University Homecoming Committee that the paper gave primary coverage to the Lodge walkout and not to his speech.

Then, on April 5, 1968, a demonstration held on campus after the death of Dr. Martin Luther King Jr. called for a boycott of classes and, according to a bureau memo, was "condoning the looting and burning of stores by Negroes in WDC." On May 2, 1968, another memo reported that "75 to 100 Negro and white students, the preponderance of which were hippies, gathered at the Hughes-McDowell lounge on the AU campus… consideration was given to taking over the university during this meeting but was abandoned due to the overwhelming presence of conservative students. The meeting disbanded without incident."

"WFO [Washington field office] has several informants…who have already furnished invaluable information concerning participation of SDS members in the student agitation at American University in May, 1968," stated a June 13, 1968 FBI memo, which went on to discuss various ways of disrupting SDS activities on campus. "It is suggested that the draft status of male activists be determined in an effort to learn if these individuals practice what they preach about the war. Such information might be useful in exposing certain individuals."

One memo from the WFO to the bureau director dated October 15, 1968, proposed a phony anonymous letter to the parents of an AU SDS leader alleging drug abuse. Letters to parents was a proven bureau practice, used by field offices across the country. "The purpose of the letter is to arouse parental concern and hopefully interference in the activities of [redacted]."

Other D.C.-area colleges also attracted the attention of the bureau. Georgetown University's May 23, 1968 sit-in that demanded classroom space for the "Poor People's University" that coincided with the district Poor People's Campaign was under marked surveillance. A July 2, 1968 memo warned that potential disruptive activity could be expected at George Washington University when classes commenced in the fall. A June 6 memo stated that there were no groups affiliated with the New Left at Catholic University.

But it was at AU that activities were of particular concern to the bureau. In a memo from Charles Brennan to the special agent in charge (SAC) of the WFO, he stated that "we should formulate a comprehensive Counterintelligence Program [at American University] and, in this regard, you should immediately submit to the Bureau your observations and specific recommendations as to how we can best achieve this goal."

The Washington SAC responded in late August 1968 with a radical idea: working with an informant, create a phony four-page, eight-and-a-half- by eleven-inch offset printed underground newspaper carefully designed to discredit the radical influences on the AU campus. Originally to be called the *Workshop*, its proposed motto was "Revolution is the religion of the masses with the *Workshop* for its bible."

"The purpose of this newsletter is to uncover domestic and foreign interests both legal and illegal concerned with the New Left," the proposal stated. "Its aim is to cause disruption among the New Left with the ultimate goal of frustrating their efforts to destroy democracy and neutralizing them."

While the bureau was impressed with the proposal, it was worried the publication was "too ambitious" if it was to be attributed to their informant, who had limited financial resources. "If it is initially published on a shoestring and with obvious amateurish touches," the director suggested, "it would then be a more credible operation."

Then, apparently alarmed by an SDS conference planned at the Kay Spiritual Life Campus Center on December 14, the WFO proposed a one-page flyer with those "amateur touches" desired by the bureau director for distribution at AU just before Thanksgiving, titled "Where do you stand AU SDS?" It was intended to introduce a moderate voice and display the hypocrisy of the student movement by comparing motives and quotations by SDS leaders with Chinese premier Mao Tse-tung.

In February, the ever-resourceful Washington field office SAC proposed another phony underground paper called *Chevara News*, which was a merger of the name Che Guevara, the Cuban revolutionary killed in Bolivia in 1967. The Washington SAC stated somewhat sarcastically on the proposal that "bureau criticisms and suggestions concerning the publication of this leaflet would be appreciated by the WFO." But in June, the WFO abruptly rescinded the proposal. "Since the AU SDS has been rendered relatively ineffective…WFO will not publish and distribute the *Chevara News*." They did, however, leave open the option to proceed with the idea in the future if circumstances on campus warranted.

Sure enough, at the beginning of the fall 1969 academic year, the WFO noted a resurgence of activity in the SDS, the Student Mobilization Committee (SMC) and other "radical groups" at AU. Again, the bureau requested permission to publish the phony newsletter, only this time instead of *Chevara News*, the proposed name was the *Rational Observer*. Bureau approval was granted, but only if it were printed on unwatermarked paper, distribution was handled by a source using a "cut-out" (non-FBI) to avoid any affiliation and a post office box was included to gauge attitudes, as "those who respond may constitute a potential font for sources."

"This [newsletter] will purportedly be from a small group of students who take exception to the developments on the American campus and who are taking an opportunity to point out some of the inconsistencies and obvious dangers posed by the New Left on the campus."

Underground Press historian James Danky wrote in a 2013 e-mail, "Everyone in the underground press knew they were being infiltrated but the idea that the FBI was producing such publications would have seemed farfetched. The FBI would have seemed too clumsy to pull it off."

The *Rational Observer* was in fact one of several phony underground papers proposed or produced by the FBI. From September 1968 through March 1969, the bureau created and distributed four editions of an "underground" paper on the campus of the University of Indiana–Bloomington called *Armageddon News*. A third phony paper, proposed by the San Antonio field office in January 1969 at the University of Texas–Austin and called the *Longhorn Tale*, never progressed past the planning stages.

"These faltering efforts speak to the cultural and political distance between the forces of repression led by J. Edgar Hoover and the seismic changes in America's social fabric," wrote Danky. "Such shoddy examples of a political press would not have been successful products in the marketplace of ideas of that time."

The first issue of the *Rational Observer* landed on the AU campus sometime around the end of September 1969. It is unknown who distributed it; alumnus Rich Pollock claimed in January 2000 that he saw copies being handed out

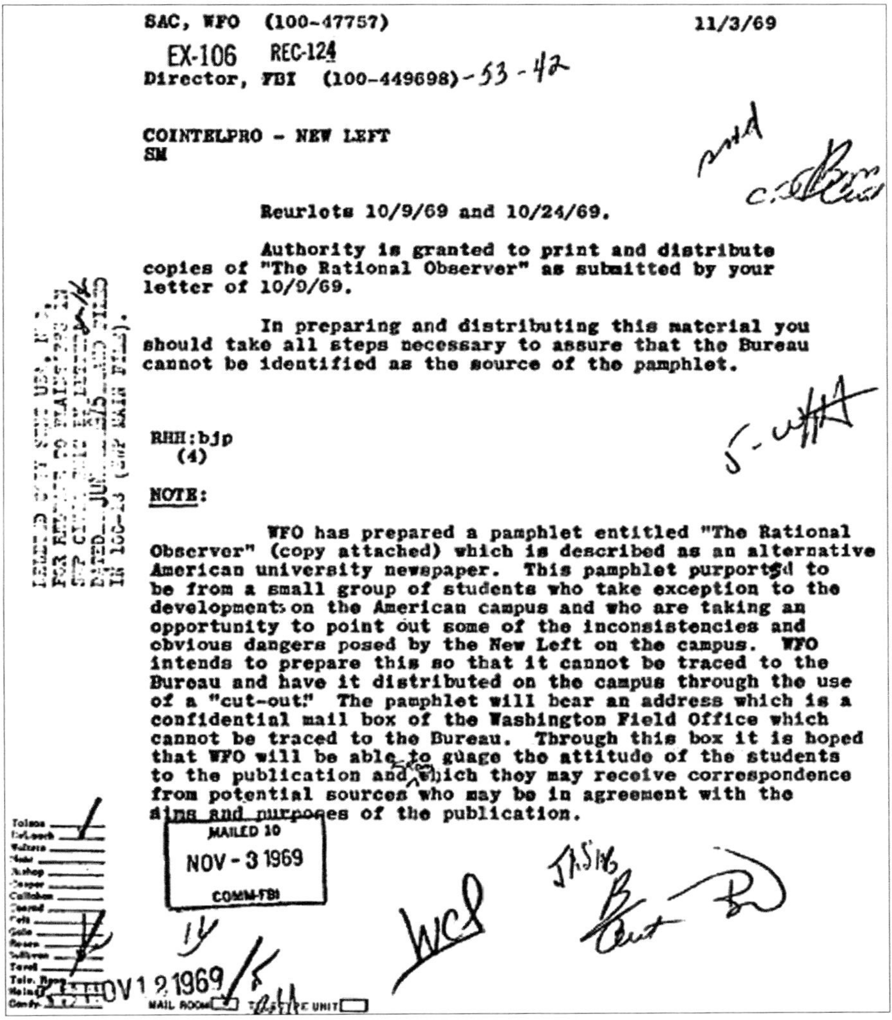

SAC, WFO (100-47757) 11/3/69

EX-106 REC-124

Director, FBI (100-449698)-53-42

COINTELPRO - NEW LEFT
SM

Reurlets 10/9/69 and 10/24/69.

Authority is granted to print and distribute copies of "The Rational Observer" as submitted by your letter of 10/9/69.

In preparing and distributing this material you should take all steps necessary to assure that the Bureau cannot be identified as the source of the pamphlet.

RHH:bjp
(4)

NOTE:

WFO has prepared a pamphlet entitled "The Rational Observer" (copy attached) which is described as an alternative American university newspaper. This pamphlet purported to be from a small group of students who take exception to the developments on the American campus and who are taking an opportunity to point out some of the inconsistencies and obvious dangers posed by the New Left on the campus. WFO intends to prepare this so that it cannot be traced to the Bureau and have it distributed on the campus through the use of a "cut-out." The pamphlet will bear an address which is a confidential mail box of the Washington Field Office which cannot be traced to the Bureau. Through this box it is hoped that WFO will be able to güage the attitude of the students to the publication and which they may receive correspondence from potential sources who may be in agreement with the aims and purposes of the publication.

MAILED 10
NOV - 3 1969
COMM-FBI

NOV 12 1969

FBI memo granting permission for the Washington field office to create and distribute the *Rational Observer*, November 3, 1969. *Courtesy the author.*

by members of the right wing group Young Americans for Freedom (YAF). The 1971 *Eagle* editor, Jinnie Rhodes, made the same claim; however, former YAF president Ken Tobin told the *Eagle*, "It was not associated or promoted by the YAF to the best of my knowledge."

Regardless of who distributed it, the *Rational Observer*'s appearance provoked a subdued response at AU. The September 19, 1969 *Eagle* published a letter to the editor by William Leonhart, who (not knowing that the paper was a FBI phony) scolded the *Observer*, writing that "your vituperation has blinded you…perhaps you will overcome your rage and begin to act reasonably-reason tempered. You are, it seems to me, duped in your rage."

While no copies of issue number 1 could be located, a single faded copy of issue number 2 contained a snarky response to Leonhart's letter: "Bill, thanks for your criticism, but we think most of it was inundated in your tidal wave of intellectual egotism."

American "leftist professor" Dr. Louis Loeb was apparently also the target of an attack in issue number 1 of the *Observer*. Loeb was a spokesman for several students who were demanding a reversal of AU president George H. Williams's refusal to allow a mock inauguration of black comedian Dick Gregory on campus, a decision that created a "hit and run occupation of campus buildings," according to the March 8, 1969 edition of the *Baltimore Afro-American* newspaper. A profile of Loeb by writer Gary Nordlinger in the December 12, 1969 edition of the *Eagle* mentioned that Loeb "finds the attack on himself in the *Rational Observer*, an AU rightist flyer, 'amusing.'"

Gary Nordlinger is today a Washington-based business consultant. He said in a 2014 e-mail that he had "no idea" the *Rational Observer* was an FBI phony.

"What is the *Rational Observer*?" the masthead of issue number 2 asked. "It is an attempt by a small group of students, who love democracy, to preserve democracy and who believe that evil exposed is evil eliminated."

"The purpose and aims of this paper are not to stifle dissent but to expose charlatans of the right, left and middle, whether they be in government, industry, clergy, labor or the academic world; to expose those who capitalize on legitimate dissent for their own selfish purposes or concede to pressure groups the rights of the orderly."

Other articles in the *Rational Observer* read more like "Hints from Heloise" than expositions of the evils of the New Left. "If you must freak out on society don't turn on with drugs," warned a news short. "Drugs offer only temporary relief…Turn on to your rabbi, minister, priest, and yes, your parents, for help in solving your hang-ups."

"President Williams," the story grimly closed, "don't turn your back on drug abuse at American University. It may come back to haunt you."

Another short article on page three warned students about the future implications of excessive Vietnam War protesting: "Remember you will be faced with joining society upon completion of your academic training. Don't do anything in haste today which could cause you embarrassment tomorrow."

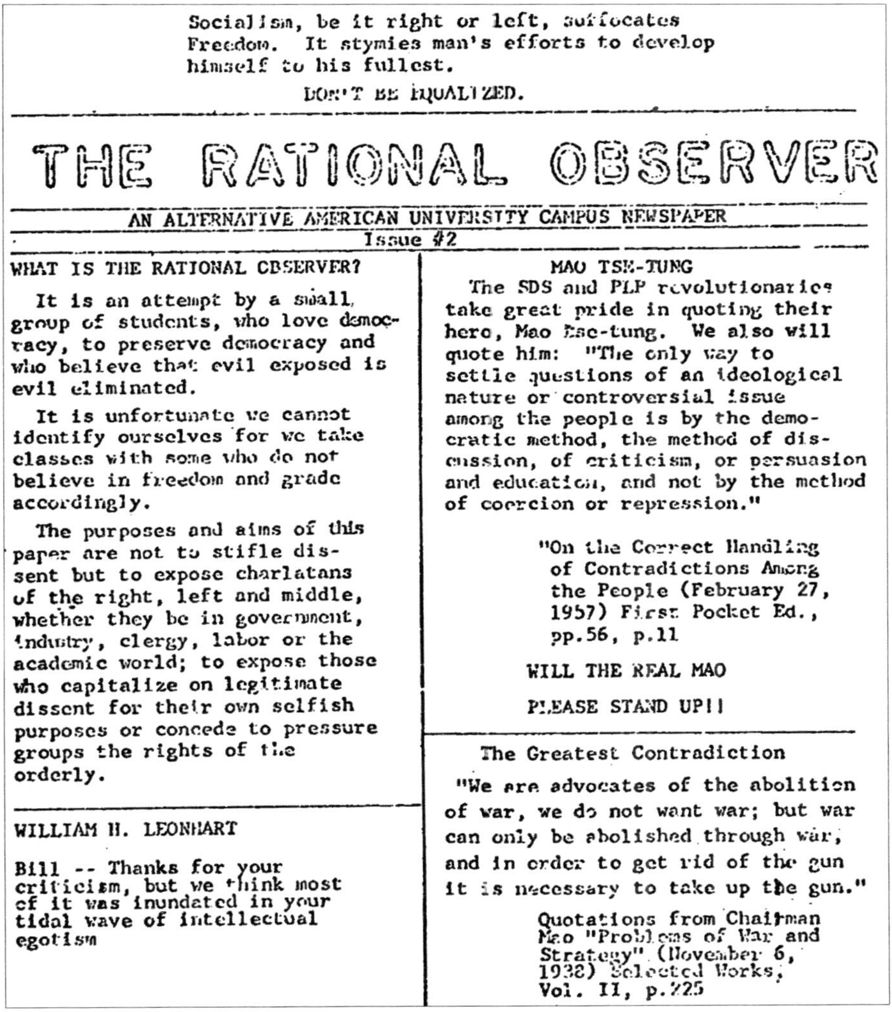

Socialism, be it right or left, suffocates Freedom. It stymies man's efforts to develop himself to his fullest.

DON'T BE EQUALIZED.

THE RATIONAL OBSERVER

AN ALTERNATIVE AMERICAN UNIVERSITY CAMPUS NEWSPAPER

Issue #2

WHAT IS THE RATIONAL OBSERVER?

It is an attempt by a small group of students, who love democracy, to preserve democracy and who believe that evil exposed is evil eliminated.

It is unfortunate we cannot identify ourselves for we take classes with some who do not believe in freedom and grade accordingly.

The purposes and aims of this paper are not to stifle dissent but to expose charlatans of the right, left and middle, whether they be in government, industry, clergy, labor or the academic world; to expose those who capitalize on legitimate dissent for their own selfish purposes or concede to pressure groups the rights of the orderly.

WILLIAM H. LEONHART

Bill -- Thanks for your criticism, but we think most of it was inundated in your tidal wave of intellectual egotism

MAO TSE-TUNG

The SDS and PLP revolutionaries take great pride in quoting their hero, Mao Tse-tung. We also will quote him: "The only way to settle questions of an ideological nature or controversial issue among the people is by the democratic method, the method of discussion, of criticism, or persuasion and education, and not by the method of coercion or repression."

"On the Correct Handling of Contradictions Among the People (February 27, 1957) First Pocket Ed., pp.56, p.11

WILL THE REAL MAO PLEASE STAND UP!!

The Greatest Contradiction

"We are advocates of the abolition of war, we do not want war; but war can only be abolished through war, and in order to get rid of the gun it is necessary to take up the gun."

Quotations from Chairman Mao "Problems of War and Strategy" (November 6, 1938) Selected Works, Vol. II, p.225

Page one of the *Rational Observer*, October 1969. *Courtesy the author.*

A bizarre and poorly drawn cartoon on page two showed AU president Williams's head on the body of a cow, holding a leash in his teeth. On the other end of the leash is an unrecognizable hairy monster with "SMC" (presumed to refer to Student Mobilization Committee) on its nose. A word balloon from Williams reads, "Alright I'll call you master."

It is unknown if AU administration knew of or was involved in the covert FBI activity on campus. It is also unknown exactly how many editions of the

Rational Observer were actually published and distributed and what the effect of the paper's presence on campus really was, if any. A December 4, 1969 FBI memo from the WFO to the director boasts with zero documentation that "as a result of this publication, sources advised that students on that campus became aware of the nature of SMC and its affiliations with the YSA [Young Socialist Alliance] and partially as a result of this, refused to participate in an SMC planned demonstration on that campus."

On March 8, 1971, while most of America was at home watching the "fight of the century" between Joe Frazier and Muhammed Ali, an anonymous private group calling themselves the Citizen's Commission to Investigate the FBI raided the bureau field office in Media, Pennsylvania, and carried away over one thousand memorandums and detailed descriptions of COINTELPRO's wiretapping and infiltration activities that included even members of Congress. Over the course of several months, the group mailed the materials to newspapers all over America.

The cat was out of the bag. On April 5, House majority leader Thomas Hale Boggs slammed J. Edgar Hoover and the bureau, stating that "when the FBI taps the telephones of members of this body and members of the Senate, when the FBI stations agents on college campuses to infiltrate college organizations, when the FBI adopts the tactics of the Soviet Union and Hitler's Gestapo, then it is time that the present director no longer be the director."

Boggs's statements provoked a verbal smack down from Attorney General John Mitchell, who said that Boggs's comparing Hoover and the FBI to the Gestapo "reached a new low in political dialogue. He should recant at once and apologize to a great American."

In October 1972, while he was still majority leader, Boggs and Alaska congressman Nick Begich's twin-engine airplane disappeared over Alaska. Presumed crashed, it was never found.

The COINTELPRO revelations prompted a terse memo on April 28 by a nervous Hoover, abruptly canceling not just the *Rational Observer* but all COINTELPRO-related operations.

NBC reporter Carl Stern initiated a Freedom of Information Act lawsuit in March 1974, compelling the bureau to produce all documentation from the COINTELPRO programs. Once exposed, and coupled with damage to its reputation due to the devastating findings of the 1975 Church Committee hearings, the bureau was dragged through court numerous times to answer for its COINTELPRO activities.

In every instance, the FBI took the high road, unsympathetically dismissing the pain, job losses, family disruptions and even deaths attributed to its unlawful program. Acting Director William Sullivan told the Church Committee on October 16, 1975, that "the Bureau people did not think that they were doing anything wrong and most of us to this day do not think we were doing anything wrong." Racial Intelligence Section chief George C. Moore concurred in his testimony on November 3, stating, "I thought I did something very important during those days. I have no apologies to make for anything we did, really."

Opinion pages in newspapers across the country offered withering denunciations of the FBI's activities. The December 11, 1973 *Toledo Blade* wrote that if the now-public memos were true, then "the FBI was in some respects not much removed from the secret-police tactics of totalitarianism."

In 1976, eight former Washington-area political activists brought suit in D.C. District Court in *Hobson v. Wilson*, claiming that their constitutional rights had been violated by the COINTELPRO program. The plaintiffs sought damages against numerous active and retired special agents of the FBI and members of the Washington and D.C. metropolitan police departments. The amended complaint, filed on October 28, 1977, alleged that each of the thirteen defendants had violated plaintiffs' constitutional rights while they were engaged in lawful political protest against government policies.

"Defendants suggest that publication of *The Rational Observer* could not constitute unlawful activity under any circumstances," stated the transcript. "But…publication of a newspaper, under Government auspices, with its true author misrepresented, which cautions peace demonstrators that they might be embarrassed later in life for their present activities, and which urges students to seek an injunction against publication of another newspaper, is unlawful."

Trial transcripts revealed that FBI security coordinator and squad supervisor Courtland J. Jones approved the creation of the *Rational Observer*, and New Left coordinator Gerald T. Grimaldi conceived and published it. Grimaldi also testified that he was responsible for the fictitious names and addresses on address cards stolen from the *Washington Free Press* office prior to the counter-inauguration in January 1972. A transcript of a February 8, 2008 oral interview with Jones made by Stanley Pimentel for the National Law Enforcement Museum contains no mentions of COINTELPRO, although Jones did call the program "wrong and childish" in Alexander Avakov's 2006 book *Plato's Dreams Realized: Surveillance and Citizen Rights, from KGB to FBI*.

Following a seventeen-day trial, a jury returned verdicts in favor of most of the plaintiffs, awarding compensatory and punitive damages totaling $711,937. Only one plaintiff, the Washington Area Women Strike for Peace, was found not to have been injured by any of the defendants' activities. An appeal by the defendants to the D.C. Circuit Court of Appeals in 1984 upheld the lower court ruling, and a 1985 appeal to the U.S. Supreme Court was refused, leaving intact a ruling that denied the agents immunity from private lawsuits.

J. Edgar Hoover never testified nor was held accountable for his role in any of the COINTELPRO programs. He succumbed to heart failure on May 2, 1972.

MAYDAY AND HARD TIMES

1968–70

In October 1968, three Washington journalists produced a weekly four-page muckraking and political commentary tabloid (printed appropriately on yellow paper) called *Mayday*.

With consumer advocate Ralph Nader listed second as consulting editor, the editors were a who's who of '60s investigative journalists that included at least one name familiar to the New Left movement—*New Statesman* correspondent Andrew Kopkind, who had also worked for the *Washington Post*, *Time* magazine, *Ramparts* and the *New Republic*. In the 1960s, Kopkind distinguished himself with excellent coverage of the civil rights movement, SDS, Black Panther Party and the birth of the New Left movement on college campuses.

One of Kopkind's co-editors was former *Wall Street Journal* correspondent James Ridgeway. Ridgeway was the *New Republic* reporter who revealed that General Motors hired private detectives to spy on Ralph Nader in an attempt to discredit him when he challenged the safety of the Chevrolet Corvair. Ridgeway's story prompted a Senate subcommittee investigation that forced an apology from GM president James Roche.

As the Washington correspondent for the *Nation,* Robert Sherrill was banned from the White House for "posing a physical threat to the president," a distinction that landed him on Nixon's infamous enemies list. Sherrill also briefly worked for journalist I.F. Stone for his self-published paper *I.F. Stone's Weekly*.

More antiestablishment and alternative than underground, the first issue of *Mayday* contained a report on "blue collar" support of presidential contender George Wallace and a detailed account of Richard Nixon's business and law associations.

In April 1969, after twenty-five issues, the owner of the trademark for the international distress signal "mayday" (from the French *m'aidez*—"help me") asked the magazine to cease using the name, so it adopted *Hard Times*, published by the New Weekly Project, Incorporated.

Hard Times continued the same hard-hitting investigative journalism that had distinguished *Mayday*. Enhanced by Samuel Antupit's sparse, text-only design, the four-page publication was more of an academic journal, on top of its form exposing waste, corruption and needless government bureaucracy, federal meddling in foreign affairs and the war against the New Left. A special issue in November 1969 highlighted, in a single long story by Robb Burlage, the Alaskan oil boom and the difficulties in piping the oil to the lower forty-eight.

Suzanne and Tom Bodenheimer wrote a frank analysis of the California grape pickers' strike, led by Cesar Chavez, in the May 12, 1969 edition. "Eventually Chavez and his followers will win the right to organize," they wrote, "and their victory will be little more than a reaffirmation of a long recognized principle of American life. If however, they come to perceive their particular battle as part of and responsible to the larger struggle being raised by America's discontents, then they could strengthen the liberation movement within the U.S."

In December 1970, just after *Hard Times* folded, Kopkind and Ridgeway joined the editorial staff of *Ramparts* and created a *Hard Times* supplement. A *Ramparts* editorial called them "the most formidable journalistic team on the American Left."

COLONIAL TIMES AND DAILY RAG

1971–74

In early October 1971, a new biweekly tabloid that promised to be "radical in content but not rhetoric" appeared in D.C. More leftist-alternative than underground, the *Colonial Times* was founded to "fill the void between the underground *Quicksilver Times* and the city's main daily newspapers," adding that the paper would resemble either the *Boston Phoenix* or the *Village Voice*.

The *Colonial* founders all had strong journalism experience. William Hobbs was once editor of two Fairfax County newspapers; Robert Hinton was a former reporter for both the *Baltimore Sun* and the *Washington Post*; Malcolm Kovacs was a freelance writer; Dorothy McGhee was a former reporter for the *D.C. Gazette*; and David Riley was former associate editor for the *Vicksburg Citizens Appeal*.

"We're going to put out a paper that covers the things people want to read, which the establishment press and the underground papers don't cover," said Hobbs.

With $500.00 of borrowed money and use of the production equipment of the women's liberation paper *Off Our Backs*, the staff produced twenty thousand copies of the free first issue. Subsequent issues cost $0.25.

The *Colonial Times* lasted only three issues. It later reappeared in late 1972 with a completely different staff as the *Daily Rag*, "a community newspaper" published by Colonial Times, Incorporated, at 2416 Eighteenth Street Northwest.

The *Daily Rag* tried to channel the antiestablishment spirit of the underground press but with less of the strident death-to-the-pigs-style vernacular. Despite its more straightforward presentation, it still managed (in the best underground tradition) to anger the U.S. Postal Service. Acting on an obscenity complaint, postal inspectors intercepted four copies of the December 8, 1972 edition and then hand-delivered them to subscribers, asking if they wished to refuse acceptance. Any refusals would be a basis to take the matter to the U.S. attorney for criminal prosecution.

The cause for the trouble was a cover illustration portraying a woman wearing a button on her shirt that said "Fuck the food tax." It was an illustration of the *Rag*'s ongoing editorial opposition to Washington, D.C.'s 2 percent tax on food, which it considered regressive and in need of appeal. Sam Smith, editor of the *D.C. Gazette*, was asked by his postman if he wanted to refuse his copy. Smith reported he was more outraged by the postal worker soliciting a complaint than he was by the cover illustration.

"They're actively trying to intimidate the free press," Dorothy McGhee told the *Washington Post* on behalf of the *Rag*. "They're harassing our subscribers and materially damaging our circulation."

Postal inspector Jason Souder acknowledged that similar words and phrases are commonly found in magazines and newspapers sent through the mail, but in this case, the word is found on the cover of the *Rag*, which was mailed unwrapped and in plain view of "unsuspecting innocents along the mail route." Souder cited federal law Title 18, Section 1463, which forbid the mailing of any material "upon the outside wrapper

THE DAILY RAG

A COMMUNITY NEWSPAPER

Volume One / Number Eighteen | Washington, D.C. | June 15 – 29, 1973

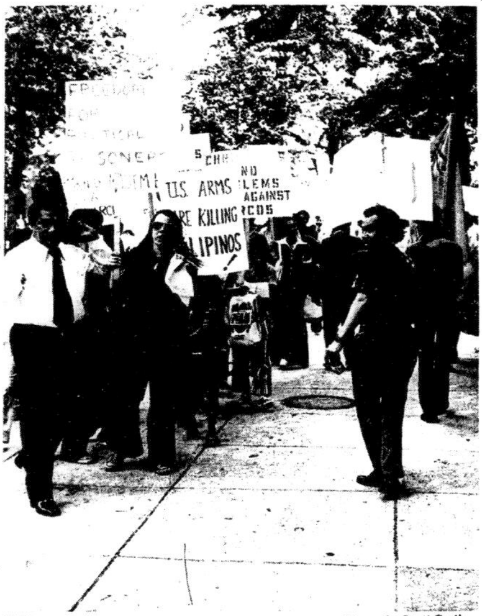

On 9 June, 200 people, nearly half of whom were Filipino, marched from Dupont Circle to the Philippine Embassy, in commemoration of kicking the Spanish out of their country in 1898. Unfortunately, the Americans moved in six months later.

They marched to demand an end to Martial Law in the Philippines, which has been in effect since September 21, 1972; the restoration of civil liberties; the release pf 20,000 people from Philippine prisons, who, the National Committee for the Restoration of Civil Liberties in the Philippines claim, have been arrested for political reasons; and the end at all U.S. military and technological aid to the Marcos regime.

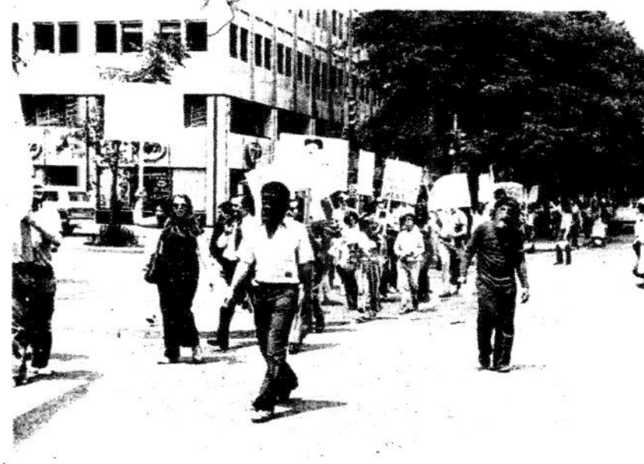

The U.S. is giving Marcos $22 million a year in military aid. Marcos recently demanded even more military support, and another $100 million in technological aid.

There are 23 military bases in the Philippines, including the headquarters of the Seventh Fleet and Clark Air Force Base which houses US B52s used in air combat in Indochina. The demonstrators claimed that US B52s are also being used to strafe political insurgents within the Philippines.

U.S. industry has invested an estimated $36 million in the Philippines, accounting for 80% of the foreign capital invested there. The Committee claims that 30% of the 39 million people living in the Philippines are either under or unemployed. Farm workers earn around 50 cents a day.

Photos by Scott Custin

Gov'ment Searched Free Press

The New York Times reported May 31 that FBI agents, assisted by men from the 116th Military Intelligence Detachment, broke into the old Washington Free Press offices without a search warrent shortly before Nixon's inauguration in January of 1969. The agents said they were looking for evidence of "overseas communist influence."

John Wagner, a former intelligence sergeant, said they "went in a second story window at night. I knew it was illegal. The Feds set it up and wanted the Army along. The break-in was part of the security operation in advance of the President's inauguration."

Another former Army intelligence officer said the FBI was concerned about counter-inauguration activities planned by the Free Press and other local radical groups.

They stole 500 postcards that were to be filled out by local Washington residents willing to house counter-inauguration demonstrators. The agents later filled them out and sent them back to the Free Press with bogus names and addresses in order to demoralize the organizers.

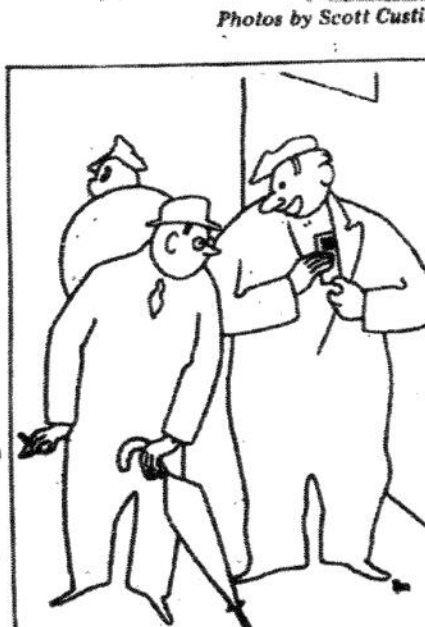

"Psst, Buddy—copy of the Bill of Rights!"

Wagner said the agents found no evidence of any foreign ties to the Freep.

Both army intelligence officers said that the clandestine operation was planned by the FBI. "When we wanted to penetrate, we just grew beards and put on fatigues and walked in the front door."

The break-in came more than two years after Attorney General Ramsey Clark ordered an end to all such FBI operations on the grounds that they were unconstitutional.

D.C. Nine to be Retried

On June 18, the retrial of two of the "D.C. Nine" defendants, Father Joseph O'Rourke, S.J., and Mr. Michael Dougherty, will begin in U.S. District Court House. The D.C. Nine, on March 22, 1969, destroyed Dow Chemical liason files with the Pentagon and the State Department in Washington, D.C., to protest Dow's manufacture of napalm, which was used to torture and maim civilians in Vietnam. As anti-war sentiment grew and public pressure against Dow mounted, led by actions such as that of the D.C. Nine and a nationwide boycott of all Dow products, Dow finally yielded and ceased production of napalm in late 1969.

O'Rourke and Dougherty are pleading "not guilty" in the upcoming trial, insisting on defending their innocence on the grounds that the illegal war in Vietnam compelled such actions to bring about its end.

The D.C. Nine were originally brought to trial on February 5, 1970. The defendants insisted on their right to defend themselves but were steadily overruled by Judge John Pratt. A jury verdict of "guilty" was handed down and the nine defendents were sentenced by Judge Pratt to terms ranging from six months to six years in prison for the same act.

The defendants subsequently appealed the trial to the Court of Appeals. The majority of the Court of Appeals ruled the original trial a mistrial on the grounds that the defendants should be permitted to defend themselves. A minority position also put forth the argument that the jury should have been advised of the right of jury nullification—namely, that if the jury feels a law was justifiably violated it can in effect nullify the law and find the defendants not guilty.

On June 18, the two defendants O'Rourke and Dougherty, will again be tried before Judge John Pratt at the U.S. District Court House in Washington, D.C. They will act in their own defense, with legal counsel as staff. As an ironic note, Tom Green, who prosecuted the D.C. Nine in the original trial, recently announced to the press that if he had the choice, he would refuse to prosecute them the second time.

Defendant O'Rourke maintains that, "there is still every reason for resistance and other efforts at challenging the institutionalized violence that controls our meaning abroad and our own powerlessness at home." And certainly, after years of struggle for peace in Southeast Asia and the right of the self-determination of nations, the participants in the bolder of the anti-war actions should not be railroaded off to prison sentences. The correctness of the anti-war struggle, while still going on, has already been proven by history. The actions which focused attention and prodded further mass movement against the illegal war in Southeast Asia should be heralded., not punished.

We urge supporters of O'Rourke and Dougherty to attend the D.C. Nine trial beginning June 18. They also ask that letters be written to Judge John Pratt requesting that charges be dropped.

Montevideo (LNS)— Uruguay's president, Juan Bordaberry, has announced plans to turn an old cargo ship into a floating prison. It is expected that the new prison will be used to hold the approxiamlely 2000 people arrested over the last year as suspected members of the Tupamaros urban guerrilla organization.

The Daily Rag, June 15–29, 1973. *Courtesy Alderman Library microfilm collection, University of Virginia, Charlottesville, Virginia.*

or cover of which, any delineations, epithets, terms or language of an indecent, lewd, lascivious or obscene character are written."

"The word certainly is not obscene in that context," argued McGhee. "The only thing obscene about this whole thing is the food tax and [postal employees'] ignorance."

Nevertheless, the *Rag* hired ACLU attorneys from the firm of Covington & Burling and took the matter to the United States Court of Appeals, D.C. Circuit, on January 3, 1975. The *Rag* alleged that in the course of hand delivery of the four copies of the December 8 edition, the post office agent not only advised the subscribers to refuse delivery but also suggested that accepting the paper might subject them to criminal prosecution. The post office vehemently denied the allegation, admitting that an agent was simply trying to recover a copy strictly for investigative purposes. The *Rag* also claimed that an assistant postal inspector informed them that the issue would be submitted to the Justice Department for review.

The trial became mired in procedural difficulties, was deferred to a later date and ultimately dismissed.

The following October, the *Daily Rag* angered the Washington, D.C. police, who claimed that their disclosures of police informants during the 1968–73 antiwar movement had jeopardized their intelligence-gathering capabilities.

Because of the *Rag*, Intelligence Division acting director Captain George Sutter was forced to confirm the identity of twenty-year-old Ann Kolego, or "Crazy Annie," who had infiltrated the People's Coalition of Peace and Justice and the National Peace Action Coalition from 1971 until early 1973. Sutter called her an "excellent" intelligence source.

The disclosure of "Crazy Annie" was leaked to the *Rag* by a D.C.-based organization called the Committee for Action/Research on the Intelligence Community (CARIC). CARIC revealed it had sources inside the D.C. police and that more revelations were forthcoming, a charge Sutter could neither confirm nor deny.

A second disclosure was Earl Robert "Butch" Merritt Jr., who worked undercover for both the D.C. police during the Mayday demonstrations and earlier did "voluntary work" for the FBI. Merritt was the agent named by columnist Jack Anderson in 1975 as the one selected to infiltrate the home of Ethel Kennedy and who had been sent into the phony Red House bookstore to steal its mail. He also admitted to breaking into the Community Bookstore to steal petitions and delivering mail stolen from the Institute of Policy Studies to the FBI and D.C. metro police. Finally, he said he was trained by D.C. police how to forge a draft card—a federal crime.

DAILY RAG NEWS
P.O. [illegible]
Washington, D.C.

The Daily Rag

July 13 to July 27, 1973
Volume 1, Number 20
A Community Newspaper
Circulation 20,000
Washington, DC

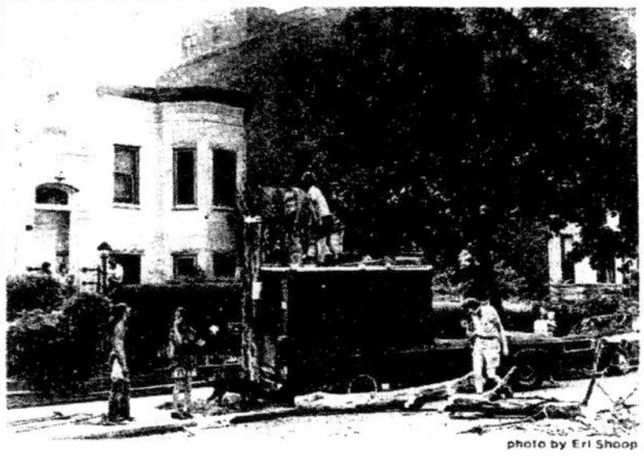

photo by Eri Shoop

The People's Tree Saga

At approximately 4 pm on July 8th, several people living on 19th St., nw, near Dupont Circle, began sawing and hacking at the cadaver of a tree that had died three years ago. Ninety minutes later, the upper portion of the 30-40 foot tree lay shattered in the street, leaving an eight foot stump. Twenty minutes later, the street was clear and traffic resumed.

The 19th Street People's Community rendered a service to the area by removing the hazardous tree in less than two hours. The city had had three years in which to do the same thing. But the police, who arrived during the cleaning up process, didn't see it that way. They issued, instead, citations to Gwen Shaub, Bud Shaub, Chasimo and Bill Burligh to appear in the Corporation Counsel's office at 9am July 12th for a hearing in connection with "cutting a tree (in Public Space) in front of 1706 19th St., nw."

Public space, apparently, is not the peoples' space in the eyes of the Metropolitan police department. But the eight foot stump, nonetheless, now wears a sign reading "People's Tree" and it is being used as a community bulletin board.

Gainesville VVAW Case Exposes Watergate Creeps

by Tim Butz

The trial of eight members of the Vietnam Veterans Against the War/Winter Soldier Organization, charged with conspiracy to create riot during the 1972 Republican National Convention, opens July 31st in Gainesville, Florida. The trial will begin at a time when an evergrowing amount of evidence points to connections between the veterans' indictment and the espionage plans of the Committee to Re-Elect the President (CREEP).

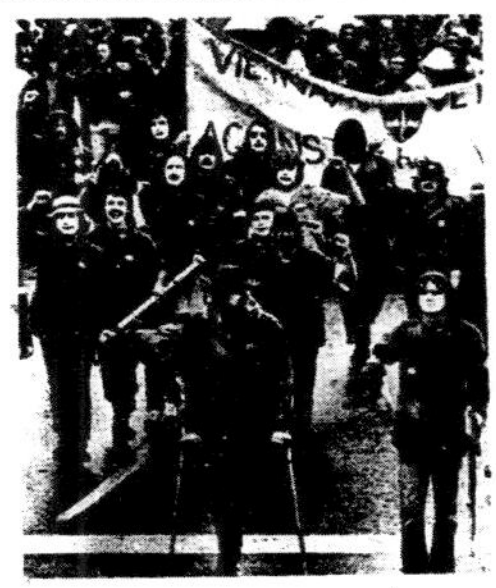

Four of the eight defendants traveled to Washington the week of July 9 to listen to the testimony of former Attorney General John Mitchell before the Senate Select Committee on Presidential Campaign Activities.

The four defendents—Scott Camil, Alton Foss, Don Perdue and Stan Michelson, hope that Mitchell's testimony will shed more light on the complicity between government agencies and the CREEP espionage apparatus as it relates to their trial.

The Washington trip was made necessary when federal judge Winston Arnow in Gainesville blocked defense attorneys from exploring possible Watergate connections during an April 25 pre-trial hearing.

One of the defendants, Scott Camil, stated "At first, we thought that these charges were another case of intimidation and political witch-hunting.

"But now," he said, "it is obvious that the government's motives were dual: they wanted to discredit the organization because of the effective political work it has done against the war *and* use it as the first step in their cover-up of criminal activities on the part of the Republican Party members."

Camil concluded that "Nixon used us in Indochina to carry out the most brutal experiment in the history of modern imperialism, and now he is trying to use us to cover his own criminal activity at home. We're being used again, and we know it."

[Camil's apartment was broken into twice in late 1971, according to syndicated columnist Jack Anderson. The robberies, which occured shortly before a series of indictments against Camil, resulted in the loss of membership lists, background questionaires and testimony sheets from vets concerning atrocities in Vietnam.

[Anderson also reported that in July 1972 the office of Carol Scott, Camil's attorney, was broken into and that her files on the Camil case were stolen.

[Anderson pointed out that the break-ins were similar to the illegal entry of the office of Daniel Ellsburg's psychiatrist, which resulted in a mistrial being declared in the Ellsburg-Russo espionage trial.

[The FBI has admitted to possessing a documentary film stolen from a VVAW member, but has yet to reveal the details of that theft.]

The first hint that Watergate figured in the Gainesville Conspiracy Case came in January, during the course of the Watergate burglary trial and a few days prior to the Inaugural Demonstration. James McCord, testifying in open court, cited the VVAW as a "violence-prone" organization that motivated him to take part in the break-in of the Democratic National Committee. Simultaneously, Jeb Stuart Magruder, a former CREEP official, went on national television and repeated the same charge in response to a reporter's question on the upcoming Inaugural Demonstration. Magruder has since been implicated as one of the CREEP officials who participated in the planning of CREEP covert operations.

In Gainesville, the trial judge lunches with the special Justice Department prosecutor, and defense efforts to gain insight on the depth of CREEP involvement have been obstructed in court. Outside the courtroom, however, the defense and the press have compiled facts tying the Gainesville trial to the Watergate affair.

—Former VVAW coordinator William Lemmer, an FBI informer and a prime prosecution witness, participated in planning meetings for the VVAW convention demonstrations at a time when the FBI's Operation Inlet was sending polit

continued on page seven

Right and Left Battle in Chile

After this report was written there was an attempted coup in Santiago, after which the El Teniente strikers went back to work and demonstrations were halted.

by Philip E. Wheaton
Daily Rag Special Correspondent

SANTIAGO, Chile, June 24—During the past two weeks in Chile, the struggle between the left and the right has become a daily battle on the streets of Santiago, a battle now marked by the right turning to open violence.

The occasion for this new tactic was a strike at the El Teniente copper mine which reduced production to approximately one third capacity as 25 per cent of the miners, supported by 75 per cent of the office personnel, protested wage and other working conditions.

This partial strike then became the battle cry of a significant rightist segment of the student body of Catholic University who barricaded the downtown campus (Casa Central), holding it as an "asylum" for some of the miners who came to Santiago because they couldn't dominate El Teniente.

Together these students and miners attempted to blockade certain downtown streets and to encircle the presidential palace, La Moneda.

These events were enough to send shock waves through the Chilean society as they potentially threatened Allende's already tentative economic position.

The Chilean economy is dependent upon copper production. It also provided the rightest majority in Congress an opportunity to move outside their "neutralist" position by allowing some of these miners to set up a second refuge on the grounds of the Congress.

But far more serious, the strike triggered open acts of terrorism by the storm troops of the reactionary Nationalist Party, the extremist front "Patria y Libertad." The result was to move Chile one step nearer civil war.

To counter these open challenges to his legal power, President Allende was forced to take extreme measures.

The first involved calmly employing the riot police (the *carabineros*) to maintain law and order, clear the street baricades, and keep the opposing bands from engaging each other in open stone-throwing clashes.

Secondly, last Friday, June 15, in a pouring rain, thousands of workers and members of the middle class left surrounded La Moneda to prevent the dissident miners and rightest students from occupying the Plaza of the Constitution.

Then, almost a week later, on June 21, the massive Chilean communist labor organization CUT (Central Unica de Trabajadores) called for a march of the entire Unidad Popular (Allende's left coalition) to close down the three principal cities of Chile: Santiago, Concepcion and Valaparaiso in order to show all Chileans where the real potential to control production lies.

The result was the most massive popular demonstration in the history of Chile. Almost half a million people, largely workers, campesinos (farmers) and the ghetto poor, along with thousands of middle class supporters and the extreme leftist organization, MIR, participated in the rally.

In four gigantic columns they converged on La Moneda and from 10 am to 4 pm turned all downtown Santiago into a people's rally of unprecedented proportions.

The dialectic of this incredible and daily struggle between the left and the right in this ostensibly democratic country keeps pushing both sides to new levels of consciousness and crisis.

On the one hand the right feels it cannot allow Allende to serve a full term (until 1976), for he is gaining more popular support every day.

To the surprise of everyone, the Unidad Popular increased its percentage in the last local elections from 36.4 per cent to 43.6 per cent, a jump of almost seven per cent.

Furthermore, local popular control of various societal functions is increasing in the countryside and in the urban ghettos (*poblaciones*) caused in part by rightest hoarding and the black market, which the Congress refuses to control.

Since the bosses' strike of last October, the government has had to set up food supply and distribution centers called "Warehouses of the People" run by neighborhood boards for supply and price control (the so-called JAPs).

A counter-dialectic is occuring among the right, which includes both the liberal and conservative Christian Democrats and their reactionary cohorts, the Nationalist Party.

Unable to stop the growing socialism in Chile, the right is desperately trying to find any issue, any economic contradiction or political weakness, in Allende's management of the government that would allow them to declare the experiment null and void.

The strike at El Teniente seemed to have that potential. On the crest of the student support of a few miners, they unleashed an extensive series of bombings and shootings aimed at producing some extreme reaction by Allende for which they could legally fault him in Congress and the courts and thus call for an intervention by the armed forces.

The use of an illegal television station (Canal 6) initiated the main ideological attack by the right, calling for people to take to the streets.

In other words, the extreme right has openly turned to fascist tactics and its vanguard, Patria y Libertad, has even employed a symbol which seems to reflect their intent.

The whole panorama of Chilean politics is, notwithstanding these clearly defined alternatives, a complex picture.

For instance, in the strike at El Teniente, 75 per cent of the miners stayed on the job and promised to make up for the copper not mined during these disturbances by offering to work additional man-hours.

Similarly, the east campus of Catholic University (Oriente) was shut down recently by the left during a march because 25 per cent of the total student body and an even larger percentage of professors were joined by most of the

continued on page six

The *Daily Rag*, July 13–27, 1973. *Courtesy Alderman Library microfilm collection, University of Virginia, Charlottesville, Virginia.*

Merritt approached the *Rag* with this information after admitting he had been "turned off" by the job.

Many advertisers in the *Rag* were holdovers from the hippie era. "Bong sale!" announced an ad by a business called Earthworks in the June 29, 1973 issue. "Regular $6.00, Now $4.00." Underneath in small type it promised "free rolling papers with this ad!" Other ads are seen in 2014 as quaint reminders of the times: Earth shoes, the Happy Trucking Company and the women's liberation–managed Bread & Roses Record Co-op, where all new albums are "only $3.57."

A special "Inaugural Handbook" issue, published on January 20, 1973, provided a play-by-play guide to the four-day Nixon inauguration demonstrations by such groups as the yippies, SDS, NPAC and VVAW. On Friday, January 19, there was announced a "Gay Dance" at the Marvin Center at Twenty-first and H Streets Northwest. "Straights invited—Free bar."

The July 27 issue carried a cover story of how on one night, July 23, three different buildings—the Washington Peace Center, Friends Meeting House and Quaker House—were all broken into and ransacked in apparent searches for political files. Oddly, only keys were stolen, despite cameras, tape recorders, typewriters and other easily fenced items lying in open view. No arrests were made.

Going into 1974, the *Rag* was averaging sixteen pages per issue with a press run of thirty-five thousand per week. But money was tight, and a house ad in the January 12, 1974 edition contained a plea for contributions in an unlikely manner—asking readers to be "unsuscribers" by buying a subscription and then having no papers mailed to them. "Then we can spend the money to pay our bills…print more pages, distribute in more places, and possibly even pay some of our writers and production workers."

Editorially, the *Rag* was a powerhouse. A November 30, 1973 cover story by College News Service editor Chip Berlet analyzed the teamster connection to the Nixon administration. Bill Peters unveiled documentation in the January 12, 1974 issue of a plan to add another one thousand inmates to the already overcrowded Lorton prison. The May 2, 1974 issue covered a march of about ten thousand to impeach Richard Nixon.

Finally, on June 13, 1974, the *Daily Rag* called it quits. "There are models of alternative papers around the country that do well," stated a farewell article ironically titled "*Daily Rag* Plans Publishing Empire." "But we are unhappy with our ability to do this while continually struggling for economic survival. We have been a small operation staffed mostly by volunteers, scrounging to pay the printer."

Columnist Jack Schwartz stated in a moment of brutal honesty that he hoped that the five members of the *Rag* who were planning a weekly newspaper in September were successful "and that they don't become as isolated and incompetent as the *Rag* has become when dealing with those not in their small circle."

Despite the admonishment, the *Daily Rag* never returned.

NORTHERN VIRGINIA FREE PRESS

1969–70

The *Northern Virginia Free Press* was a tabloid paper that appeared sometime in 1969 or 1970 out of Springfield, Virginia. Only about two editions were published, selling for fifteen cents.

Staff members were listed collectively, with no titles and hierarchies, including founders Skip Smith and Jim Battista.

While seeming to struggle for an identity with underground powerhouse *Quicksilver Times* publishing so close by, the paper appeared to have large aspirations: volume 1, number 1, published with no date, carried several Liberation News Service stories. The centerspread on pages six and seven carried the travails of navy underground publisher Roger Priest, page

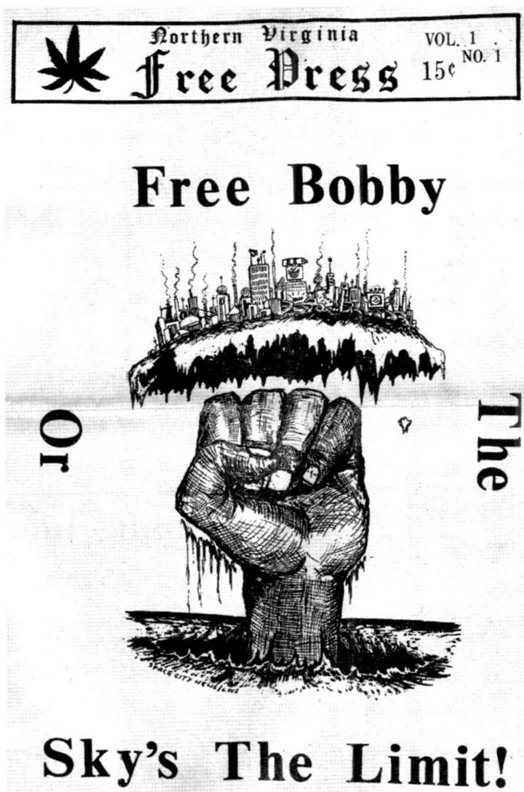

Northern Virginia Free Press, volume 1, number 1, no date. *Courtesy Bonnie Atwood and the VCU Cabell Library Special Collections, Richmond, Virginia.*

ten carried a story titled "Torture in Brazil" and the cover featured a popular illustration (originally published by Houston's *Space City News*) of a black fist bursting from the ground with the phrase "Free Bobby [Seale] or the Sky's the Limit," all from LNS. A syndicated "Fabulous Furry Freak Brothers" cartoon graced page eleven.

There were a few original stories in the debut issue as well. A story by civil rights activist and SSOC member Sue Thrasher titled "Political Repression" was about the gruesome deaths of SNCC leaders Ralph Featherstone and William Payne near Bel Air, Maryland. Page four contained an uncredited story on the D.C. 9 and another by staff member Monty Neill about America's use of chemical weapons in Vietnam, titled "Poison Gas in 'Nam."

Although there was no paid advertising in this issue, the back page contained a full-page (unpaid) ad pulled from *Police* magazine for "Street Cleaner" brand pepper spray: "You know how fast rioters move out when a Pepper Fog© tear smoke generator moves in."

2
CHARLOTTESVILLE AND CENTRAL VIRGINIA

THE NEW VIRGINIA

1965–66

The Southern Christian Leadership Conference's 1965 SCOPE project brought hundreds of northern college students and Freedom Movement supporters into black communities in Alabama, Georgia, North and South Carolina, Florida and Virginia to encourage voter registration and community organization prior to the 1965 Voting Rights Act. In Virginia, some students formed an offshoot called the Virginia Students' Civil Rights Committee (VSCRC), with their connecting device a newsletter called the *New Virginia*.

Some of those working for the VSCRC and contributing to the *New Virginia* would later become active in Virginia's underground press, making this mimeographed newsletter the direct link between Virginia's civil rights and New Left movements. Those members and contributors include Bruce Smith, who was an SSOC co-founder and original editor of the *Richmond Chronicle*; Howard Romaine, who co-founded the *Virginia Weekly* in Charlottesville and the *Great Speckled Bird* in Atlanta; and Bob Foley, who also co-founded the *Richmond Chronicle* and *Bragg Briefs* at Fort Bragg, North Carolina.

Appearing in July 1965, the *New Virginia* was created by Nathaniel Hawthorne, president of the Lunenburg County branch of the NAACP.

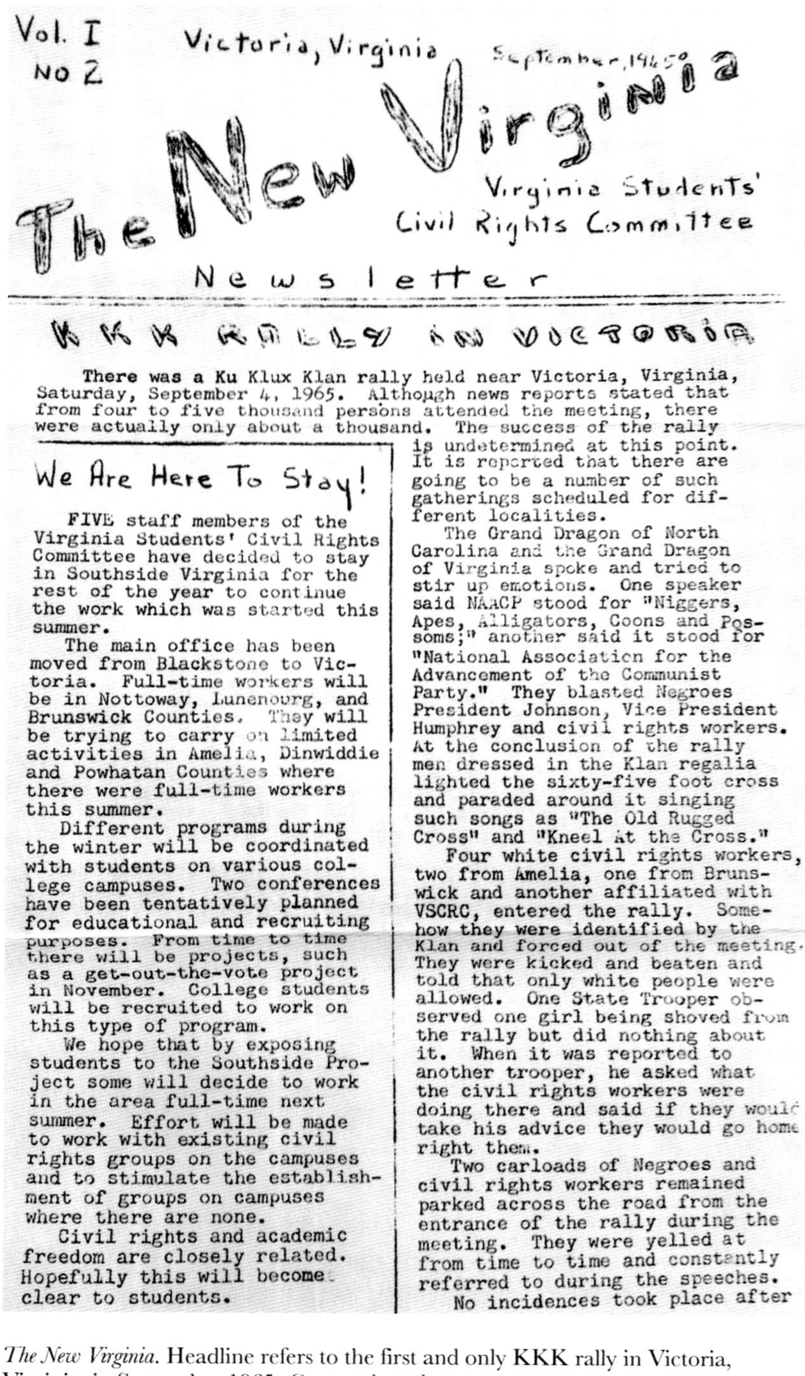

Vol. I
No 2
Victoria, Virginia
September, 1965

The New Virginia

Virginia Students' Civil Rights Committee

Newsletter

KKK RALLY IN VICTORIA

There was a Ku Klux Klan rally held near Victoria, Virginia, Saturday, September 4, 1965. Although news reports stated that from four to five thousand persons attended the meeting, there were actually only about a thousand. The success of the rally is undetermined at this point. It is reported that there are going to be a number of such gatherings scheduled for different localities.

The Grand Dragon of North Carolina and the Grand Dragon of Virginia spoke and tried to stir up emotions. One speaker said NAACP stood for "Niggers, Apes, Alligators, Coons and Possoms;" another said it stood for "National Association for the Advancement of the Communist Party." They blasted Negroes President Johnson, Vice President Humphrey and civil rights workers. At the conclusion of the rally men dressed in the Klan regalia lighted the sixty-five foot cross and paraded around it singing such songs as "The Old Rugged Cross" and "Kneel At the Cross."

Four white civil rights workers, two from Amelia, one from Brunswick and another affiliated with VSCRC, entered the rally. Somehow they were identified by the Klan and forced out of the meeting. They were kicked and beaten and told that only white people were allowed. One State Trooper observed one girl being shoved from the rally but did nothing about it. When it was reported to another trooper, he asked what the civil rights workers were doing there and said if they would take his advice they would go home right them.

Two carloads of Negroes and civil rights workers remained parked across the road from the entrance of the rally during the meeting. They were yelled at from time to time and constantly referred to during the speeches.

No incidences took place after

We Are Here To Stay!

FIVE staff members of the Virginia Students' Civil Rights Committee have decided to stay in Southside Virginia for the rest of the year to continue the work which was started this summer.

The main office has been moved from Blackstone to Victoria. Full-time workers will be in Nottoway, Lunenburg, and Brunswick Counties. They will be trying to carry on limited activities in Amelia, Dinwiddie and Powhatan Counties where there were full-time workers this summer.

Different programs during the winter will be coordinated with students on various college campuses. Two conferences have been tentatively planned for educational and recruiting purposes. From time to time there will be projects, such as a get-out-the-vote project in November. College students will be recruited to work on this type of program.

We hope that by exposing students to the Southside Project some will decide to work in the area full-time next summer. Effort will be made to work with existing civil rights groups on the campuses and to stimulate the establishment of groups on campuses where there are none.

Civil rights and academic freedom are closely related. Hopefully this will become clear to students.

The New Virginia. Headline refers to the first and only KKK rally in Victoria, Virginia, in September 1965. *Courtesy the author.*

Headquartered originally in Blackstone, then Kenbridge and then Victoria, Virginia, the *New Virginia* was a neatly typed, four-page legal-sized mimeographed newsletter that described the activities of the VSCRC staff across Southside Virginia, home of not just some of the poorest blacks in the state (the county's population ranked 405th out of 435 nationwide in annual income, and only 18 percent of the county's blacks were registered to vote) but also the heart of support for massive resistance to school integration during the '50s. The paper eventually had 1,200 subscribers.

The *New Virginia*'s specialty was reporting public harassment of blacks and VSCRC workers in violation of Title II of the 1964 Civil Rights Act. For example, on July 8, a VSCRC and a SCOPE worker, along with "four local Negroes," entered Nelson's Drug Store in Victoria. "They had to wait thirty minutes before they were waited on," the report stated. "The proprietor took the orders of the Negroes but refused to serve the whites."

On July 9, four VSCRC staff members were refused gas at a Texaco station in Amelia Courthouse. "They were then followed by two cars, one with a Mississippi state decal."

On July 10, an integrated group of VSCRC workers were overcharged nineteen cents for each food item at Dick's Place in Amelia County after being told the new higher prices were not yet on the menu. They and thirty-six others returned on July 14 and were charged the normal prices.

But the reporting also covered more sinister events. North Carolina Ku Klux Klansmen were alarmed at the rate of gains by the VSCRC and therefore came into the area to intimidate the organization members and local blacks into abandoning the movement. North Carolina Grand Klokard (lecturer) Marshal Kornegay transferred to Virginia and became Grand Dragon, establishing headquarters in South Hill before launching a recruiting drive throughout the area.

Issue number 2 of the *New Virginia* headlined a KKK rally in Victoria on September 4—the first in that part of the state and attended by between one thousand and four thousand people. The Klan even distributed a brochure stating it would "Make Virginia a hell-on-wheels to the New York, Communistic, racial agitators who seek to use our peaceful Negroes in their filthy 'Black Revolution.'"

At the rally's conclusion, a sixty-five-foot-tall cross was set on fire, and men in full Klan regalia paraded around it singing "The Old Rugged Cross." Despite the nearby presence of VSCRC members and other civil rights workers, no incidents were reported.

Issue number 3, published in October, reported that the local Negro community and the VSCRC responded to the presence of the Klan in Victoria by boycotting businesses. A leaflet circulated throughout the town read, "Negroes unite: don't spend a nickel to support cross-burners and race-haters!"

"A Negro is rarely seen on the downtown streets of Victoria," stated a page-two article on the boycott. "One merchant claims that his business has been reduced $400–$500 every weekend."

The December issue headlined the November 18 shooting of a black Victoria man named Alfonzo Stokes by two white men in a car near the VSCRC headquarters. "We saw a shotgun sticking out of the front window on the left side of the car. The car went about 200 feet past a building, stopped, and fired at us," reported Robert Beverly, who was standing beside Stokes when he was hit. A second shot missed.

Stokes was treated for a head wound. "It was a narrow escape," said Beverly. Another black youth named Edward Glasgow was shot at two nights later. He was uninjured.

Despite local police claiming they had two suspects, no arrests were made in either shooting. The *New Virginia* reported, "Most Negroes feel as though the local police are dragging their feet on the case."

"The night-riders are still loose," Beverly said, "and we wonder who will be next."

The April 1966 issue contained a cover story on the formation in Farmville of a central coordinating committee, made up of students from around the commonwealth. There was news of planning commissions and other dissident publications appearing on Virginia college campuses, including the *Irresponsible Sensationalist* at Old Dominion College in Norfolk and the *Voice*, an independent paper published by high school students in Farmville.

The VSCRC, however, did not enjoy the successes in the summer of 1966 that it had in 1965, as focus was shifting away from civil rights to the war in Vietnam. According to Gregg Michel in his 2004 book *Struggle for a Better South*, the students were "frustrated by the petty disputes that were undermining the VSCRC…believing that the war had become the most salient national issue, wanted to return to campus to help organize student opposition."

New Virginia founder Hawthorne continued his tireless work for racial equality and even continued to sporadically publish the paper himself until 1969. In September 1968, he protested against the weekly *Kenbridge Post* for "discriminatory practices in its classified sections and with segregating its news columns."

"White politicians will try to buy you, scare you or kill you," Hawthorne told a group of blacks and whites at a voter registration kickoff rally at Lunenburg Courthouse in July 1971. "Poor black people and poor white people must get together and be united." He died in 1974.

"I did spend time with Nathaniel, mostly here in Richmond helping him on problem-solving and making allies," wrote Virginia civil rights pioneer Dr. Edward H. Peeples in 2014. "He was sometimes in danger down there."

THE AGITATOR

1969

The *Agitator* was published by Lynchburg SSOC chapter co-founder Jim Lee Scott, and a single issue cost twenty-five cents. At least two mimeographed editions appeared in and around the Lynchburg College area in the spring and early summer of 1969 before Scott went to Charlottesville to publish another paper called *Osawatomie's Soul*.

While little is known of the *Agitator* (the Lynchburg College library did not locate any copies until 2015), it is known that beloved history professor Sheldon Vanauken was a contributor, penning a piece titled "A Position Paper" in issue number 2 in May 1969.

A friend of author C.S. Lewis, an orthodox Catholic and faculty adviser for the Lynchburg SSOC, Vanauken was a staunch advocate of women's rights, even coining the term "sexist" in a letter to the *New York Times* in 1967 (he wrote his own obituary for the *Times* in advance to make sure his creation of the term was noted). He wrote in the *Agitator* that the negative dynamics between the SSOC and the more well-known SDS evolved because of a misconception of the nature of liberalism: "Although liberals are at least a little left of center, there runs through the movement a mindless though understandable hatred of liberals…because of what establishment liberals, such as Rusk and Johnson, are."

"If the radical Movement in America is to be anything more than sound and fury, like an angry child beating on the wall," Vanauken concluded, "we have got to recognize our potential allies as well as what we are really fighting. Heresy, like that of the whole Movement against all liberals, is the surest way to get a Hitler in America."

the all-newed

Ω AGITATOR

MAR-APR 19&69

112

take this brother n may it sWerve you well 25¢

To overthrow the Government of the United States of America by force or by sedition or by firebombs or by draftcard-burnings would be considered a serious crime--especially if it should fail to overthrow the Government of the United States of America. Moreover, even to casually suggest to your friends that you should all get together and overthrow the Government of the United States of America by force or by sedition or by shotguns or by agitational pamphlets would be considered a serious crime. Furthermore, to call for the overthrow of the Government of the United States of America by force or by sedition or by karate or by marijuana-smoking on a Monday would be just as serious a crime as to call for the overthrow of the Government of the United States of America by force or by sedition or by revolvers or by long hair on a Tuesday--or on any other day of the week, for that matter.

If any of you, dear readers, have finally reached the point where you've said to yourself that this present Government of the United States of America has gone too goddamned fuckin far now--with just one too many Vietnamese persons murdered, and with just one too many American young men imprisoned or exiled for refusing to murder those Vietnamese persons, and with just one too many American citizens kept underemployed and underpaid because the present capitalist economy requires it to be that way, and with just one too many American millionaires who do not pay any personal income taxes and damn few corporate income taxes because that's the way the laws in the present Government are set up, and with just one too many fascist oligarchies in Latin America and in Asia and in Africa and in Europe (especially Greece--"the glory that was ______" currently being pillaged by U.S. corporations with the help of U.S. guns) being backed up by the present Government of the U.S.A., and with just one too many Peoples' Revolution against oppressive Governments around the world being barbarously and savagely delayed by the present Gov't. of the U.S.A.--if any of you, dear readers, have thought about these kinds of things long enough to finally come to the logical conclusion that the present Government of the United States of America should and must be overthrown now by whatever means prove necessary--if any of you, dear readers, have reached that conclusion, <u>be careful</u>.

Be careful of what you do and say. Smile at <u>policemen when</u> you see them. Write patriotic letters to the editor of your hometown newspaper. Participate in the two-party-system's democratic process. Attend loyalty parades--or, better yet, march in them. And if you should chance to overhear any kind of talk against the Government, stop up your ears and flee quickly from those people. Take every precaution. You cannot be too careful. For to even <u>think about</u> overthrowing the Government of the United States of <u>America by force</u> or by sedition or by riots or by folksongs (if you happen to be crossing a state line at the time) would be considered a serious crime. Be careful what you think. For God's sake, for the sake of your loved ones, and for the sake of the Free Enterprise System (for "God, Home and Country"--as the National Guard poster so beautifully puts it), be careful what you think. be careful what you think. be careful what you think. be careful what you think. be careful what you think. be c areful what you think. be careful what you think. be careful what you think. be careful what you think. be careful what you think. be caref ul what you think. be careful what you think. be careful what you thi nk. be careful what you think. be careful what you think. be careful what you think. be careful what you think. be careful what you think. be careful what you think. be careful what you think. be careful what you think. be careful what you think. be careful what you think. be c areful what you think. be careful what you think. be careful what you think. be careful what you think. be careful what you think. be caref ul what you think. be careful what you think. be careful what you thi nk. be happy in your work. be careful what you think. be careful what you think. be careful what you think. be careful what you think. be c areful what you think. be careful what you think. be careful what you think. be careful what you think. be careful what you think. be caref ul what you think. be careful what you think. be careful what you thi

The Agitator, March–April 1969. *Courtesy the David M. Rubenstein Rare Book & Manuscript Library, Duke University, Chapel Hill, North Carolina.*

Former student David Hartman wrote at theimaginativeconservative.org that "Vanauken said if any of us was arrested for anti-war activities—which at that time consisted of picketing the Lynchburg post office, the only federal building in town—all we had to do was call him and he would post bond."

"Sheldon Vanauken was a good friend and often went to bat for students who challenged the administration," wrote former Lynchburg student and SSOC co-founder Bruce Smith in 2014. "He was the most active faculty sponsor of a SSOC chapter that I am aware of."

"If any of you, dear readers, have…finally come to the logical conclusion that the present government of the United States of America should and must be overthrown now by whatever means prove necessary," warned Scott on the front page of the March–April 1969 debut issue, "be careful."

Osawatomie's Soul

1969

Bearing no relation to the Weather Underground newspaper *Osawatomie*, which was published in 1975, *Osawatomie's Soul* (*OS*) was created by Jim Lee Scott under the pseudonym James Lee Jackson (presumably after the civil rights protestor killed by an Alabama state trooper in 1965) and published in July 1969 by the Virginia Organizing Committee in the Community, University and Elsewhere (VOC-CUE) in Charlottesville, Virginia.

OS's fourteen boisterous mimeographed pages were packed with countercultural news and quotes by Castro, Mao, the Bible and Helen Keller. There were reprints from Liberation News Service and other topical publications including *Hard Times* and *Anarchos*. There was even room for bold insider humor and poetry, including a powerful antiwar poem by *Richmond Chronicle* editor Nina Sabaroff titled "Coming Home."

The lead story in a surviving issue chronicled the June 1969 Mt. Beulah meeting of the SSOC, which voted to disband itself—a move that left the writer (one of the founding members) cold. "Personally, I'm going to be listening to Bob Dylan and Johnny Cash and smoking what I want and writing what I want and just generally intercoursing with mine [*sic*] fellow revolutionary brothers and sisters."

Page three contained a reprint of a Barry Barkan story from the *Richmond Afro-American* of a disturbance in Petersburg involving over four hundred

Osawatomie's Soul

a publication of the Virginia Organizing Committee in the Community, University & Elsewhere (VOC-CUE)

Volume I, Number 1, Revolution #4, July 1969. Price-10¢ or so...

"...but his soul goes marching on..."
--Olde Civil-War Song

Could any whites join his OAAU? 'If John Brown were alive, maybe him.' ... 'He smiled and chuckled, but he was in dead earnest.'"
--The Autobiography of Malcolm X, pages 416-7.

"You figure it out."
--"Snake," in conversation.

* *
$ $
? ?

<u>The Arbitrator</u>,
a Regular Red by
James Lee Jackson.

("Every Communist must grasp the truth, 'Political power grows out of the barrel of a gun.'"--Mao Tse-tung, <u>Little Red Book</u> page 61.

'And ye shall know the truth, and the truth shall make you free.'"--Jesus Nazarene, <u>John</u>8:32.

Now I've got one more quote to do, and if there are any super-radical "Marxist" types out there who want to charge "tailism!", or any super-literary types who wish to label my literary style as "derivisionist"--well, all of you types should get together and have a pure ball; in other words--voc-cue! So here's another quote:

"The revolution is not made for the sake of revolution itself... Revolutions are made only with the purpose of creating a happier man."--Fidel Castro

And I wish to report that I came away from the Mount Beulah thing in Mississippi June 5-10 feeling <u>everything except</u> happy. And I strongly suspect that I was far from alone in that regard. I noticed that the PL-SDS leaders held another of their innumerable closed caucuses on the last day of the Beulah thing. This was after the "vote to dissolve SSOC" had been pulled off. This final, post-mortem caucus had as its purpose, I suppose, to discuss the tactics which they used to pull it off, and "how we could have done it better," etc. I sure hope that the PL-SDS leaders went through some meaningful and fruitful self-criticism in their final closed caucus of the convention, because I for one <u>will not abide</u> any more

(continued on page 2)

The Washington Free Press says that Bob Dylan and several of his friends are going to give a free concert at Bob's farm near Woodstock, New York, on or about August 13. We are chartering three ocean liners to make the trip. We shall be sailing from Charlottesville on or about July 28, passing by way of Oyster Bay, and so should dock in Woodstock well in time. Tickets are free as thee. Interested people should contact us here at the VOC-CUE House by letter, phone, telegraph, wireless, telepathic ESP, smoke signals, or drums. Yall come. A good time will be had by all.

--(for the Committee)
James Lee Jackson

* * * * * * * *

SCEF WARNS AGAINST FASCISM

EDWARDS, Miss. (LNS)--The board of the Southern Conference Educational Fund (SCEF) says that "a repressive, fascist-like society and police state is an ominous, threatening possibility. Let us all who advocate social change reject factionalism and infighting, and unite instead against the common foe of reaction and repression in all its guises," the board urged.

The statement was made in one of several resolutions adopted at a recent meeting here. SCEF is a South-wide interracial group working to end war, poverty, racism, and denial of civil liberties in the South.

The board declared that more and more people see the need for ending the war in Vietnam and using the money to feed the hungry, guarantee a living wage and a decent income to all Americans, and redistribute the power and wealth now held by a few people.

Osawatomie's Soul, no date. *Courtesy Social Movements Collection, Small Special Collections, University of Virginia Library, Charlottesville, Virginia.*

demonstrators, "some as young as 10 or 12," following an alleged rape of a fourteen-year-old black girl by a white Petersburg police officer.

Pages seven through ten contained a long article titled "Counterinsurgency Research and War Profiteering in Virginia" by A.P. Long, which diagrammed a hierarchy of companies all branching from a Falls Church, Virginia firm called Melpar, Incorporated, which provided chemical and electronic warfare research.

Scott blamed his embrace of the Youth International (yippie) Movement for the paper's bad financial situation. "Komrades…unless we can get some bread from sales and contributions for this first issue, the chances are slim indeed there will be a second issue…We're trying to get a job, but damn if it don't look like they got a ban on hiring yippies around here."

The yippie movement was in fact not a movement at all but a media myth created by Abbie Hoffman, Jerry Rubin, Ed Sanders, Stu Albert and a few friends. But their actions were reported by the mainstream press as though it was a movement of thousands.

OS almost unbelievably got traction across the United States. Scott's close friend Bruce Smith said in 2014 that after attending the Black Panther convention in Oakland during late summer 1969, they stopped by Delano, California, to support the striking United Farm Workers. "When they heard the editor of *Osawatamie's Soul* was at the door, everyone came out to meet Jim Lee," wrote Smith.

Scott died in 2013.

THE ICONOCLAST AND THE VIRGINIA WEEKLY

1967–72

This is the way civilizations begin to die.
—President Richard Nixon on student agitation, reported in Commonweal *magazine, April 11, 1969*

From the mid-'60s into 1971, the University of Virginia (UVa) at Charlottesville was Virginia's civil rights and New Left activism headquarters. Composed of rights advocates, local and university-affiliated liberals and students, it was the center of operations for the Students for Social Action (SSA) and the SSOC, an organization that developed out of the Student Nonviolent Coordinating Committee in 1964. University

THE ICONOCLAST

OUR PURPOSE
by Robert Dewart

This being the first issue of the Iconoclast, it seems proper to include a statement of the editorial policy to be pursued by this paper, its origins, its means, and its objectives.

The paper grew out of general dissatisfaction with the other publications at the University, primarily the Cavalier Daily. It is felt that the vital social and political issues of the day find no public expression at the University. The Cavalier Daily virtually ignores issues which arouse lively debate elsewhere: the undeclared war in Vietnam, racial discrimination in all phases of life, academic freedom at American universities, lack of responsible student government, the collateral existence of poverty and the affluent society, substandard public education, lack of justice in our legal system, and as many others.

We hope to help rectify this condition by offerring an open forum where students and faculty members can debate these issues. The Iconoclast is published by the Students for Social Action, but not merely for that group. It is hoped that other members of the University community will read it and submit articles for it. All opinions expressed in the Iconoclast are only those of the author of each particular article and do not necessarily reflect the opinion of any member of the S.S.A. or the editor.

The Iconoclast is distributed on the grounds without charge. Contributions will be needed in order to support future editions. Checks should be made payable to the Iconoclast, c/o Robert Dewart, 167 Chancellor St., Charlottesville, Va.

TOKENISM AT UVA
by Steve Wise

The heritage of racial segregation confronts us in practically all phases of life. Now in the sixties when partial efforts have been made to tear away the legal barriers, the social, economic, and political barriers stand out more clearly for those who care to look. Perhaps the most critical barrier to a full participation in American society is that of education. As the technological and cybernetic revolutions threaten to move out of control, segregation's victims face a bleak future without the necessary education to take advantage of the new cybernetic society just dawning.

The University, as the foremost institution of public education in Virginia, ought to play a major role in the eradication of the gross inequities inherited from past segregation. Is the University meeting this responsibility? The existing racial imbalance here provides mute evidence that this responsibility has not yet begun to be faced.

Official policy states that no segregation exists; that all qualified applicants will be admitted; that UVA has done all that it can do. Yet there is no strenuous effort being made to encourage Negroes to enter the University. Very little is done in the way of recruiting. Recruiters go to "white" high schools, not to "Negro" high schools. Negro students may be invited (though not

The Iconoclast, no date. *Courtesy Social Movements Collection, Small Special Collections, University of Virginia Library, Charlottesville, Virginia.*

students were also instrumental in founding the Virginia Students' Civil Rights Committee, an original group that did critical civil rights work in 1965 in southern Virginia.

Like most similar student organizations, the SSA realized that it could not rely on the relatively conservative student newspaper the *Cavalier Daily* to accurately communicate its message, so the founders created the university's first "insurgent newspaper," the *Iconoclast*.

Editor Robert Dewart wrote in volume 1, number 1 that the paper "grew out of general dissatisfaction with the other publications at the University, primarily the *Cavalier Daily*...[which] virtually ignores issues which arouse lively debate elsewhere."

"Dewart and some other history students were the main authors," said Thomas Gardner in 2014 of the *Iconoclast*. "I think it was mimeographed in the basement of Westminster church."

Other articles in that first issue included Gardner's "Student Council: A Serious Critique" and a piece by Steve Wise titled "Tokenism at UVA," which addressed the university's virtually nonexistent recruitment of black students.

Dewart's article "Direct Democracy in Action" described the SSA's first on-campus Vietnam protest, held on February 12, 1966, in front of Alderman Library. The story reported how two policemen watched from a car while three hundred "hostile" students surrounded the twenty-three protestors and pelted them with snowballs while other members of the academic community "restrained themselves to the extent of shouting profanity at the women and taunting others with racial slurs."

The second and final issue featured an article by Roger Hickey highlighting the hypocrisy of the university for hosting the all-black Harlem Globetrotters yet refusing to recruit "Negro athletes."

The *Virginia Weekly*, first appearing on February 13, 1967, was not a direct offshoot of the *Iconoclast*. The premiere issue appeared less like an underground paper and more a traditional old Virginia tabloid, steeped in a seersucker conservative look. Founded by Howard Romaine, Donald Watson and Franklin Delano, the paper stated it was an "independent, student-operated newspaper at the University of Virginia," with offices at 2256 Ivy Road and printed at the *Orange Review* newspaper in Orange, Virginia.

"We hope that our little paper can be an outlet for opinion and news that other, more tradition-oriented media around the Grounds may miss or, perchance, ignore," stated an editorial in volume 1, number 1 in defiance of its own traditional appearance. "We do not seek to cast aspersions on those who admire what is venerable and heavy with tradition. We just like newness."

Romaine said that the SSOC's Ed Hamlett gave a $300 grant to the UVa chapter to start the *Virginia Weekly*, "to turn the staid University of Virginia into a Berkeley of the South." "[The paper] was primarily my idea," Romaine wrote, "although it was conceived in the living room of my

The Virginia Weekly 10c

Volume I, Number 2 | Charlottesville, Virginia | 10 Cents | February 20, 1967

Charlottesville Peace Lobby Organized

A group of Charlottesville citizens recently announced the formation of a local peace lobby. Mrs. Dieta Jehle and Mrs. Carolyn Worrall are co-ordinating transportation and housing for the group's planned trip to Washington on Tuesday, Feb. 28. They plan to talk with Senators and Congressmen about peace in Viet Nam.

The program is sponsored nationally by thirteen different church groups. Transportation will be available for anyone desiring to participate in the program. Free overnight accomodations will be provided by the Friend's Committee on National Legislation. The Committee will also coordinate meals, provide an orientation session and discussion sections on the war.

Interested people may contact Mrs. Jehle at 293-3328 or Mrs. Worrall at 293-1074.

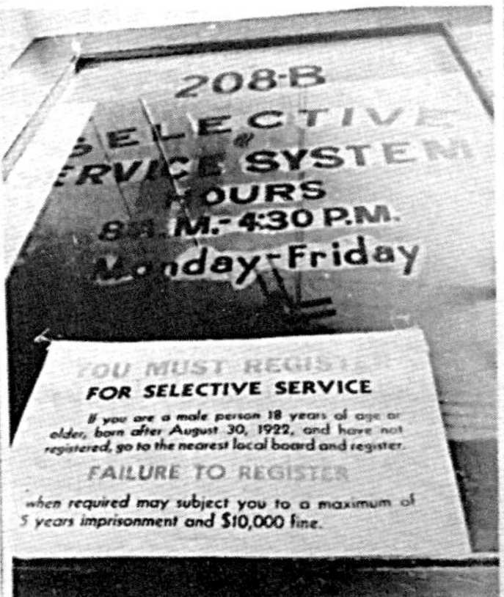

Virginia Weekly Photo by Dick Johnston

Leaders Demand Draft Changes

Compiled from CPS

Seventeen youth leaders representing the political spectrum from the left-wing Students for a Democratic Society (SDS) to the right-wing Young Americans for Freedom (YAF), called early this month in Washington, D.C. for abolition of the draft and the creation of new programs for voluntary national service.

They charged that "the present draft system with its inherent injustices is incompatible with traditional American principles of individual freedom within a democratic society."

The meeting marked the first time that such a diverse group had reached agreement on a statement of major policy. Although the participants signed the statements as individuals, it was expected that most of the organizations represented would adopt the position taken. These organizations must meet in convention to adopt statements of official policy.

In introducing the conference statement, Sherman B. Chickering, the publisher of Moderator magazine, stated, "No one in government seems aware of how widespread and deep runs the resentment toward the draft among young people."

Chickering, whose magazine sponsored the meeting, said government officials did not realize "that the country is in danger of losing the loyalty of an entire generation of Americans." He suggested that President Johnson's State of the Union address "didn't have a word for young people on any subject."

In calling for a program of voluntary national service, the conference participants said, "An urgent need exists within our society for young people to become involved in the elimination of such social ills as ignorance, poverty, racial discrimination and war."

Chickering announced the creation of a Student Serving Society to act as a registry of individuals willing to serve voluntarily to correct social problems. A 50-cent fee will be charged to help maintain the registry.

The magazine hopes that at least 500,000 students will enroll in the program "to total up the individual commitments to serve, and to make known the willingness of thousands of students to serve their society."

One of the signers of the statement, Joseph Higdon, Southern recruitment director for the Peace Corps, commented that as a southerner he saw voluntary national service "as a means of uniting the South with the rest of the country on a basis other than militarism."

Viewing "service as the way and volunteering as the means," Higdon said he came to the meeting "with Ferlinghetti, the poet, to say that I am 'waiting for the American Eagle to spread its wings and straighten up and fly right'."

Another statement was issued by nine religious student groups that said, in part, "We believe that the draft should be abolished not only because it supports our extensive use of military force, but also because conscription, by its coercive nature, stifles growth and freedom of conscience."

VA. STUDENT LEADER JOINS RADICALS

John Witeck, sole U. Va. student at the conference, represented the Roman Catholic Newman Student Foundation as its national affairs vice president. He said the present draft system is "inadequate with regard to conscientious objection" because of the stipulation that objection to military service must be based on religious belief. He also signed the more militant statement introduced by SDS which reaffirms its "opposition to conscription in any form" and encourages all young men to resist the draft. It also proposed a union of draft resisters, utilizing direct action tactics including "anti-war education for potential inductees."

Witeck explained, "If the program is immoral, as we all agreed it was, then it follows logically that it must be actively opposed." He said, "it is also impossible to separate the issue of the war in Viet Nam, for its immorality dictates a similar obligation of resistance."

Witeck plans to implement opposition locally by calling on the Student Council to sponsor an educational program on the draft. He says, "it's urgent at least to get the issue raised, students' views aired and student opinion mobilized before the Congress takes up the issue in June."

He stated further that "many students do not want to raise the issue of the draft, for they are cloaked in the protective apathy provided by their 2-S status. It's legalized draft dodging. Many of them are all for the war as long as someone else will do their fighting for them."

Those on record as favoring voluntary national service are representatives from the U.S. Youth Council, NSA, SDS, YAF National Newman Club Federation, UCCF, Union Theological Seminary, University Christian Movement, Young Men's Christian Association, College Young Democratic Clubs of American Friends Service Committee, National Association for the Advancement of Colored People, the Peace Corps, and Young Women's Christian Association.

Most of the organizations represented at the meeting are members of the United States Youth Council (USYC), which will stage a national meeting to discuss voluntary service in Washington in early March.

Bureaucratic Secrecy Fails To Hide Facts

Matters of direct interest to students do not concern them, implied Robert J. Harris, Dean of the Faculty of Arts and Sciences, when interviewed by The Virginia Weekly last Tuesday.

Harris refused the press a copy of the agenda for the next faculty meeting, scheduled for February 23 in Room 202 of Rouss Hall at 4 p.m. Harris stated that these faculty meetings are for faculty alone. He admitted that student opinion would be a valuable consideration in such matters, but he had no answer when asked how there can be student opinion if students are uninformed.

Continuing his objections, Harris said that some faculty members had not been informed of the meeting and might resent seeing their business in the Weekly. He insisted that the agenda be kept secret until after the meeting and refused to allow members of the press to attend the meeting.

Obtaining an agenda from one of the faculty, it is apparent that the proposals to be discussed are of important concern to the students. These are the topics for consideration that Harris says "concern faculty alone":

Library Proposals

The Library Committee headed by Professor Lester Beaurline of the English department, recommends that the normal check-out period "for undergraduates and graduate students should be two weeks." Doctoral candidates, faculty and staff would have semester privileges but would be required to return everything at the end of each semester." "Bound and unbound periodicals" should not leave the building overnight." Additional, inexpensive copying machine should be installed"; "a door-check. . .should be maintained on the building as soon as feasible." Citing that no student had ever been convicted of an honor violation for removing books from the library, that the faculty are "often the worst offenders" in failing to check out books, that one hundred books on Shakespeare and about a thousand in American history, that many popular reference volumes have to "be hidden" behind the reference desk, the Committee recommended, in full agreement with Mr. Wylie, the head librarian, that these steps be taken.

Educational Policy

The Committee on Educational Policy, Chairmaned by Alfred Fernbach, professor of government and foreign affairs, "in order to strengthen the work of the college and assure that the ROTC programs do not absorb too many of the elective courses of students enrolled in their programs," recommended that a maximum of twelve semester hours of ROTC courses be credited toward the degree requirement of 120 hours.

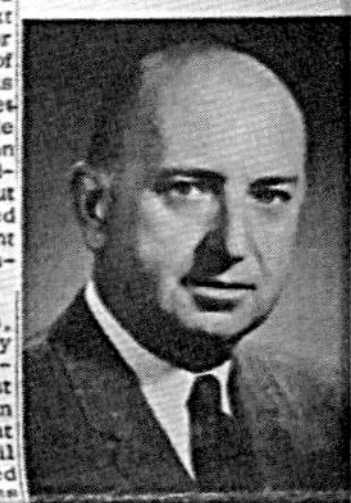

Harris

Also recommended, after a study of similar programs at universities with which Virginia likes to be compared, was a special program for incoming first-year men who show promising scholarship but whose backgrounds "require special academic preparations to meet our standards." Special summer sessions prior to unconditional admission and tutorial programs after admission are features of the program.

New Courses

The Committee on Academic Legislation recommends the addition on two courses in American government, which will be concerned with the role of public administration in contemporary government and with the contemporary relations of national, state, and local governments; two courses in history which will focus on the major trends in ancient and modern Chinese thought; and three courses in advanced undergraduate psychology - an introduction to the experimental study of the psychological and physiological bases of behavior, a course in which an original experimental project will be undertaken, and a seminar in a current problem area of psychology.

These are the major points to be acted on by the Faculty of Arts and Sciences and problems of major concern to students interested in their library, the academic curriculum, and the University in general. It seems impossible to understand the secrecy of Dean Harris concerning these matters.

The Virginia Weekly, February 20, 1967. *Courtesy Small Special Collections, University of Virginia Library, Charlottesville, Virginia.*

off-campus house, with my wife, and fellow UVa grad student Anne Cooke Romaine, now deceased. The first issues were laid out and typed on our apartment living room floor."

"It was deliberately conservative in presentation to make its astounding claims more credible," he added, explaining that the look better reflected their own scholarly and "culturally imbibed conservatism" at the time.

Romaine said since the "frat-party oriented" *Cavalier Daily* was published Tuesday through Friday, the *Weekly* came out on Mondays.

Stories in that first auspicious four-page issue pushed forward the gains made by pioneering civil rights and New Left groups led by people like Romaine (who had served as national chairman of the SSOC), Steve Wise, Tom Gardner, David Nolan and Anne Cook Romaine, among others. A page-one story about the "radical middle" featured former student body president Alan Friedberg, who, with a contingent of thirty-eight other non-UVa students, met with Secretary of State Dean Rusk regarding U.S. foreign policy in light of the Vietnam buildup.

"The *Virginia Weekly* was 'conscious' of a world ethical rejection of the various 'rationales' for segregation and voting rights discrimination," Romaine said of the relationship the paper shared with the civil rights movement. A striking example of that awareness was its coverage of the Thomas Wansley trial in Lynchburg, called "the most atrocious case in south history" and highlighted in the March 13, 1967 issue. Wansley was a twenty-two-year-old black male convicted and sentenced to three death sentences in 1963 for the rape and robbery of two women. The Virginia Supreme Court of Appeals threw out the convictions due to civil rights violations and ordered a new trial on March 18, 1967. Wansley's attorneys were William Kunstler and Philip Hirschkop—familiar names to the New Left. "This is one black life that Virginia is not going to get," Hirschkop declared in a legal forum in the UVa Law School lounge.

Wansley was again found guilty and sentenced to life plus twenty years by an all-white jury in the rape of the fifty-seven-year-old white woman. He was released by U.S. District Court judge Robert Merhige Jr. in 1973, stating that "shockingly prejudiced and highly-inflammatory" newspaper coverage in 1963 jeopardized his chances of getting a fair trial. Despite being told to "get out of Virginia" for his own safety by several acquaintances, Wansley stayed, becoming a truck driver in Harrisonburg. He died in 2012.

In May 1967, UVa's Patrick Henry society—objecting to the *Weekly*'s analysis of a Barry Goldwater speech—mailed threatening letters to its

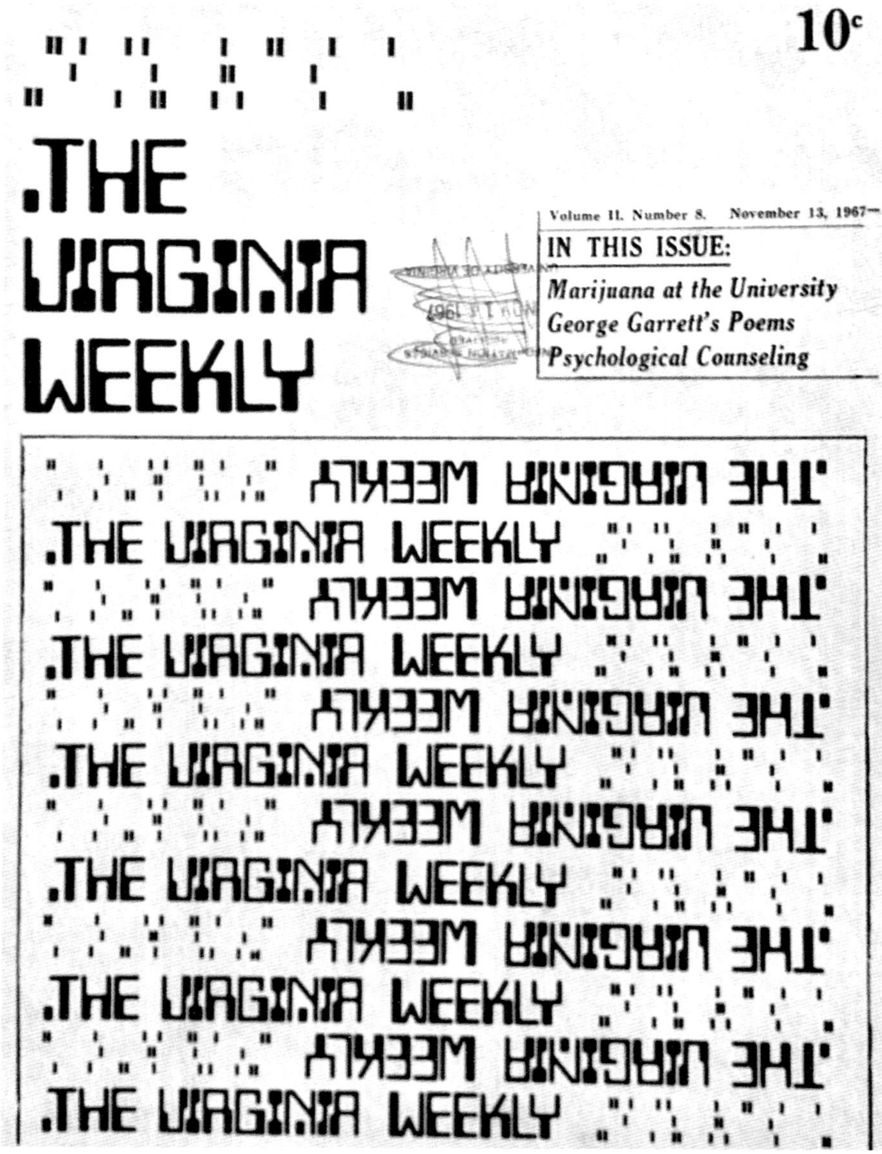
10c

THE VIRGINIA WEEKLY

Volume II. Number 8. November 13, 1967

IN THIS ISSUE:

Marijuana at the University

George Garrett's Poems

Psychological Counseling

The Virginia Weekly, November 13, 1967. *Courtesy Small Special Collections, University of Virginia Library, Charlottesville, Virginia.*

advertisers, including Aunt Jemima's Pancake House, Gus' Steak House and Brookwood Nursery and Kindergarten. "Advertising in a journalistically irresponsible publication can have harmful effects on your business because people will tend to associate you with the nature of the publication," stated the letter in part.

After a summer off, the September 11, 1967 edition of the *Weekly* promised less straight news and "more book reviews, and more and longer pieces of opinion, analyses and commentary." Undaunted by the Patrick Henry Society letter, all its previous advertisers seemed to have returned, including many new ones.

"The *Weekly* remains unabashedly liberal in its editorial views but stands ready to publish meritorious articles from those of contrary opinions."

Throughout the rest of 1967, each edition focused on campus events mixed with headlines from the rapidly emerging New Left movement, including the 1967 march on the Pentagon and the escalating antiwar fervor on campus, the USS *Pueblo* crisis and articles and interviews on LSD and marijuana.

The April 4, 1968 assassination of Dr. Martin Luther King Jr. had a lasting impact on UVa and the Charlottesville community. At a rally near the university campus, Charlottesville SNCC chairman James "Rat" Brown told students that to respect Dr. King's memory, they should demand union wages for all campus employees and support their right to organize—words that drew the attention of Charlottesville Commonwealth attorney J.T. Camblos. Then on April 22, Brown gave a speech directed at angry black students at newly integrated Lane High School, who felt they were being ignored by the white faculty and administrators during SSOC's "Ten Days of Secession." Brown concluded the controversial speech by saying, "I don't teach violence, but I don't teach turning the other cheek either. And if it should come down to the question of living or dying, make it 'even Steven.' I say, if you are going to be killed, take a white with you."

That fall, state police had to be called in to stop rioting in black neighborhoods. Two black policemen's homes were attacked, and a fire bomb was thrown into a white-owned business and inside Lane High School, causing minor damage.

Galvanized by racial tensions, the assassination of Robert Kennedy and the brutal behavior of the Chicago police at the Democratic convention, the Charlottesville chapter of the SSOC sought recognition as a legitimate UVa student organization. Al Long and Don Fleck wrote on the application that the goal of the organization was "the destruction of the University as a perpetuator of traditional social values and creation of a University that can lead to a revolutionary movement in Virginia."

The December 9, 1968 issue featured an article by Arthur "Bud" Ogle about the unjust arrest of "Rat" Brown when he was charged with stealing a bag of nickels from the Charlottesville Post Office that had supposedly been bugged with an electronic tracking device. "The warrant, the paucity of evidence, the total lack of eye-witnesses, the strange behavior and the large number of eager law enforcement officers involved all indicate a tip-off, a frame-up, an innocent man," said the *Weekly*. "Let's hope we don't 'kill a Mockingbird' or allow one to be killed."

While the FBI declined to take legal action, Brown was prosecuted by Camblos and convicted in state court of federal mail theft—a first. Obviously Brown had been singled out: in previous years, several Charlottesville postal employees had allegedly been charged with stealing U.S. mail, but they were fired or transferred to other post offices, neither arrested nor charged with felony theft.

In March 1971, Brown was sentenced to five years in the state penitentiary. After serving ten months, he went on work release at the Richmond city jail. On parole, he was hired and trained as a staff member of Rubicon, a drug treatment program.

In the spring of 1969, Tom Gardner returned to UVa to complete his degree requirements just as a new group called the Radical Student Union (RSU), along with the SSOC, was organizing a protest against the university's board of visitors' refusal to embrace campus racial equality. They also demanded the ouster of board member and Danville attorney C. Stuart Wheatley, who, in the late 1950s, was a proponent of massive resistance to school integration. In a June 19, 1969 *Washington Post* interview, Wheatley disagreed that he was a racist, "especially not a racist pig as they wrote on my car." University student council ultimately voted down Wheatley's removal from the board.

Emboldened by several successful protests, students formed the Virginia Progressive Party (VPP), and their slate of delegates, headed by Tom Gardner, won the largest margins of victory in student council history. This new council immediately went to work with the ACLU to recruit more black and female students.

UVa's New Left had thus created a formidable student movement: the VPP controlled the student council, the RSU was strong and well organized and the *Virginia Weekly*, under editor Judy Wellman, was looking (and sounding) more and more like an angry metropolitan underground paper and enjoying wide readership.

Despite the *Weekly*'s financial troubles (it began publishing biweekly as a result), writers such as Tom Gardner turned in remarkable in-depth stories on such controversies as unionizing UVa employees, the 1969 post office strike and the massive class boycott by nine hundred students at Mississippi Valley State College on February 10.

The UVa administration and board of visitors got so upset at the surging New Left activity that Rector Frank Rogers said at his retirement that "eight years ago you couldn't conceive of that terrible bunch of thugs that now make themselves so articulate at the university."

While planning a protest against President Nixon's ordered invasion of Cambodia in May 1970, news of the shootings of four students at Kent State resounded across every campus in America. The refusal of Shannon to sign a student-drafted telegram to Nixon led eighty students to temporarily occupy the ROTC offices at Maury Hall. A firebomb thrown that night through a window in Halsey Hall caused no damage.

After a memorial service for the victims of Kent State, supporters of a proposed student strike met at Newcomb Hall to draw up a list of nine demands. They included prohibiting university police from carrying firearms for the duration of the strike, removing all ROTC from campus, terminating research sponsored by the defense department and demanding that administration set a goal of 20 percent black enrollment.

Armed with the slogan "Shut it down, open it up," as much as 80 percent of the student body picketed and skipped class on "Freedom Day," May 6, which, in a remarkable coincidence, also included joint appearances by renowned ACLU attorney William Kunstler and yippie co-founder Jerry Rubin. An estimated nine thousand students heard Kunstler implore the students to "shut down the University in order to stop the war," and a minor scuffle broke out when he was booed by five members of George Wallace's American Independent Party. Jerry Rubin's speech was a rambling, incoherent tirade "laced with obscenities," according to the *Charlottesville Daily Progress*, but it didn't stop a huge crowd from marching to President Shannon's house and then back to again occupy Maury Hall. Around 1:30 a.m., smoke chased the students from Maury, with some speculating a mattress was set on fire in the basement by the administration to force the students out.

The next day, two hundred police in full riot gear clashed with one thousand students at Routes 250 and 29. Dean Alan Williams and some other administrators convinced the police to pull back to avoid a full-blown riot after two officers and a WINA news reporter were injured by flying rocks.

On Friday, after a full day of picketing and skipping classes, Commonwealth attorney Camblos invoked the "Riot Act," which outlawed any gathering of three or more people. Mistakenly thinking that the approaching riot police would not attack them on university property, hundreds of students massing on Emmett Street in a "honk for peace" rally fled into unlocked university buildings only to be dragged out and taken into custody.

Sixty-eight arrests were made, including former student council president and ordained Presbyterian minister Bud Ogle, a frat brother's father visiting for the weekend, a groundskeeper and a pizza delivery driver. Camblos told the *Daily Progress* the extreme measures were necessary but admitted "we arrested some we shouldn't have arrested."

On Saturday, while many students were in D.C. for an antiwar rally, President Shannon convinced the state police to leave the grounds. On Sunday, he surprised everyone with a forty-five-minute speech. "This week has brought us to the brink of disaster," he told a crowd of about four thousand, "but we are still intact as a university."

He drew strong applause declaring "unequivocal support for full access, opportunity and participation in the university for women and black students." He was met with the loudest cheers and raised fists of solidarity when he said he had conveyed the frustration and alienation of the students in a letter to Senators Harry F. Byrd and William Spong.

The conservative board of visitors, the *Richmond Times-Dispatch* editorial page and even Governor Linwood Holton castigated Shannon's "appeasement" of the demonstrators, with Holton even threatening to yank state funding. The student movement rallied behind Shannon, however, and he became the strike's most unlikely hero.

Because of publishing schedules, the *Virginia Weekly* missed the events of May 1970, having to settle for editorializing them when it resumed publication the following September. "Last fall Edgar F. Shannon…held candles with peace marchers in front of his home," reported the September 14, 1970 edition, months after the goodwill had faded. "But now that students have begun to demand an end to university complicity in the war machine, his tune has changed."

During the strike (and with the absence of the *Weekly*), some students anonymously published an alternative underground paper called the *Sally Hemings*, named for the female slave with whom Thomas Jefferson allegedly had a family. "This strike has brought to many of us an awareness of the need for better relations with the community," stated an undated volume 1, number 10.

On May 11, the student strike was approved with 68 percent of the vote. Six of the nine demands were accepted, ensuring the continuation of the strike for the remaining few weeks of the semester. At that point, President Shannon proposed options for students, including accepting whatever grade they had on May 1 or finishing the work and taking exams if desired.

Some students were rescued by the strike. "The Strike of 1970 saved my academic ass; given how unsophisticated I was about things political at the time," said former student and 1973 publisher of *AAIEE!* magazine Orlan Cannon in 2013.

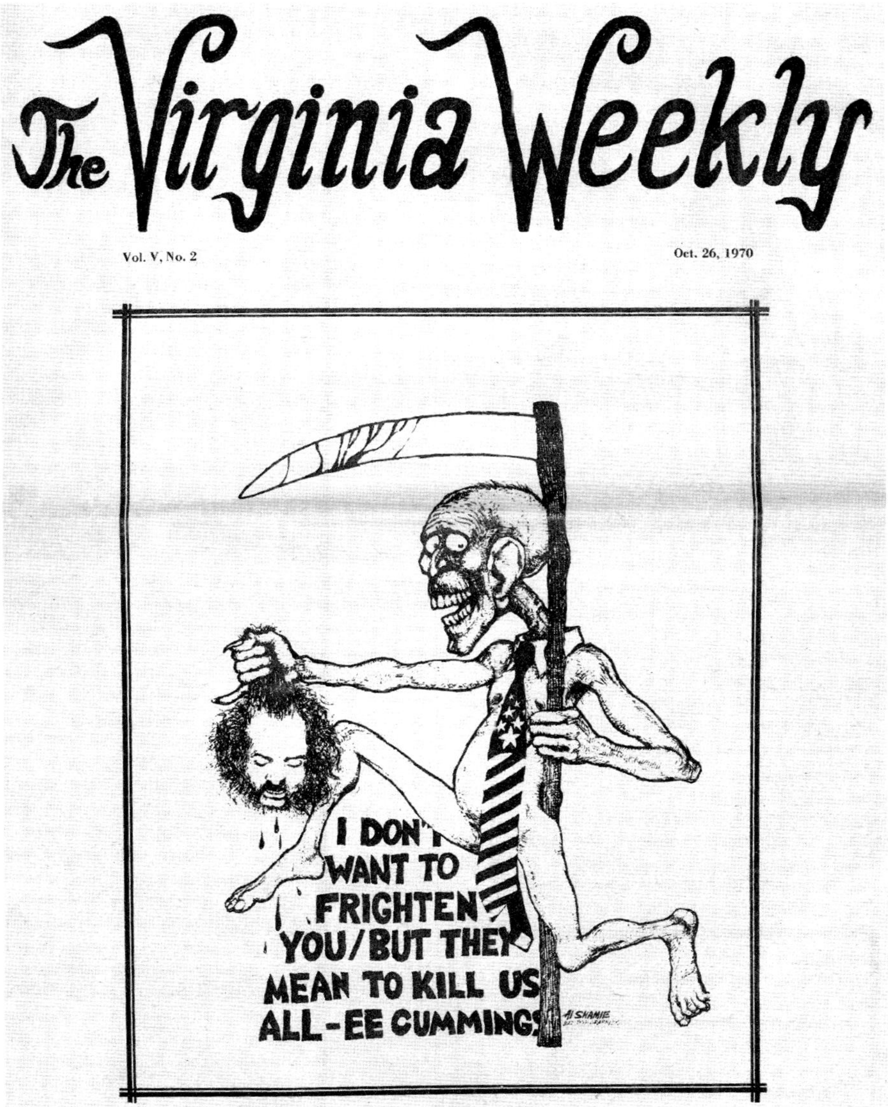

The Virginia Weekly, October 26, 1970. *Courtesy Small Special Collections, University of Virginia Library, Charlottesville, Virginia.*

Three students were formally charged with incitements related to the strike, with *Weekly* staff member Tom Doran taking the worst hit (for allegedly breaking windows and perjuring himself). Doran was a former student reapplying to the university when he participated in the strike, bolstering the university's argument that "outside agitators" were primarily responsible for the disturbances. The *Weekly* set up a defense fund for him at the Prism Coffee House on Rugby Road. Incredibly, within one month, the $5,000 bail was raised and Doran was cleared.

From the fall of 1970 into the spring of 1971, the demonstrations died down, but the *Virginia Weekly* became more antiauthoritarian and reflective of the plight of indigent Virginia blacks, coal miners, striking General Electric employees, gays and working poor.

The December 7, 1970 edition described how UVa complicated a proposed speaking invitation offered by the *Weekly* to Black Panther Huey Newton by insisting on onerous charges for its facilities and refusing to allow members of the Black Panther Party to frisk people attending the speech. Also with this issue, the paper began exposing FBI agents, informers and undercover narcotics officers around campus.

With the February 8, 1971 issue, the *Weekly* found itself in deep trouble with the Commonwealth of Virginia over an advertisement on page two placed by the Women's Pavilion in New York City that stated, "Unwanted Pregnancy Let Us Help You. Abortions are now legal in New York." The ad went on to offer abortion placement and information in accredited hospitals and clinics "at low cost."

Weekly editor Jeffrey Bigelow was charged with violating Virginia statute 18.1–63, which made it a misdemeanor for any person, "by publication, lecture, advertisement, or by the sale or circulation of any publication, or in any other manner, [to] encourage or prompt the procuring of abortion or miscarriage."

The court found him guilty, fining him $500, with $350 suspended. Bigelow appealed to the Supreme Court of Virginia, which rejected his claim that the advertisement was purely informational and thus was not within the "encourage or prompt" language of the law and affirmed his conviction in a four to two vote.

Bigelow appealed again in 1973, but in light of the pending *Roe v. Wade* and *Doe v. Bolton* legislation, the United States Supreme Court deferred the case back to the Virginia higher court, which agreed to reconsider it. Again, it found him guilty.

Undaunted, Bigelow appealed once more to the United States Supreme Court. On June 16, 1975, he finally won: "The Virginia courts erred in assuming that advertising, as such, was entitled to no First Amendment protection and that appellant had no legitimate First Amendment interest," stated the majority opinion, delivered by Justice Harry Blackmun. "Speech is not stripped of First Amendment protection merely because it appears in the form of a paid commercial advertisement."

Throughout 1971, the *Virginia Weekly* covered strikes at Richmond newspapers, Alliance Manufacturing in Shenandoah, GE and Brown and Williamson Tobacco, but like with many underground papers, the legal troubles and law enforcement hassles began piling up. In addition to the abortion ad difficulties, a reporter was arrested for "illegal picketing" at the Alliance workers' strike. Bigelow was forcibly ejected from a courtroom during the trial of fourteen-year-old "black revolutionary" Matthew Johnson. Finally, two Charlottesville policemen, David L. Pleasants and T.J. Robertson, sued the *Weekly* for $200,000 in damages, claiming a September 1970 article titled "Racist Justice in Charlottesville" impugned their reputations with allegations of racism and police brutality. The *Weekly*'s lawyer was Gail Marshall, whose husband was a direct descendant of Chief Justice John Marshall.

Marshall said the best defense for libel was the truth. "We did more digging, and it seemed like there was no end to stories of blacks in Charlottesville who had been harassed, insulted, beaten or otherwise disrespected by these two cops," wrote Gardner of the suit in 2014. "She let their lawyer know that we were looking forward to going to trial to get all this out in public. They dropped the suit."

Throughout the fall of 1971 and into the spring of 1972, the *Weekly* became a staunch advocate of prisoners' and women's rights and spoke out for black liberation while exposing racism in the university, the public school system, prisons and even in city and state governments.

While the abortion ad case was a huge win for the *Virginia Weekly*, the paper was out of business by the time it was settled, with the last issue appearing in September 1972. "For many of us on the staff of the *Virginia Weekly*, this will be the last issue we'll actively participate in," stated a "goodbye" editorial on page two. Still, the rest of the issue was typically powerful, with a well-written update on the Wansley case, coverage of a black boycott in Suffolk against Rose's and Leggett's department stores, the Richmond penitentiary and the Norfolk Foam Plastics strike and two articles on the upcoming presidential race.

"Those friends leaving the staff will be working in factories and hospitals, taking part in union struggles," stated the final editorial. "All of these activities will be directed toward what we see as our principal responsibility: that of forging a revolutionary party capable of leading the working class to socialism."

3 THE SHENANDOAH VALLEY AND SOUTHWEST VIRGINIA

THE ANT HILL

1968

The writers of this paper believe in freedom of speech. That is why this paper was conceived. We hope we are creating a new channel of communication representative of the uncensored truth. The freedom of speech issue is here—we could picket.
—The Ant Hill, *volume 1, number 1, March 31, 1968*

New Left and antiwar sentiment on a sleepy western Virginia campus such as Radford College may have been smaller in scope than those protests in the larger metropolitan areas but was no less passionate. It's not that social protest was unheard of in rural southwest Virginia; in 1963, an integrated group of high school and college students marched through the streets of Roanoke to city hall, demanding a complete desegregation of public accommodations. Unfortunately, the white students dropped out of the protest when an undocumented rumor spread that "communists were behind the civil rights movement," according to Lansing Rowan, a nearby Hollins College student.

Students at the small, all-female Radford College, an hour west of Roanoke in Virginia's southwest Shenandoah Valley, grew increasingly frustrated that the college administration, led by President Dr. Charles K. Martin Jr., was unwilling to compromise on campus issues that concerned them, such as censorship, dress and conduct codes and vocal opposition to the war in Vietnam. Subsequently, a few of them broke ground as the first group of students who would publicly demonstrate against that school's outmoded and suffocating social policies.

With 3,300 students by the mid-1960s, Radford College may have been the second-largest women's college in the United States but still grasped its "finishing school" past. Not only did the students endure ultraconservative social regulations and authoritarian dorm rules, enforced with an iron fist by "dorm mothers," but the school still maintained a "home economics house," with classes and seminars that prepared them for careers as housewives and mothers.

The first actual protest on the Radford campus occurred in 1964, when some students initially called for a demonstration against antiquated dress regulations and socially repressive measures on dating. The organizers decided at the last minute, however, to call it off because they feared that two faculty advisors might lose their jobs. Unfortunately, about one hundred students did not get the memo and silently marched without incident around the dormitories anyway.

Students were not allowed to have locks on their dormitory doors, have cars on campus, walk on the grass or consume alcohol within a fifty-mile radius of campus. They were expected to subserviently abide by old-fashioned curfews and dating rules, with no exceptions. They were also aggravated by the school's creaky honor system, which had not been updated in decades and could still get a student expelled for attending a party but not for stealing.

But it was the college's dogged insistence on enforcing dress codes straight out of the 1940s that raised the most frustration. According to the 1967 handbook, Radford women were not allowed to leave their dorm rooms in hair rollers. They were required to wear dresses on campus, downtown and on Sundays, when hats and gloves were also required. Bermuda shorts were permitted only if they were "appropriate for the occasion," otherwise they had to cover themselves with a knee-length jacket. If students wanted to wear shorts in their dorms, they could only do so in the upper, rear levels of the building. When going off-campus in shorts, they had to take the "most direct route" from the campus using back entrances, "thus minimizing the public's view."

There were harsh dress regulations for men who dared venture onto campus for a visit. Male visitors had to approach the dorm proctor's desk "properly dressed" in a "dress shirt, tie or ascot, coat or sweater, and slacks (no jeans)."

Boyd Glover, a 1971 VPI graduate, today attests to the strictness of the Radford dress code. "I showed up on the Radford campus for my date at the beginning of the fall 1967 semester in a jacket and tie, just like they wanted," he said, "but it was hot, and I don't wear socks when it's hot. Anyway the dorm mother noticed I wasn't wearing socks, called the security guard and escorted me off campus."

A second protest occurred one month later when the student snack bar known as "the Cove" was ordered closed by Dr. Martin at 9:00 p.m. on weeknights. One night, some fed-up students and their dates refused to leave, lingering in the Cove and singing "We Shall Overcome" and "God Bless America." When the local police showed up, the women scattered back to their dorms and the guys back to VPI to avoid arrest.

When student complaints were printed in the April 1967 *Radford News-Journal*, Dr. Martin waved them off, telling the paper that "some of the student charges simply are not true" and attributing the students' unrest to "spring fever," trivializing their concerns and making them even angrier.

Finally, during the spring 1968 semester, a few students decided they had had enough of the smothering rules, lack of academic freedoms, alleged censorship, editorial direction of the school newspaper *Grapurchat* and even the Vietnam War. So following in the footsteps of their cosmopolitan counterparts up north, on March 31, they launched somewhere off campus their own mimeographed dissident newspaper, the *Ant Hill*.

"The purpose of this publication is to give expression to the ideals of free and responsible thought about the quality and direction of life in the Radford College community," stated the mission statement in volume 1, number 1. "The opportunity of submission of articles for publication is open to everyone."

While an advisory board consisting of local business and religious leaders was listed on the front page of the first issue, all contributors to the *Ant Hill* elected to keep their identities secret. "We fear administrational reprisals to our participation in this free press," stated the third and final issue. "[But] we encourage contributors to challenge expressed views. We would not be true to the purpose of *The Ant Hill* if we did not."

The *Ant Hill* claimed it was *not* "an organ for students and others to voice their discontent with Radford College and its administration—in particular, its president," but an "outlet for creative literary expression." Nonetheless, the articles expressed dismay with the way the college conducted itself. One in particular expressed hope that a bill before the Virginia House of Delegates would allow at least limited undergraduate co-educational opportunities. "Radford College ought to begin to move into the field of

THE ANT HILL

VOL. 1 NUMBER I — MARCH 31, 1968

THE PURPOSE of this publication is to give expression to the ideals of free and responsible thought about the quality and direction of life in the Radford College community. The opportunity of submission of articles for publication is open to everyone. The editorial board, composed of Radford College students, oversees the selection and publication of articles. Information concerning contributions may be obtained from any of the advisors. Unless specifically requested to the contrary, names of contributors will be withheld from publication and will remain confidential with the editorial board. No article will be accepted for publication, however, without the writer's signature.

ADVISORS: Carolyn Crawford, Joseph A. Dunaway, William Gardner, Geneva Metzger, Deborah Prenger, Richard Ray.

A REACTION TO A TALK DELIVERED BY THOMAS J.J. ALTIZER

This reaction is based on Dr. Altizer's talk delivered March 1, 1968, at Radford College. I had one overriding reaction. It seemed to me that Dr. Altizer would construct "straw men" which he would present as Orthodox Christian positions and would then proceed to tear down those straw men with his "radical theology," his "Christian Atheism." My reaction was that the positions which he proposed as part of the "New Theology" were nothing more or less than what responsible Christian theology has been saying for centuries. In other words, Dr. Altizer presented positions which he called orthodox (which in point of fact was not a fair presentation of Orthodox Christianity, but a perversion) and then he would propose an alternative position to what he described as "Orthodox Christianity" (which was not a "new theology").

My sharpest criticism was that he presented Orthodox Christianity as holding only a concept of a transcendent God out there. His comment that "the Resurrection and Ascension means that Jesus leaves the realm of man and 'goes back' out there" is the major thing that sticks in my mind. That, as I understand it, is precisely what the Doctrines of the Resurrection and Ascension do not mean.

CO-EDUCATION?

A bill was offered in the Virginia House of Delegates recently which, if passed, would bring at least limited co-education to Radford College at the undergraduate level.

On February 7, Delegate Alan Diamondstein of Newport News offered House Bill No. 692 which would amend the Code of Virginia, adding to paragraph 23-7.2 the following: "Notwithstanding any other provisions of this title to the contrary, every state educational institution which grants an education degree or education certificate shall extend its admission privileges to both male and female students."

This bill has been put to rest in the House Committee at the present time which means that in effect it will likely not be considered this year. But there may be other bills in other years and anyone interested in such a change, can write her state Senator or Delegate and encourage her parents to do so, making known your wishes in the matter.

Following are some excerpts from an editorial which appeared in the Richmond News Leader in February:

"Simply, the bill would have admitted men to the institutions that train teachers. This, according to the American Association of State Colleges and Universities, is something which every other state-supported college in the nation now does, except for one school in Texas. Affected would have been Longwood and Radford and, possibly, the Woman's College of the University of Virginia, Mary Washington. Mr. Diamondstein's argument that this would help reduce the shortage of men teachers makes good sense. Moreover, the present policy denies equal protection of the law to the tax-paying parent with a smart son. Imagine,

The Ant Hill, volume 1, number 1, March 31, 1968. *Courtesy Radford University Special Collections, McConnell Library, Radford University, Radford, Virginia.*

undergraduate co-education, simply because a college education on any other basis is incomplete and unrealistic," stated the story on page one. "We live in a bisexual world, and then to isolate a man or woman during his or her active and formative college years is quite unnatural and ill-preparing for the rest of life."

While the writers of the *Ant Hill* embraced the participatory nonobjective journalism practiced by the larger underground papers, they shied away from their inflammatory language. Calling the Radford police "pigs" would have been rather irresponsible in such a small southern Virginia town.

The *Ant Hill* also accused school administrators of censoring a rather nondescript humorous political column called "Over the Picket Fence" written by sophomore English major Trudy Stephenson. "The style and content of *Grapurchat*'s most popular column has been altered," the writer observed. "Conscientious readers have noticed the radical shift of emphasis from a liberal critique of college policies to an ultra-conservative silence concerning major issues previously mentioned in the 'Picket Fence' column."

"Our college newspaper is subject to censorship," the *Ant Hill* continued. "I guess the staff and advisor would not want to bring 'disgrace' to the college."

The article drew condemnation from former *Grapurchat* editor Trish Moore, who stated in an editorial that "Dr. Martin doesn't sit down with a red pencil and strike out all objectionable stories." The *Ant Hill* agreed that may be true, however, but they believed that many articles and letters submitted to the *Grapurchat* were simply not printed, sometimes for "nefarious reasons."

America's presence in Vietnam provoked conflicting campus opinions. A story titled "The Defense of the Offended" in the *Ant Hill* purported to be an interview of an anonymous inspector working in Vietnam, whose job included inspecting morgues. "These morgues contain the bodies of not only U.S. servicemen, but also those of the VC, Vietnamese regulars and Vietnamese civilians," the article stated, describing "unnecessary cruelties" committed on both sides.

"I would, placed in the position of many Vietnamese, join forces with the VC, not because they are fighting for my ideals, but because they are my people fighting against these strangers who show no feelings for the worth of our lives," the article continued, slamming America's role there. "Of course, the VC perform these same actions, but they belong to Vietnam. They are fighting for home rule."

On October 14, 1969, the student body showed solidarity against the war when about four hundred students and professors joined in a candlelight

THE ANT HILL

VOL. I NUMBER 2 APRIL 21, 1968

TO REITERATE. The Ant Hill has come into being through the efforts of some students who feel the need for a free press in the Radford College community. Not a "house organ" of the College, The Ant Hill is accessible to everyone who desires to do creative and critical writing on any subject matter. This paper pledges to be fearless and free, liberal and positive in approach, and it will print opposing opinions on any subject. Please contribute to it if you have strong feelings on anything. Articles must be signed but names do not appear unless by request. The source of each contribution remains confidential with the student editorial board.

ADVISORS: Carolyn Crawford, Joseph A. Dunaway, William Gardner, Deborah Prenger, Richard Ray, Edward Andrews.

A LETTER TO THE EDITOR

Dear GRAPURCHAT Editor,

As members of the student body and patrons of the Radford theater, we would like to air a complaint about the only theater within walking distance of the college campus. While we realize the quality of the movies presented is usually excellent, the interior of the the theater leaves much to be desired. Despite popular belief, the Radford theater could become a place we are proud of if it were swept, recarpeted, painted and the seats were re-cushioned. New projection equipment also seems to be in order.

As loyal supporters of the Radford theater, we suggest written complaints be sent by each concerned student to Mr. R.H. Carpenter, Radford Theater, Radford, Virginia.

Sincerely,

EDITORIAL NOTE: The editorial staff feels that the students of Radford College are also a part of the greater Radford community and believe in the necessity of speaking out in the public interest. *See page 3

PALM SUNDAY REFLECTIONS

Today is Palm Sunday--a day of mourning for Dr. Martin Luther King, Jr.. The Radford churches held a community service in memory of Dr. King. We stood together; we walked together; we talked and sang together; we were as brothers and sisters of Christ and of each other! Can it--will it last? We must do more than want it to last. We must live as we did those few hours today; but, it must be active, not passive living. We were friends--brothers and sisters in Christ and it felt good. It was not hard--no one was inconvenienced. St. Paul is right--no matter what we do or for whom we do it, if we have not love in our hearts, minds, and souls, it does no good.

THE KING IS DEAD!

The King is dead!
He has sparked the consciousness of men;
He has lived by the peace and love of God;
He has died by the violent hand of an assassin.
The King is dead!
He had a dream;
A dream of peace, a dream of love,
A dream for Protestant, Catholic, Moslem and Jew,
A dream for black, for white, for yellow, and for red.
The King is dead!
Tell me black man, who killed the King?
Tell me white man, who killed the King?
Who was it?
Was it Indifference? Was it Hatred?
Was it Fear? Was it Insanity?
Was it Me? Was it You?

The Ant Hill, April 21, 1968. *Courtesy Radford University Special Collections, McConnell Library, Radford University, Radford, Virginia.*

observance as part of the national Vietnam Moratorium, walking slowly around campus and singing "Give Peace a Chance."

An article entitled "Apathy '68" in the second issue of the *Ant Hill* complained of the political indifference on the Radford campus. "The Young Republican and Democrat clubs along with 'Choice '68' are trying wholeheartedly to create enthusiasm," stated the article. "It seems we will soon owe them an apology for our disinterest."

"Choice '68" was a student primary sponsored by *Time* magazine and the Univac Division of Sperry-Rand Incorporated that, like state presidential primaries, tended to show voter preference. "More response is given the 'beauty contests' on campus than our own student elections," groused the *Ant Hill* about the students' lack of conviction.

"Our campus' involvement in national politics is pathetic in comparison to other Virginia schools, much less other national campuses," chastised the uncredited writer. "I think that it is time we put aside our negativism and apathy and do something so that we won't apologize every time we're asked 'Where do you go to school?'"

By May 19, 1968, the third and final issue of the *Ant Hill* had gotten at least tacit attention of the college students and administration, to the point that a letter to the *Ant Hill* editor questioned the validity of an advisory board composed of "local ministers and denominational workers" rather than university personnel. That prompted a response from those advisors, who said, "We are the pastors of local congregations or religious campus workers…but we serve as an advisor as persons designated to work with college students, and feel very strongly in the right of every student to express her views freely and without fear on any issue…so long as they are not obscene or profane."

"We are not happy with the *Ant Hill* as it now is," the answer continued. "We hope for improvement in many ways as it strives to become an effective, constructive tool for dialogue."

Despite the optimistic response that more issues were forthcoming, the *Ant Hill* instead, for unknown reasons, stopped publishing entirely. In an August 22, 1968 *Radford News Journal* interview, Dr. Martin addressed rumors of student unhappiness and apathy toward those campus rules and regulations. When asked about how that administration viewed the *Grapurchat* and "the clandestine *Ant Hill*," Dr. Martin stated, "The newspaper (*Grapurchat*) is a college function. It's not my business," and then said, "I don't wish to criticize *The Ant Hill*…but some of its attacks are false."

There was more campus unrest in 1970, but whether it was due to issues raised by the defunct *Ant Hill*, the long list of dress regulations in the handbook was reduced to a single paragraph. The Radford College campus was full of promise for those students who had actively participated in initiating change. Conferences shifted away from topics such as housewifery and home management to civil rights, women's liberation and opposition to the war. Then in July 1972, under Dr. Donald N. Dedmon, Radford went co-educational, and the dress code was abolished.

All the challenges to the status quo raised by the *Ant Hill* staff were done not out of spite for Radford but because they cared so much about the school and its future. In a May 24, 1968 letter to President Martin's secretary Sara Hall, an unnamed *Ant Hill* editor wrote, "We do not consider ourselves radical…We would not be members of *The Ant Hill*'s editorial board if we did not love Radford College."

ALICE

1968–72

The fact that this campus…must fully face the issues of the "world out there," and see that there is a definite need for a focal point of free exchange and presentation of ideas at VPI. Thus the conception and birth of Alice.
—Alice, *volume 1, number 1, May 18, 1968*

It is not surprising that a college with as rough and tumble a past as Blacksburg's Virginia Polytechnic Institute (VPI) would embrace New Left radicalism so far from its urban counterparts to the north. The school started as an all-male institution in 1872, and its distant location and rampant testosterone led to random acts of rowdiness that sometimes threatened to shut the school down. The first group of women was not admitted until 1921 (the first female graduate, Mary E. Brumfield, class of 1923, was the daughter of the college physician Dr. William Brumfield and a distant relative of this author). The first black male was admitted in 1953 and the first black females in 1966.

In January 1968, four students—Bob Greenawalt, Jane Baldwin, Ben Lawten and Cecil Pettus—decided to challenge restrictive dress regulations. Despite vague assurance by the dean of students, Dr. James A. Dean, that nothing prohibited them from conducting a poll of student opinions on the regulations, the dean's staff approached them during the polling and took their names.

After the poll, Dr. Dean informed the four students they were on disciplinary probation until graduation for violation of the solicitation clause, which prompted a petition requesting the student government association (SGA) intervene in the case. After collecting almost two thousand signatures, a select committee only accepted the administration's story, throwing out the student petitions and claiming the name "Nikita Khrushchev" appeared on one of them, despite scrupulous checking for false names before the petitions were turned in.

With great pressure applied from students, faculty and even some administrators, a faculty review board for the first time in VPI history reversed the dean's decision, and only Bob Greenawalt drew conduct probation. All other disciplinary actions were stricken.

Several curious students then approached the staff of the VPI student paper the *Virginia Tech*, asking why it ran no coverage of either the petition incident or the reversal of the dean's decision. While numerous reasons were offered, the students suspected that subtle pressure might have been applied by the administration affecting future funding or to the possible replacement of certain editors at the *Virginia Tech*.

In fact, when Lucy Minogue stepped down as editor of the *Virginia Tech*, she allegedly had in her possession several letters from administrators, even at least one dean, requesting she refrain from covering certain events that could reflect negatively on the college.

It was apparent to that handful of liberal-religious students that a second newspaper was now needed, so Everett Hogg, along with Thomas Saunders, Bryan Ackler and a few others, founded the Blacksburg Free Press during the 1968 spring break and created their new newspaper, *Alice*.

Alice technically was the second Blacksburg underground paper—a single anonymous issue of *FREE! Blacksburg Underground Newsletter* appeared sometime in late 1967. *FREE!* was an undated, typewriter-produced two-column newsletter that copied the editorial model of the larger underground papers around the country, with bold outbursts about cops, the Vietnam War, capitalist pigs, oppression and the "Establishment," almost all lifted from Chicago 7 activist Jerry Rubin's book, *Do It!*

The staff of *Alice* differed on the role of a college newspaper when asked why they chose to start a whole new paper and not to work on the staff of the *Virginia Tech*. They asserted that the *Tech* did not properly represent the diversity of the student body, that competition was healthy and that the

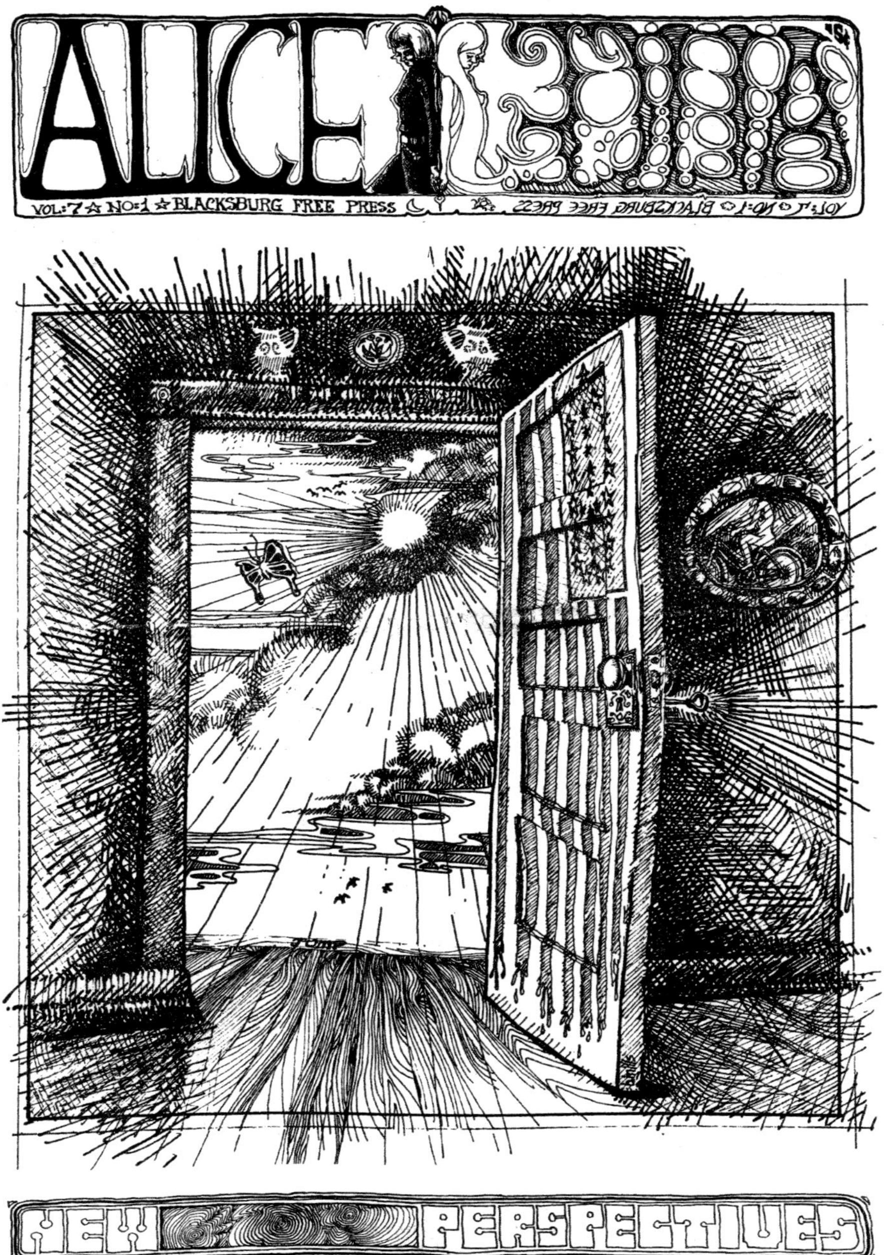

Alice, May 18, 1968. *Courtesy the author.*

college administration was too heavy-handed in its editorial and financial supervision of the student paper.

Alice appeared on May 18, 1968, on tabloid-size newsprint. Its four pages were so voraciously snatched up that almost no copies of that issue exist in 2014. "What is 'Alice'?" asked the headline on the cover. "Alice, from 'Alice in Wonderland,' Alice a girl I once knew, Alice a cat, Alice a dwarf Russian olive, Alice the mother of a friend, and the Alice that runs a restaurant, and various and sundry other Alices that one finds, comes 'Alice,' a free newspaper."

Like most free community publications, it meant "free" from institutional control, not free to read—at first, it cost ten cents per copy, raised to fifteen cents a few issues later.

"The administrative system that the *Tech* is committed to does not allow the staff the amount of voice in the paper that we feel it should have," stated staff member Bryan Ackler in the first issue of *Alice*. "Finally the point arises as to how can an official portion of the University turn around and ethically attack the university of which it is part and from which it is accepting approval and funds."

The staff of *Alice* was listed in the first issue according to their job duties: Everett Hogg, editor; John Pendleton, business manager; Jans Appel, art editor; and Ackler, copy editor. The planning, creation and production of volume 1, number 1 of *Alice* was done in secret—if the college was willing to discipline four students over a dress code poll, how would it react to an unapproved newspaper circulated on campus?

"Our group was nurtured in the student programs by the Methodist and Episcopal churches, whose leaders provided space for people to meet, discuss current issues and otherwise provided an ethical framework to review our concerns with both current politics and the immediate situation around us," former student Thomas Saunders reported in a 2014 e-mail.

Alice appeared just after the assassination of Dr. Martin Luther King Jr., when, according to Saunders, some students started openly cheering in classrooms. On the day of the shooting, and after the honor guard customarily raised the U.S. and Virginia flags at Burruss Hall to full staff, a group of students led by Saunders petitioned the campus to lower the flags to half-mast, which was refused. "Together with one of the ministers on the campus a group of approximately thirty lowered the flags and sat in beneath [them]," said Saunders. "The result was a counter-demonstration; very ugly and hateful, shouting racial epithets and celebrating the assassination of King." According to Saunders and *Alice*, it was a large, intimidating group, and eventually some of them forced their way in, wrestled the ropes away and fully raised the flags "to the cheers of the crowd."

Within minutes, however, word came that President Lyndon Johnson ordered all flags at half-staff. The demonstration broke up, and the VPI honor guard lowered the flags.

Coverage of this event varies wildly between *Alice*, the *Virginia Tech* and the current Virginia Tech website; the latter two chose not to describe the racial animosity reported by the participatory journalism style of *Alice*, the contributors of which were thick in the center of the altercation and offered firsthand reporting.

Alice's life was marked by extreme highs and almost desperate lows, fighting constant battles against finances, student apathy and small-town antipathy. "The idea of free speech, the ability and willingness to look at views that were not considered acceptable by authorities kept students from accepting leaflets, listening to discussions or engage with anyone who was in any way 'different,'" said Saunders. *Alice* subscribed to Liberation News Service when it could afford the membership and published its first LNS story on the cover of its first issue, about the Southern Christian Leadership Conference Poor People's Campaign.

In addition to LNS copy, there was an article called "Putting It Down" reprinted from volume 1, number 15, of the Richmond underground paper the *Sunflower*. On page two was a long letter from a "non-combatant draftee" named Rob about the pitfalls of the draft. Bruce Smith, who was the Virginia liaison of the SSOC and future co-founder of another Richmond underground paper, the *Richmond Chronicle*, wrote an appeal for any VPI students interested in helping organize poor and middle-class whites for the Poor People's Campaign. *Alice* also reported a campus presentation Smith gave on the purpose and mission of the SSOC and of the demonstrations at University of Virginia, Virginia Union and Virginia State Universities.

The first issue contained two small ads—for Books, Strings & Things ("We don't advertise our record prices") and Carver's on College Avenue.

Issue 2 also reported six Blacksburg people arrested for marijuana possession. "We thank [the police] for removing this evil," stated an uncredited commentary.

Despite the quick disappearance of every copy, the staff was disappointed by the poor response of the VPI community. They decided after the first issue to change the mission of the paper from an open forum for dialogue to an educational presentation, hoping it would spur more student interest.

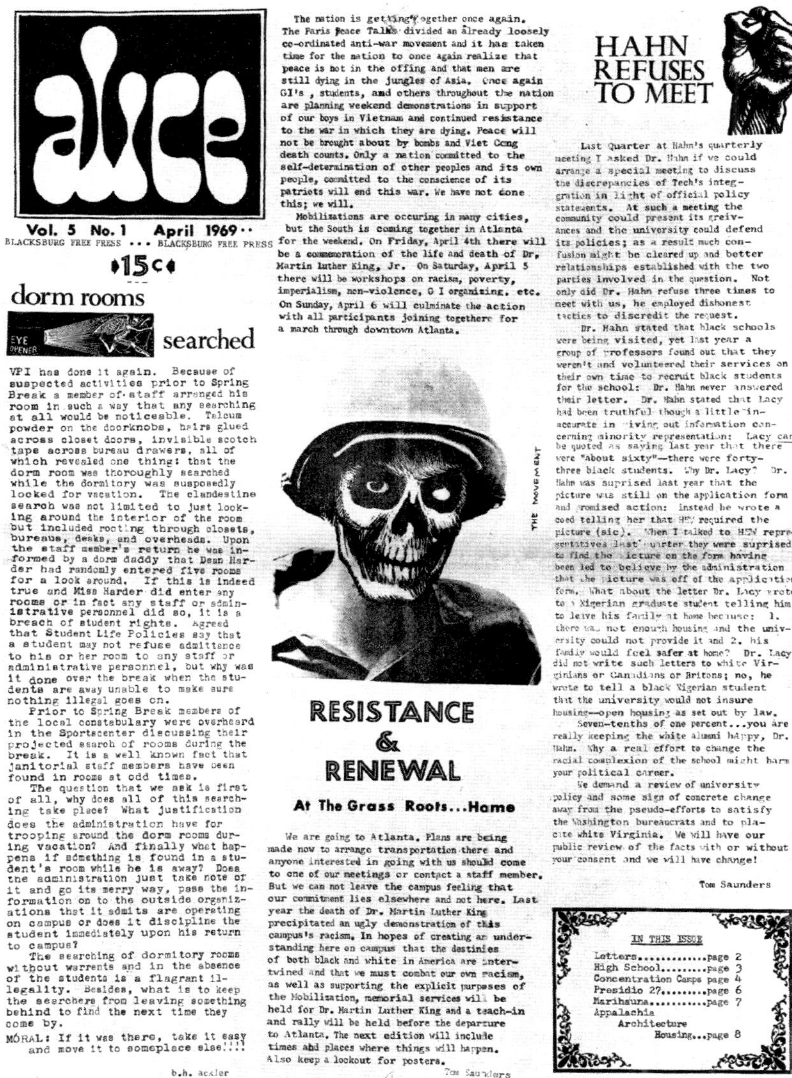

alice

Vol. 5 No. 1 April 1969

BLACKSBURG FREE PRESS ... BLACKSBURG FREE PRESS

15c

dorm rooms searched

VPI has done it again. Because of suspected activities prior to Spring Break a member of staff arranged his room in such a way that any searching at all would be noticeable. Talcum powder on the doorknobs, hairs glued across closet doors, invisible scotch tape across bureau drawers, all of which revealed one thing: that the dorm room was thoroughly searched while the dormitory was supposedly locked for vacation. The clandestine search was not limited to just looking around the interior of the room but included rooting through closets, bureaus, desks, and overheads. Upon the staff member's return he was informed by a dorm daddy that Dean Harder had randomly entered five rooms for a look around. If this is indeed true and Miss Harder did enter any rooms or in fact any staff or administrative personnel did so, it is a breach of student rights. Agreed that Student Life Policies say that a student may not refuse admittance to his or her room to any staff or administrative personnel, but why was it done over the break when the students are away unable to make sure nothing illegal goes on.

Prior to Spring Break members of the local constabulary were overheard in the Sportscenter discussing their projected search of rooms during the break. It is a well known fact that janitorial staff members have been found in rooms at odd times.

The question that we ask is first of all, why does all of this searching take place? What justification does the administration have for trooping around the dorm rooms during vacation? And finally what happens if something is found in a student's room while he is away? Does the administration just take note of it and go its merry way, pass the information on to the outside organizations that it admits are operating on campus or does it discipline the student immediately upon his return to campus?

The searching of dormitory rooms without warrents and in the absence of the students is a flagrant illegality. Besides, what is to keep the searchers from leaving something behind to find the next time they come by.

MÓRAL: If it was there, take it easy and move it to someplace else!!!!

b.h. ackler

The nation is getting together once again. The Paris Peace Talks divided an already loosely co-ordinated anti-war movement and it has taken time for the nation to once again realize that peace is not in the offing and that men are still dying in the jungles of Asia. Once again GI's, students, and others throughout the nation are planning weekend demonstrations in support of our boys in Vietnam and continued resistance to the war in which they are dying. Peace will not be brought about by bombs and Viet Cong death counts. Only a nation committed to the self-determination of other peoples and its own people, committed to the conscience of its patriots will end this war. We have not done this; we will.

Mobilizations are occuring in many cities, but the South is coming together in Atlanta for the weekend. On Friday, April 4th there will be a commemoration of the life and death of Dr, Martin Luther King, Jr. On Saturday, April 5 there will be workshops on racism, poverty, imperialism, non-violence, G I organizing, etc. On Sunday, April 6 will culminate the action with all participants joining togethere for a march through downtown Atlanta.

THE MOVEMENT

RESISTANCE & RENEWAL

At The Grass Roots...Home

We are going to Atlanta. Plans are being made now to arrange transportation there and anyone interested in going with us should come to one of our meetings or contact a staff member. But we can not leave the campus feeling that our commitment lies elsewhere and not here. Last year the death of Dr. Martin Luther King precipitated an ugly demonstration of this campus's racism. In hopes of creating an understanding here on campus that the destinies of both black and white in America are intertwined and that we must combat our own racism, as well as supporting the explicit purposes of the Mobilization, memorial services will be held for Dr. Martin Luther King and a teach-in and rally will be held before the departure to Atlanta. The next edition will include times and places where things will happen. Also keep a lookout for posters.

Tom Saunders

HAHN REFUSES TO MEET

Last Quarter at Hahn's quarterly meeting I asked Dr. Hahn if we could arrange a special meeting to discuss the discrepancies of Tech's integration in light of official policy statements. At such a meeting the community could present its greivances and the university could defend its policies; as a result much confusion might be cleared up and better relationships established with the two parties involved in the question. Not only did Dr. Hahn refuse three times to meet with us, he employed dishonest tactics to discredit the request.

Dr. Hahn stated that black schools were being visited, yet last year a group of professors found out that they weren't and volunteered their services on their own time to recruit black students for the school: Dr. Hahn never answered their letter. Dr. Hahn stated that Lacy had been truthful though a little inaccurate in giving out information concerning minority representation: Lacy can be quoted as saying last year that there were "about sixty"—there were forty-three black students. Why Dr. Lacy? Dr. Hahn was suprised last year that the picture was still on the application form and promised action: instead he wrote a coed telling her that HEW required the picture (sic). When I talked to HEW representatives last quarter they were suprised to find the picture on the form having been led to believe by the administration that the picture was off of the application form. What about the letter Dr. Lacy wrote to a Nigerian graduate student telling him to leave his family at home because: 1. there was not enough housing and the university could not provide it and 2. his family would feel safer at home? Dr. Lacy did not write such letters to white Virginians or Canadians or Britons; no, he wrote to tell a black Nigerian student that the university would not insure housing—open housing as set out by law.

Seven-tenths of one percent...you are really keeping the white alumni happy, Dr. Hahn. Why a real effort to change the racial complexion of the school might harm your political career.

We demand a review of university policy and some sign of concrete change away from the pseudo-efforts to satisfy the Washington bureaucrats and to placate white Virginia. We will have our public review of the facts with or without your consent and we will have change!

Tom Saunders

IN THIS ISSUE

Letters..............page 2
High School..........page 3
Concentration Camps page 4
Presidio 27..........page 6
Marihsuna............page 7
Appalachia
Architecture
Housing...page 8

Alice, April 1969. *Courtesy Bonnie Atwood and the VCU Cabell Library Special Collections, Richmond, Virginia.*

In keeping with underground tradition around the country, *Alice* made no apologies for practicing its own form of nonobjective, advocacy journalism. "Every staff member has his own prejudices and we make no attempt to cover them up by saying that we are objective," stated an undated issue. "When the reader picks up *Alice* he knows beforehand what he is about to read is biased to some degree. We are at least honest about it." Reflective also of the paper's open submission policy, many of the articles were written in first-person, reflecting the writers' personal feelings and experiences.

Throughout its uneasy three-year existence, *Alice*'s format and printing varied widely as finances and circumstances dictated. The first two issues were tabloid-size newsprint. Starting on June 24 and up to November 25, 1968, the paper published sixteen issues (one about every ten days) on eight-and-a-half- by fourteen-inch mimeograph paper, each edition averaging between two and four pages each and in press runs between 1,000 and 1,400 copies. Each issue stated at the top, "This is a limiting printing, please read and pass on." In January 1969, the paper returned to tabloid size.

Tom Saunders took over as editor during that first summer of 1968, and the staff learned the hard lessons of underground newspaper publishing. "It requires a lot of work, there are no immediate rewards, and that you cannot make money in the underground newspaper business," wrote Ackler in 1969. He went on to describe other pitfalls of alternative publishing in the Blacksburg area that echoed similar situations in larger metropolitan areas, such as Washington, D.C.: "Shop keepers throw you out of their shops while you are soliciting ads, hate notes are nailed to your door, and a lot of people call you a communist, and even though they don't know what one is, they know what he looks like."

Indeed, even though the students who became involved with *Alice* were an interdisciplinary assortment of "Vietnam veterans, seminary students, military brats, liberals, moderates, ministers," maybe even a few misfits and weirdos, none professed to being communist.

Stories appearing in the summer issues included Ackler's blistering critique of VPI administrative staff who conducted a dorm room search while students were away on break. He pointed out that an *Alice* staff member had intentionally rigged their room by placing Scotch tape over dresser drawers, talcum powder on interior doorknobs and hairs glued across closet doors. "What is to keep the searchers from leaving something behind to find the next time they come by?" he asked.

Despite the early negativity, the paper clung to life in the smaller mimeograph form and, by the spring of 1969, became a lifeline in the VPI community. Shortly thereafter, it was the only liberal action agency in the entire Virginia southwest. Money appeared from somewhere, and the issues went back to tabloid size and grew fatter, ranging from eight to eighteen pages, with the October 14, 1969 issue topping out at a record twenty pages.

People began calling the paper looking for draft counseling, abortion services or a free lawyer when a "friend" got busted.

During the spring 1969 semester, *Alice* editor Tom Saunders left VPI and then was readmitted in May 1969. The next month, he participated in a peaceful anti-Vietnam demonstration during the ROTC commissioning exercises, where General William Westmoreland was the invited speaker. Suddenly in August, he was informed that his readmission was denied because he had participated in the campus demonstration as an "unmatriculated" student. The ACLU agreed he had the right to peaceably assemble at a public event on campus and won his legal battle when the Fourth Circuit Court of Appeals ordered the university to readmit him. Unfortunately, the university froze his application and scholarship money, so he was without funds to complete his degree.

"The student body will be faced with the fact that due process can be ignored by the administrators to rid themselves of any person they choose," Saunders warned in *Alice*. He went on to earn a law degree without a bachelor's degree and in 2014 still practices law.

By the late spring of 1969, the paper was again back to the smaller size, and the May 20 issue contained a poignant plea for money. "With this printing *Alice* is nearly broke," read the page-one appeal. "We have made many appeals in the past for aid, but they have had hardly any effect. One appeal drew only two dollars…We do not have the 25 dollars needed to incorporate the paper, nor the funds to rejoin the Underground Press Service…Businesses will rarely advertise and the price charged for the paper will rarely cover printing costs alone."

In the fall of that year, however, this paper with nine lives again started publishing biweekly. Though the local response was still muted, the VPI student government slowly began picking up and responding to several articles that pertained to campus activities. After an article appeared in *Alice* about institutionalized racism, students tried to get a Confederate flag removed from the coliseum. A committee was formed to investigate the presence of firearms on campus after an *Alice* story. Two years after the Blacksburg Free Press community established a legal aid fund and lawyer referral list, the college established its own legal aid clinic. And almost one year after the liberal community set up a free university, with fifteen courses offered, the college did the same, although students complained the course offerings were merely recycled graduate-level courses.

"With this special 'birthday' issue, *Alice* is taking a short rest," said a mimeographed letter to "Subscribers, patrons and friends" written by

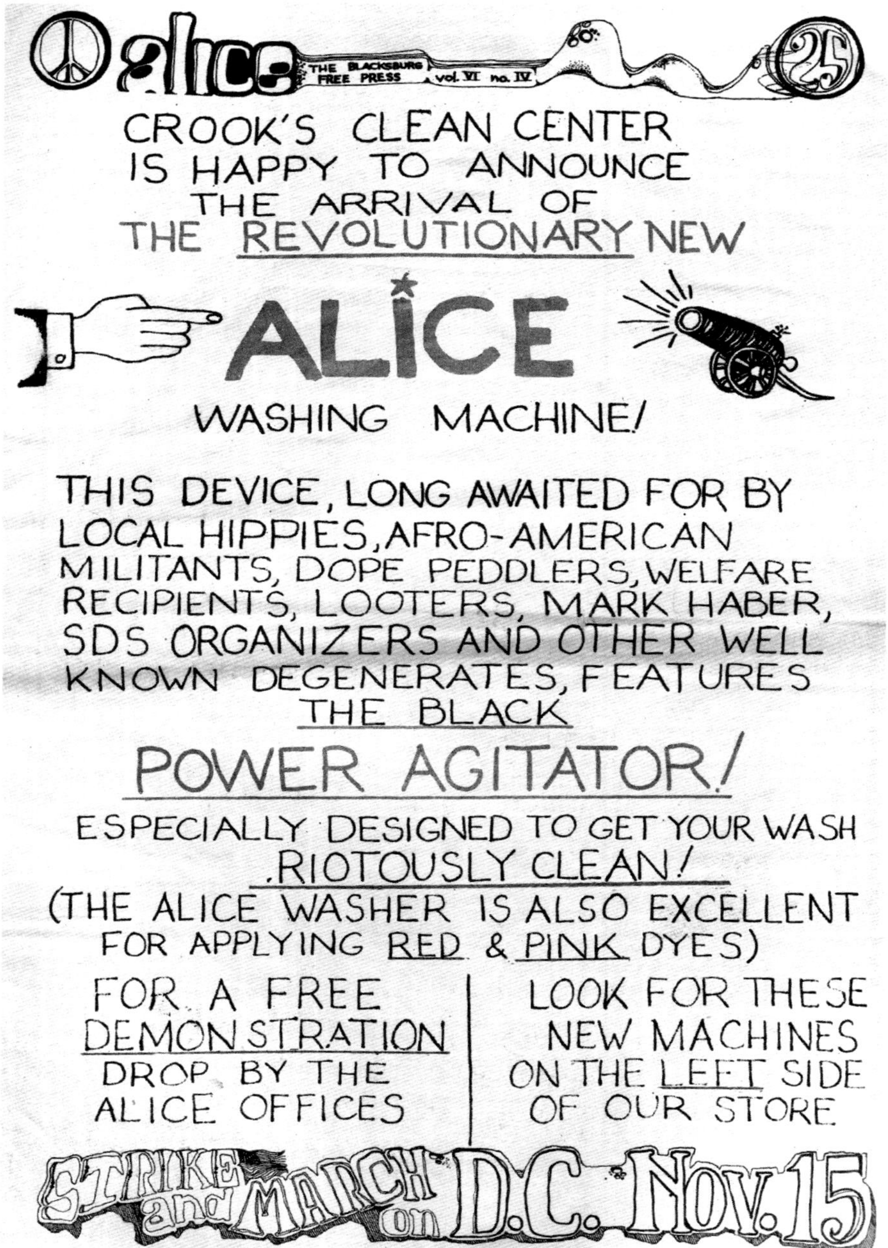

Alice, November 1970. *Courtesy Bonnie Atwood and the VCU Cabell Library Special Collections, Richmond, Virginia.*

subscription manager Carole Hunt in June 1969. "But we will not be idle during the summer. The *Alice* is planning ahead for a better paper next year."

Alice (and its radical reputation) indeed returned, and by October 1969, selling *Alice* on the nearby Radford College campus became almost as perilous as hawking the *Washington Free Press* in downtown D.C. An article by an unnamed Radford student in the undated October issue stated that a sign in her dorm window announcing that *Alice* was available for sale there was immediately removed by the dean of women, who also told them they could not sell or solicit *Alice* on campus. "We reminded her that students sell books, guitars and various other items without being told they could not sell or solicit," the student told *Alice*.

Entering into the new decade, the staff of *Alice* (with a maddening habit of not dating their issues) balanced its local VPI and Blacksburg coverage with the good fight of the national New Left movement, with both feet now firmly planted as pro–women's liberation, pro–civil rights and anti-Vietnam as any other underground paper in America. Even the staff was listed as a collective. Volume 6, number 4, contained a two-page spread on the November 14, 1969 march on Washington, an LNS feature on the conspiracy trial of the Chicago 7 and a piece on the financial solvency of the recent Woodstock Art and Music Fair. Locally, it also contained a feature prepared by the Radford ACLU chapter president on the unfair treatment of a student after alcohol was found in her dorm room after someone pulled a fire alarm. There was an article on the inequities of the VPI honor court and another on the difficulties faced by Blacksburg high school students in trying to get their own underground newspaper published. "Undaunted by Mr. Gray's opposition to a similar paper last year and his statement that 'as long as he was principal, he wouldn't allow it,' the students are still planning to press their case."

Around early February 1970, *Alice* speculated in a special "Drug Issue" that federal and state authorities were active on campus following a marijuana bust. The drug issue was a big one: sixteen pages printed in color on oversize tabloid newsprint. Long academic articles on marijuana, mescaline, speed and LSD and a blinding center spread of Virginia's drug laws set in seven-point type were all reprinted from other sources, such as LNS, the *Berkeley Barb*, *Chicago Seed* and others. These were interspersed with a few shorter articles of local interest, including an "open letter to Clark Kent," which may or may not have been written incoherently on purpose.

In the undated volume 7, number 3, the women's liberation issue, a very un–women's liberation sentiment was expressed by an editorial writer

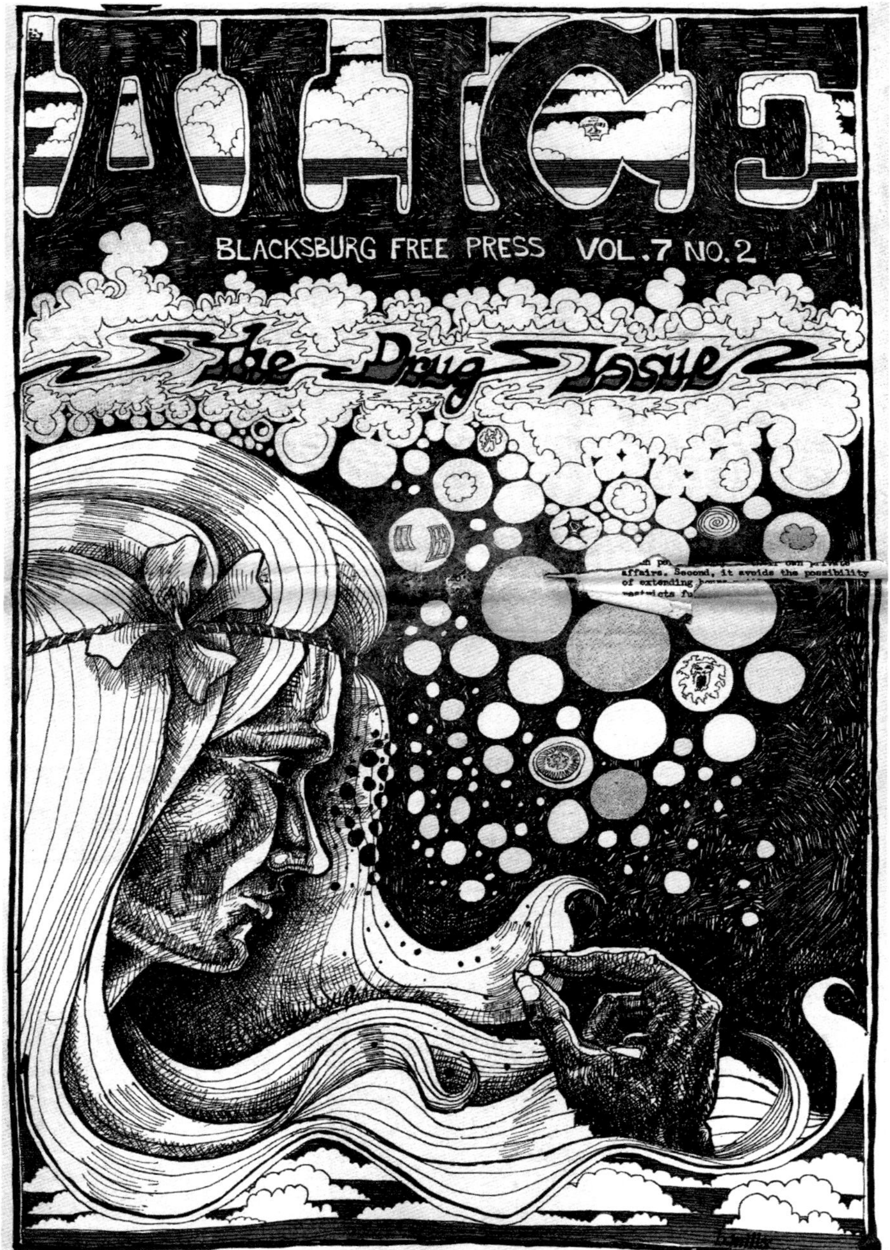

Alice, "The Drug Issue," February 1970. *Courtesy Bonnie Atwood and the VCU Cabell Library Special Collections, Richmond, Virginia.*

listed only as "Frodo." "There's a sense of brotherhood with *Alice*, and it's kind of latched on to me…I met a couple of chicks. They had caught hell at the teach-in when they tried to talk about 'women's liberation,' whatever that was."

"So I liked them as people, 'cause we worked on the paper together, besides as chicks."

A horrific account of the alleged sexual assault of a freshman female at a fraternity party under the title "Sisters Unite" was censored from the women's liberation issue by *Alice*'s printer but was inserted as a legal-size typed insert in the issue in the blank space left by the exclusion. According to the insert, the young lady was reportedly assaulted at an Episilon Pi Sigma party after passing out from numerous strong drinks made for her by a fraternity brother. Waking with bruises on her thighs in the infirmary the next day, a doctor reportedly told her that if she was not a virgin, then it was not rape, but a lesser charge of sexual assault. The college called in her parents, and the results of her pelvic exam were reportedly never divulged to her. Several frat brothers reportedly came to apologize to her, but none could (or would) identify the guilty parties. No resolution to this story could be located.

Alice ran into money problems yet again and called an emergency staff meeting to address that constant headache. "Several pressing problems have reared their heads in the production of *Alice*—and some basic decisions must be made concerning financing, type of printing, and so on. All *Alice* staffers are urgently needed to participate."

By the spring of 1970, antiwar sentiment had exploded at this rural college started and built on military tradition. A group of students and two faculty members interfered with a cadet drill, forcing the university to seek an injunction against further disruptive activities by them. That prompted a demonstration by about three hundred students at Burruss Hall. Then, on May 12, twenty-three students occupied and chained shut Cowgill Hall in support of a student strike against Vietnam and the deaths at Kent State.

Articles in the sparse spring 1970 issues of *Alice* include those on the thirty arrests at Harrisonburg's Madison College during a sit-in protesting the dismissal of several professors, gay liberation and the proliferation of black lung disease in the mountainous areas west of Blacksburg.

No issues of *Alice* published in 1971 could be located—the year the most intense demonstrations at VPI's campus occurred over a university council decision requiring students' dorm room doors to be open at least six inches whenever a visitor of the opposite sex was inside. Over the next several days, up to two thousand demonstrators marched through downtown Blacksburg not once but twice, blocking traffic and breaking store windows.

A fire suspected but not proven to be arson on May 29 heavily damaged a former on-campus apartment house, and a homemade tear-gas grenade detonation in the Squires snack bar finally put an end to the violence.

Troubled by the severity of student agitation, VPI president Thomas M. Hahn Jr. moved off-campus in late 1971. His former on-campus home was converted into offices.

The presumed last issue of *Alice*, published in 1972, makes no pleas for contributions nor announces that it is the final issue. It does list the names of fourteen staff members, including original founding member Bryan Ackler.

The dissident papers that appeared in southwest Virginia—including not just *Alice* and the *Ant Hill* at Radford but also the *Steamtunnel* (a four-page legal-sized news sheet that appeared for a few issues in 1980) and the *New River Free Press* (1983)—created forums where like-minded residents could share leftist political concerns and countercultural expressions in a mountainous part of Virginia not generally recognized for its radicalism.

As a testimony to the camaraderie of the *Alice* staff, "stowaway" contributor Bonnie Atwood said in 2014 they still get together twice a year.

THE FIXER

1969–72

This paper is like a joint...it needs to be passed around!
—The Fixer, *December 11, 1969*

Between 1966 and 1972, the student body at Harrisonburg's conservative Madison College (now James Madison University) campus seemed too apathetic for even the most benign extracurricular activities. The March 18, 1968 student newspaper the *Breeze* stated that the student government association (SGA) had to solicit students to run for even minor offices. Then, on May 7, the *Breeze* suspended publication for the remainder of the year due to a lack of student interest.

"It was a pretty quiet campus," said 1972 music graduate James Sheldrake, adding that their biggest protest was when a small entourage went out to the

WSVA [television channel three] studio "to protest the removal of *George of the Jungle* from Saturday morning broadcasting."

When men were first admitted in the 1966–67 academic year, female students were chafing under *in loco parentis*, which enforced stifling dress and behavior regulations, with micro-managing curfews and even lists posted in dorms of local food and drink establishments off-limits to them. Women could not wear sweatshirts, jeans or slacks in any school building; nor could they smoke, wear shorts or go downtown without makeup. Deviance from any of these rules resulted in warnings, suspension or expulsion.

Alexandria, Virginia native Jay Garland Rainey was one of the first males admitted to the school in 1966; however, his shoulder-length hair and hippie-style fringed poncho, made by his wife, were apparently too threatening to the conservative Madison administration, so they informed him at the end of his sophomore year that he was not welcome to return in the fall of 1968.

Rainey took Madison to court over the dismissal and won, returning to campus in the fall of 1969. "I had a Yankee Jewish liberal lawyer from Alexandria, and he just ate it up," he said in a 1998 oral interview with Jeremy Turner. Once back, he met Les Hammond, and they, along with a couple of other students, formed an organization named Harambee, for a Swahili term meaning "people working together for the betterment of all."

According to the 1970 Madison yearbook *The Bluestone*, Harambee's mission was to "further student rights on campus, unify the student body, and arrest student apathy in matters which concern Madison."

Needing a campus voice against what they considered backward social and academic policies, the twenty members of Harambee on November 20, 1969, created a mimeographed "moderate mouthpiece," the *Fixer*. One contributor said that if more students took an interest in alternative activities, like Harambee or with the *Fixer*, it would suck more control away from the elite SGA, which they claimed represented only the popular students.

Rainey served as the *Fixer*'s first editor, and his wife, Tina, did most of the art. All students were invited to contribute. "Everything that came to mind was printed," Rainey said in the 1998 interview. "If it was an issue on campus, or at least to us, then it was printed in the *Fixer*."

"This paper's purpose is not to polarize the Madison campus," stated the lead editorial in that first product of the "Madison College Free Press." "The sole purpose of this paper is to reopen needed channels of dialogue."

Articles in the first issue dealt mostly with the unequal application of college policies. One titled "Disappearing Act" was about a student who was tossed out of school and an entire semester expunged after it was

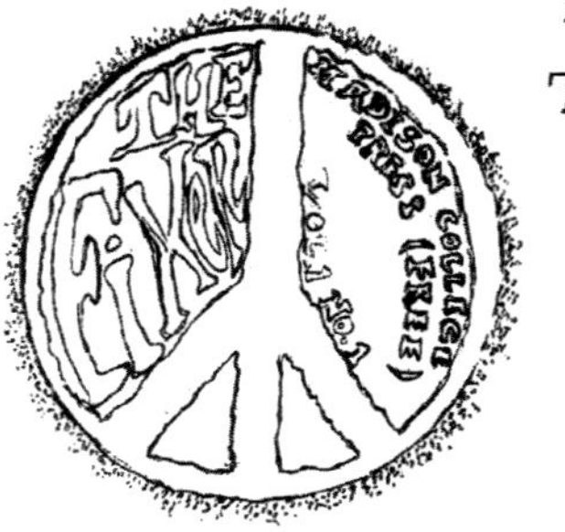

If you're not part of the
solution,
Then you're part of the
problem.

20 November 1969

This paper is written, edited, and published by SIG, a non-political, non-sectarian, non-sexual, non-racial, non-national, non-affiliated, non-profit aggregation.

OUR PURPOSE

This paper's purpose is not to polarize the Madison campus. The few interested students who made this publication possible do not reflect one absolute philosophy. We have no common goal, save to express ourselves. We do not expect everyone to agree with what we say. We do not want readers to accept our word as being above question. We are striving for a meaningful exchange of ideas, a confrontation of minds. If we fail in our objective, it is not because of what we say, but how it is received. The lines of communication at Madison have been cut, if they ever existed, and the sole purpose of this paper is to reopen these needed channels of dialogue, not only between student and administration, but also between student and student, between the student and faculty, and within the faculty itself.

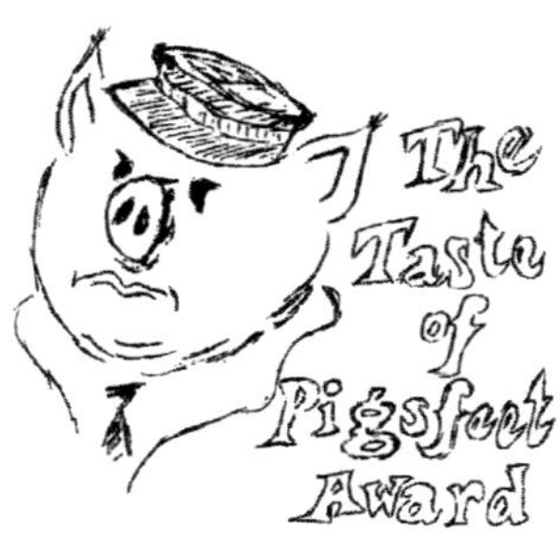

The award this week goes to the campus cop who, at a recent mixer, referred to one of Madison's Black students as "that nigger." Hang in there, humanitarian!

So you say: 80 per cent of the address labels on last week's <u>Time</u> covered Spiro Agnew's mouth. Hmmmm. . . .

Pouff! Disappearing Act

<u>Student Handbook</u>: "Failure to correct an application form submitted prior to entry to Madison which contains falsification is a violation of the Honor System, if not corrected within thirty days after registration at Madison College." (p. 67)

Dear Friends,

To those of you who are unaware of the strange disappearance of your fellow student, Toni Flitter, let me inform you.

When I applied for admission, I falsified my records by not acknowledging my attendance at West Chester State College. I did this knowing that otherwise I could not have been accepted here due to poor records from West Chester. But I have been accepted and have made the grades here. I took the opportunity to make something of myself and make something decent of my life. My education has become a part of my life; it is not just something that everyone else does. I have been pursuing this goal for the past three years in spite of one bad experience at West Chester. Now, President Miller is making it virtually impossible for me to achieve my goal anywhere. He, along with the Administrative Council, has decided to take away all my credits, saying I was never a student here at Madison. I have nothing to show for my hard work, so that if I wanted to transfer to another college, it would be impossible. By doing this, President Miller has denied me one year of my life. How can I explain my one year of disappearance?

Being a concerned parent, my father called President Miller, who was in Richmond. My father contacted Mr. James Fox telling him of my situation. He explained about my one bad year at West Chester and expressed my most sincere desire to pursue my education. He asked Mr. James Fox to help me at my hearing before Administrative Council, not to deny or hold me back from obtaining my education. My father begged Mr. Fox to show some kind of mercy so

The Fixer, volume 1, number 1, November 20, 1969. *Courtesy Special Collections and Research Services, Carrier Library, James Madison University, Harrisonburg, Virginia.*

discovered she applied with an incomplete application. Les Hammond wrote a long regular column titled "Digging the Weeds" about not just that "disappearing student" but also about committee inequities, including the case of three girls hauled before honor council for allegedly stealing an orange crate.

Issue number 2 included the paper's first paid advertisement, for Harrisonburg's "hip" clothing store, the Rag Bag, at 66 East Market Street. "Bells, vests, body shirts, Carnaby Street dresses, etc."

In January 1970, Harambee (despite having the reputation of being composed of campus radicals) was recognized as an official campus organization with Les Hammond as president. The student body started responding to *Fixer* articles of national importance, like drugs, women's liberation and Vietnam. The paper's use of "colorful" language drew much criticism: "Profanity…is in poor taste," wrote freshman SGA representative J. David Leaman in the January 12, 1970 issue, claiming he would never work on a "free" press. "I do not want to in any way jeopardize my college experience."

In the spring of 1970, three popular faculty members—Houston Rogers, James McClung and Roger Adkins—lost their teaching contracts. According to the *Fixer*, the decision was based solely on their liberalism (and their hair and moustaches) and not on scholarly merit. Attempts by students to meet with Madison president Dr. George Tyler Miller were continually rejected, leading to frustrated charges that the school was not being accountable to its student body. The *Fixer* stated angrily that "letter campaigns, marches, strikes, petitions, boycotts and other means (if necessary) will be used in this struggle to stop the school's attempt to dehumanize both its faculty and its students."

By the end of February, the *Fixer* had grown to twelve pages, listed fifty-six contributors in the staff box and had become a subscriber to Liberation News Service. It also ratcheted up its criticism of the college, the *Breeze*'s editor Frank Humphreys and especially Dr. Miller's handling of the fired faculty.

Student response to the *Fixer* and the faculty firings escalated: a March 18, 1970 letter to the *Breeze*, signed by eight students and one professor, Dr. Ralph Napp, complained, "The language and content of the article was the lowest level of communication possible. Is this the way you wish to communicate with the faculty and administration?"

Another letter in the same issue, signed by twenty-two seniors, expressed the need for changes at Madison but registered "disgust" with Les Hammond and nine other students for walking out of the Founder's Day Convocation. "There is no reason to disrupt the observance of traditions that have no bearing on student and faculty rights."

Scowling at the local campus unrest, hugely popular WSVA personalities Arnold Felcher and Wip Robinson expressed their displeasure in a March 27, 1970 broadcast editorial lifted (as claimed by the *Fixer*) from a 1920s communist party brochure, comparing demonstrating college students with communists "for the purpose of infiltrating the youth and consequently undermining the entire society."

There was no edition of the *Fixer* published on April 7, 1970, because the Madison administration and the SGA cut them off from their mimeograph machines. "Even though the students have paid for this machine they may not use it," stated an angry story in the April 15, 1970 "Screwed Awards" issue, which was printed off-campus. "We could not, and would not, allow Madison's administration, aided by the Student Government Association, to take freedom of the press and speech away from us and those students who have used and might use this publication."

The *Fixer* staff scrounged $100 for their own machine from a local Sears store, with the promise they would make it freely available to all students and organizations without fear of censorship. "We are now $90 in the hole," said a short notice. "Please give what you can."

Believing that peaceful assembly was the best way to express their concerns about the dismissed faculty—which now numbered five, after psychology instructor James Black resigned before Madison could fire him—a group of students were denied permission to hold a vigil in the administration building.

Undeterred, on Sunday, April 26, about 40 students gathered around Keezell Hall to speak with Dr. Miller about the firings. When Miller never showed, about 38 students moved next door inside the unlocked Wilson Hall, and about 250 students gathered outside. Dr. Fox arrived shortly thereafter, waving a student handbook, warning everyone that the police were being contacted.

Around 1:15 a.m., police in riot gear showed up to jeers of those gathered outside. Although most of the students returned to their dorms, thirty people—including Jay Rainey and Dr. McClung, one of the fired professors—were arrested and taken in a borrowed moving van to jail.

"This type of Gestapo tactic has got to stop," wrote Debbie Darr in the *Fixer*. A "Madison 30 Defense Fund" was established to offset the arrested students' expenses.

All of the demonstrators were found guilty of trespassing in Rockingham County Court and all paid a $100 fine but seven, who appealed to a jury trial in Rockingham Circuit Court. They were again found guilty, and unfortunately, the sentences were far worse. Dr. McClung received nine

Vol. 3 No. 13

THE FIXER

Vol. 3 No. 13 Feb. 20-26

A community without power is not a community, it is merely a collection of individuals.

H.R. Shapiro

PLEASE PASS THIS PAPER AROUND

WE ONLY RUN OFF 1000 COPIES

As Student "Government" elections approach we face a choice of alternatives. First, since this organization has not lived up to any but the most modest of expectations, we can ignore the elections. Indeed, we can activly ignore them so that no one can claim that this sluggish animal called S.G.A. is a legitimate voice of the students; so that the decision--makers cannot claim to be responding to the students when they only hear a few and listen to even fewer. This alternative would seem to demand other vehicles of student voice: civil disobedience, petition, public demonstration and the like.

The second choice, the one I would favor, is to take S.G.A. by the reins (maybe by something else). Students could, if they wished, turn out in relatively large numbers, elect their representatives on the basis of issues (rather than photographs or gimmicks) and make their presence known. If it stopped with elections it would be futile; the energy must continue. Those elected must know that everything they do is being watched, that if they are not acting for the students they will be removed from their throne. The student constituency should make the S.G.A. act for the students.

Elect an S.G.A. intelligently, keeping in mind everything on this campus that makes the student a "nigger." Then get on its ass and stay there. Don't let anything slip by you just because the Breeze doesn't publish it. The S.G.A. has an office on the first floor of the campus center. Take your complaints and questions there. If you don't get action raise hell about it. The same tools used to move any government bureaucracy can be appled to S.G.A. Maybe if enough of us push we can make this snail into a sprinter. Stop pissing and moaning about things and blaming the S.G.A. Make it work or get rid of it. It's about time the student nigger became militantly "uppity!"

David Grimes

(staff note-David was Legislative Vice President of S.G.A., he resigned in December, 1971.)

Fixer readers

Hopefully, by now, you're all aware of the upcoming election for SGA President on Tuesday Feb. 22, 9:00am--5:00 pm in the PO lobby. Hopefully, you will all exercise your rights and priviledges and vote for the one candidate that will do the best job. Hopefully, you will vote for me!

Allow me to present myself: my name is Kathy Uhler. I'm a sophomore Early Childhood major and I consider Arlington, Va. home.

OK. Now that you know who I am...let me tell you what I stand for as the only female candidate for the office of SGA President.

First-of-all, I don't plan to make any promises. Other than the one that I will work very hard and willingly for the students. I have a very sincere but simple platform. (Hopefully, some of you have read it!) I will work hard to:

1) rid Madison of the unequal, unjust, illegal rules that apply to women and <u>not</u> men;
2) make Madison a better place to stay at for the weekend, i.e. have more and better quality entertainment such as concerts, mixers, parties, etc.;
3) encourage a more natural and humane "open dorms" policy;
4) involve more student in more of the campus affairs, i.e. encourage more people to run for offices such as this one, have more participation by and for students;
5) make the SGA more of an organization and tool of the students' wishes <u>not</u> just of a select clique;
6) encourage intellectual pursuits at Madison for those that are really interested.

I feel qualified as any of the other canidates. I know the feminine point of view most intimately and am naturally anxious to achieve total equality between the sexes at Madison.

I'm presently President of the

(Please turn to page 3)

o

12% of Americans are "heavy" drinkers.

The Fixer, February 20–26, 1972. *Courtesy Special Collections and Research Services, Carrier Library, James Madison University, Harrisonburg, Virginia.*

months in jail and a $1,000 fine; Steve Rochelle, Jay Rainey, Edward Johnson, Robert Evans, William Massie and Lewis Sword were each fined $500, with Rainey and Rochelle also getting six months in jail.

The harsh sentences reflected Madison College's (and Harrisonburg's) "take no prisoners" approach to radical student behavior. Retired history professor Dr. John Wood told Jeremy Turner in a 1998 oral interview that "the town acted as if Madison had exploded into some sort of riot."

To compound the matter, on May 6, mere weeks after the Madison 30 debacle, the school administration refused to cancel or even suspend classes for three hours in memory of the students shot dead at Ohio's Kent State University.

Not all students were supportive of the radical minority. "The Madison 30 and their followers are acting like a bunch of very immature spoiled brats," wrote an anonymous student in the May 19 issue of the *Fixer*. "If [they] are suspended, good riddance. Maybe they'll grow up one day."

During the summer of 1970, Dr. Miller declared final war against the *Fixer*, informing all dormitory hostesses, resident advisors and post office employees that the paper was no longer approved for campus distribution. "Any copies found on campus will be placed in the trash."

The *Fixer* also dryly noted that Virginia attorney general Andrew Miller "has religiously collected all back copies," thoughtfully provided to him by the Madison administration.

Despite the edict, the *Fixer* roared into the new academic year looking and sounding more and more like a metropolitan underground newspaper, with articles on Vietnam, abortion rights, women's liberation poetry and edicts to boycott Safeway grocery stores for selling scab grapes. There was no word on the administration's reaction to their presence.

By the end of 1970 and into 1971, the layout, artwork and mimeograph resolution improved, but the paper became less about Madison and more about national issues, with articles reprinted not only from LNS but also other underground papers around the country, such as Atlanta's the *Great Speckled Bird* and the *Chicago Seed*. Madison students may have been eager to pick up and read the *Fixer* but were less likely to contribute to it.

Then in February 1971, the *Fixer* and Harambee caused a local uproar when they invited Jane Fonda to speak on campus to help raise funds for the Virginia Chapter of the ACLU.

In a letter to the *Harrisonburg Daily News-Record*, a group calling itself the "Defenders of Constitutional Government" voiced great indignation that such a "notorious troublemaker" was being allowed on campus.

They expressed hope that a "groundswell of opposition" would cancel her appearance.

No groundswell occurred, and Fonda appeared on February 15. In a calm discussion the *Breeze* and college administration found almost refreshing, Fonda (flanked by ACLU attorneys Philip Hirschkop and John Lowe) discussed GI rights, the war in Vietnam and the oppression of the American Indian. Fonda also gave a private interview to a group of female reporters from the *Virginia Weekly* in Charlottesville.

By November 1, 1972, the *Fixer* had lost its original staff and most of its personality, reverting back to its original, haphazard appearance. "*The Fixer* is back. For how long, I'm not sure," stated the opening sentence in the November 19 issue, typed possibly on an Old Royal typewriter with a clogged "o."A shining spot was a back-page article expressing joy that the enactment of the Virginia eighteen-year-old vote and legal adult status finally repealed *in loco parentis*, finally giving college students the rights of ordinary citizens.

The final issue was an undated volume 4, number 6, presumed to be published in late 1972 or early 1973. On the front page, Diane Huddle—perhaps unwittingly being metaphorical about the fast rise and equally fast descent of the *Fixer*—wrote that "whenever you eat too fast you get heartburn or you puke."

4

TIDEWATER

THE IRRESPONSIBLE SENSATIONALIST AND THE ODC FREE PRESS

1966–68

The *Irresponsible Sensationalist* (*IS*) was one of Virginia's first campus-based dissident papers, produced by Old Dominion College professor Dr. Willard Frank and students Allen Phemister, David Lawson, Sylvia Lynn, Margaret Nix and others, on the ODC campus in the spring of 1966.

Dr. Frank said in a 1998 oral interview with Jay Gaidmore that the name derived from ODC president Dr. Lewis Webb, who tried to temper his and other young professors' "radical" tendencies by calling them "irresponsible sensationalists…making sensationalism just for itself."

"The Irresponsible Sensationalists advocate thinking about and discussing the actual, complex problems men face," stated a May 2, 1966 cover story. "Does this make us sensationalists? Perhaps, for the problems are sensational, and we refuse to cloud them in euphemisms, oversimplifications and patriotic hogwash."

Published by "Peace Creep Cruds, Bonded Ltd," the *IS* was a scholarly combination of civil rights and campus commentaries mixed with absurdist humor bonded to a central core of opposition to America's expanding presence in Vietnam. An anonymous essay in issue number 2 entitled "Marx and Alienation" scolded the conservative establishment for taking the writings of Karl Marx out of context to twist them against the growing New the Irresponsible Sensationalist

Published by - PEACE CREEP CRUDS, BONDED LTD

MOTTO - "If you don't agree with the views expressedherein - start your own damn paper!"

C A L E N D A R   O F   E V E N T S

April 17,
A clean-shaven man answering to the name of Innocent III will be drafting all able-bodied children between the ages of 6 and 9½ to spearhead a crusade aimed at driving the infidels from the Holy Lands. All interssted children are asked to assemble at the west gate of the Physical plant no later than 7 a.m.

April 18,
At 9:30 in the parking lot adjacent to the Social Studies Building Senator Kitchener will deliver a speech on the "domino theory" entitled: "If we'd a stopped 'em in the Boar War, boys, there'd be no damn Vietnam today!" Public invited.

April 19,
Between the hoursof 10:00 - 12:00 and 1:00 - 1:30 posthumus peace demonstrations will be held protesting American involvement in the Spanish-American War (San Juan Hill, "Teddy the Stick", Manila Bay, etc.). The demonstration will be led by exotically bedecked agitators carrying colorfully ornamented placards while winding in snake-like procession around periphery of the Physical Plant. Refreshments will be served on the sidelines to pacify hecklers, demonstrators, and innocent bystanders alike.

June 1,
All interested students will meet before the west facade of the Physical Plant to clean up the mess left by Innocent's crusaders and the Peace Creep Cruds. Having done this the remaining students will form an illegal fraternity.

AN EDITORIAL: AMERICAN CONTRADICTIONS AND THE STUDENT RESPONSE

In our country today is a growing movement of students and adults who are reacting in many different ways to what they feel are profound moral contradictions in the structure of our society. There is a widespread malaise about the fact that what our moral sense and our political heritage dictates should be the relationship between man and man, between governed and the governors and between the people and the resources of this country is not what is in fact the state of the Union. We wantto focus in this issue of the newsletter on some of the conflicts that are sparking this movement, as well as attempts to capture the spirit of and basis for the student response.For the most part our opinions about contemporary America are unsystematic responses to the relationships or events that we consider wrong. But perhaps, as we sketch these opinions out and try at the same time to respond creatively to what we consider an unjust system we will move closer to a more complete analysis of today's America.

Contradictions

What are these contradictions that concern us? Here are a few from one perspective: In our country people starve and freeze in the midst of the greatest wealth the world has ever known. Billions are spent to burn

The Irresponsible Sensationalist, April 1966. *Courtesy Special Collections & University Archives, Patricia W. and J. Douglas Perry Library, Old Dominion University, Norfolk, Virginia.*

Left movement: "Marx would be appalled if he knew how neglected and distorted his insights have become," the treatise concluded. "His writings are quoted out of context in order to make him appear the devil who is guiding Russian state capitalism and Chinese Totalitarianism."

Breaking up the serious analyses was an off-the-wall calendar of events. "April 19:…posthumous peace demonstrations will be held protesting

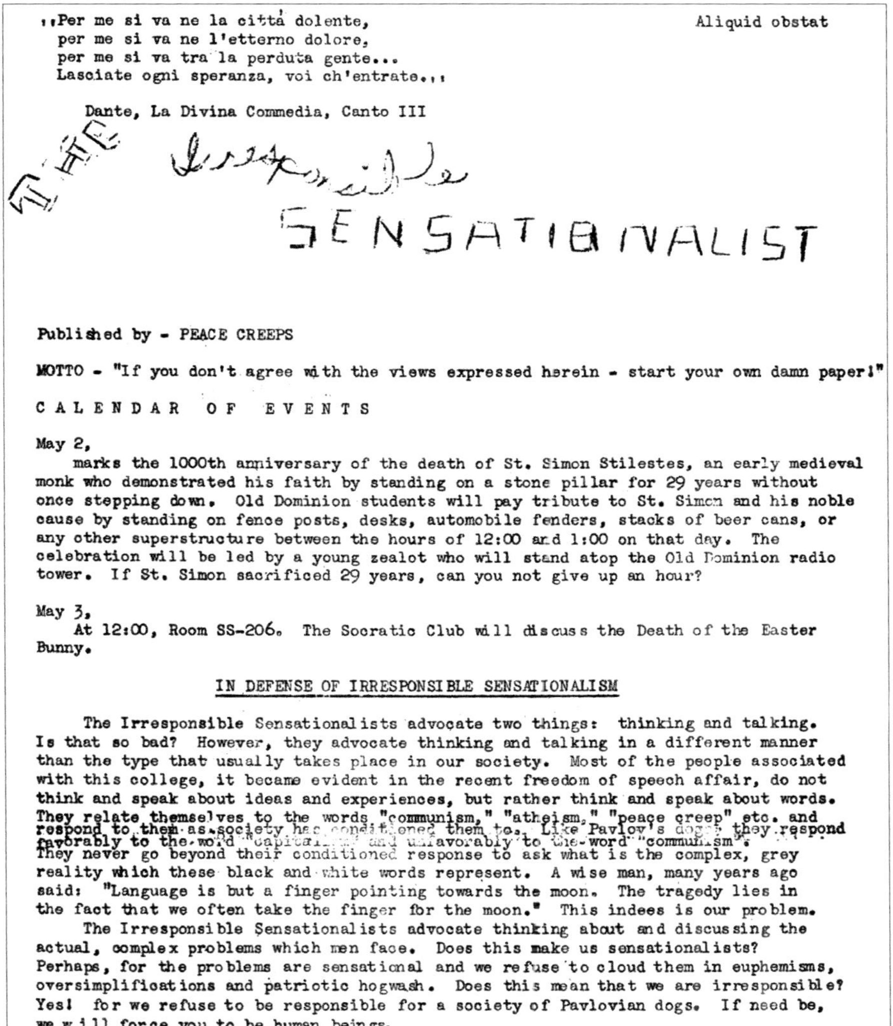

„Per me si va ne la città dolente,
per me si va ne l'etterno dolore,
per me si va tra la perduta gente...
Lasciate ogni speranza, voi ch'entrate.„

Dante, La Divina Commedia, Canto III

Aliquid obstat

The Irresponsible SENSATIONALIST

Published by - PEACE CREEPS

MOTTO - "If you don't agree with the views expressed herein - start your own damn paper!"

C A L E N D A R O F E V E N T S

May 2,
marks the 1000th anniversary of the death of St. Simon Stilestes, an early medieval monk who demonstrated his faith by standing on a stone pillar for 29 years without once stepping down. Old Dominion students will pay tribute to St. Simon and his noble cause by standing on fence posts, desks, automobile fenders, stacks of beer cans, or any other superstructure between the hours of 12:00 and 1:00 on that day. The celebration will be led by a young zealot who will stand atop the Old Dominion radio tower. If St. Simon sacrificed 29 years, can you not give up an hour?

May 3,
At 12:00, Room SS-206. The Socratic Club will discuss the Death of the Easter Bunny.

IN DEFENSE OF IRRESPONSIBLE SENSATIONALISM

The Irresponsible Sensationalists advocate two things: thinking and talking. Is that so bad? However, they advocate thinking and talking in a different manner than the type that usually takes place in our society. Most of the people associated with this college, it became evident in the recent freedom of speech affair, do not think and speak about ideas and experiences, but rather think and speak about words. They relate themselves to the words "communism," "atheism," "peace creep" etc. and respond to them as society has conditioned them to. Like Pavlov's dogs, they respond favorably to the word "capitalism" and unfavorably to the word "communism". They never go beyond their conditioned response to ask what is the complex, grey reality which these black and white words represent. A wise man, many years ago said: "Language is but a finger pointing towards the moon. The tragedy lies in the fact that we often take the finger for the moon." This indees is our problem.

The Irresponsible Sensationalists advocate thinking about and discussing the actual, complex problems which men face. Does this make us sensationalists? Perhaps, for the problems are sensational and we refuse to cloud them in euphemisms, oversimplifications and patriotic hogwash. Does this mean that we are irresponsible? Yes! for we refuse to be responsible for a society of Pavlovian dogs. If need be, we will force you to be human beings.

The Irresponsible Sensationalist, May 1966. *Courtesy Special Collections & University Archives, Patricia W. and J. Douglas Perry Library, Old Dominion University, Norfolk, Virginia.*

American involvement in the Spanish-American War. The demonstrators will be led by exotically bedecked agitators carrying colorfully ornamented placards while winding in snake-like procession around the physical plant."

In 1966, Dr. Frank worked to create the "Intercollegiate Forum" in conjunction with Norfolk State University to bring contemporary and controversial speakers to bridge the two ethnically opposite campuses and expose ODC students to minority interests. "ODC was all white. No African American students or Asians," he said in the oral interview.

The third and final issue of *IS* appeared in May 1966. Sprinkled between long commentaries on Marxism (again) and the use of Vietnam pacifism were more examples of the paper's 1966 humor. "May 13, 3:00 p.m.," stated another calendar entry, "Three angry and bearded young men will burn their zip code numbers in front of the Norfolk Post Office."

The following winter, the first issue of the *ODC Free Press* appeared, coinciding with the first organizational campus meeting of SDS on February 14, 1967. Sixteen students formed a campus chapter that same month.

Sponsored by "students and faculty committed to the free expression of all ideas," the *ODC Free Press* picked up where the *IS* left off, concerning itself in its slim six issues with campus free speech concerns and the exploits of Dennis Ciesielski, who was listed as a staff member along with Michael Bottino, Dr. Frank and Dr. Lauren Selden. The paper also reprinted articles from such publications as *WIN*, *National Guardian* and *Downdraft*.

Ciesielski was originally a military Vietnam protestor, serving nine months in a Portsmouth, New Hampshire navy brig for refusing to board a Vietnam-bound ship. Upon his discharge, he was sent back to Virginia, where he also worked to get the antiwar paper *Rough Draft* distributed at Williamsburg's Fort Eustis.

On March 7, 1967, the *Free Press* reported that Ciesielski was suspended and Dr. Webb banned all SDS publications because of "obscene language" in a newsletter containing the e.e. cummings poem "I Sing of Olaf." Issue number 6 of the *Free Press* was a response to the banning, calling Webb "Le Grand Lewie; Usurper of Academic Freedom, Paternalistic overlord, Censor."

The May 15 issue carried Ciesielski's story and republished the offending poem. "Olaf is not obscene by standards for judging obscenity laid down by the US Supreme Court," the *Free Press* said. The reprint was a "reaffirmation of our determination that students at ODC shall not be denied a constitutional right guaranteed to all other Americans."

In 1968, the *ODC Free Press* gave way to *Brown Shoes*.

Brown Shoes

1968–69

SHOES is not going to talk about the war. There will be enough death around here without our telling you more of it. We might talk about ODC (Old Dominion College), but ODC is a bastard and a crippled bastard at that…We'll probably talk about nothing since that's our most important function.
—Editorial, Brown Shoes, *September 23, 1968*

Quit school, why fake it? Brown shoes don't make it.
—Frank Zappa & the Mothers of Invention, "Brown Shoes Don't Make It," from the album Absolutely Free *(Verve), 1967*

An underground newspaper almost as cryptic and mysterious as its Frank Zappa–inspired namesake song, *Brown Shoes* first appeared around the campus of Old Dominion College (now Old Dominion University) in Norfolk, Virginia, on September 28, 1968.

"Dear President Webb," stated a letter by editor and founder Will Galloway, addressed to ODC president Dr. Lewis Webb Jr. on the cover of volume 1, number 1, "*Brown Shoes* is the title of a forthcoming newspaper which we intend to publish bimonthly…our purpose is simply to present journalism in a creative way."

The open letter went on to address the decision of the ODC board of visitors granting Webb the "unconstitutional" authority to "take any measures necessary to relieve the College of disruptance caused by unauthorized assembly" in response to student violence at other colleges around the country.

"We at *Brown Shoes* do not feel like students today; we feel like prisoners," the letter concluded. "We are asking you, sir, for our freedom."

Brown Shoes was big, brash and had little in common with its two ODC forefathers, the *Irresponsible Sensationalist* and the *ODC Free Press*. It embraced the look, language and many of the ideologies of larger underground papers around the country yet in its short history seemed unable to create a distinct, cohesive campus voice because of continuously changing formats, layout and typestyles and a revolving door of leadership and staff members. Its paper stock even varied widely from issue to issue, printed on cheap, pulpy newsprint one issue and expensive, slick stock the next.

TIDEWATER'S UNDERGROUND NEWSPAPER

Affiliate of Liberation News Service

volume 1

number 5

BROWNSHOES

FEEL FREE THE WHOLE DAY LONG

manufactured & printed in u.s..

Published by Norfolk Cooperative Newspaper Project

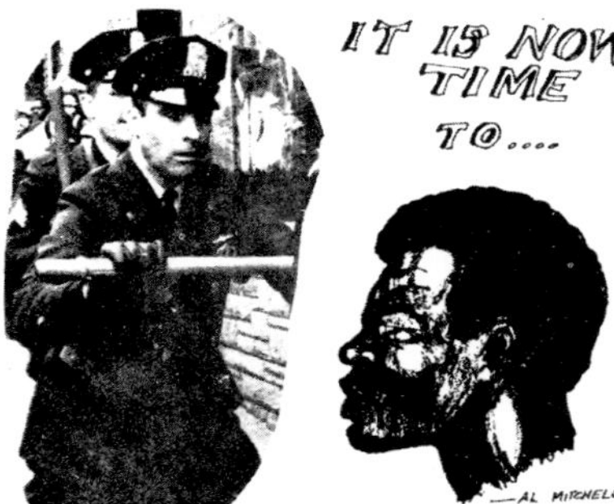

IT IS NOW TIME TO.... ...INTENSIFY THE STRUGGLE.

ALL DAY ORGY AT O.D.C.

TIME OUT pg.7 ARMY OVERKILL AT **PRESIDIO** pg.2

BOWERS BUST—16 years p.8

GRAPE AID page 1 in Hampton (SEE P.8)

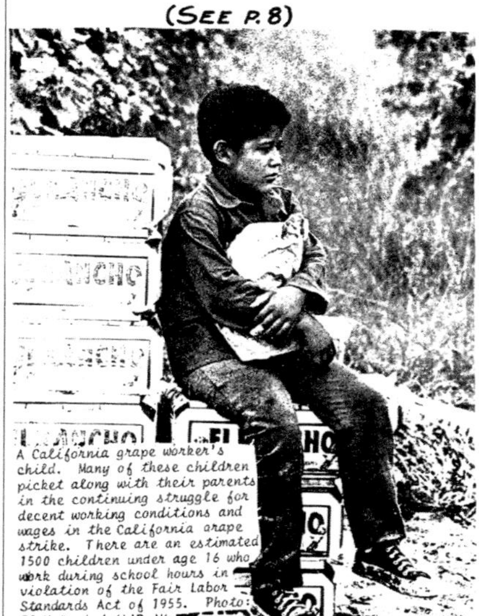

A California grape worker's child. Many of these children picket along with their parents in the continuing struggle for decent working conditions and wages in the California grape strike. There are an estimated 1500 children under age 16 who work during school hours in violation of the Fair Labor Standards Act of 1955. Photo: El Malcriado/LNS-N

EVEN BENEATH THIS BITTERNESS

AT THE BOTTOM OF THE NIGHT
THE FOOTSTEPS DESCEND AND RETREAT

SHADOWS SURROUND THEM
STREETS, DRUNKS. BUILDINGS.
SOMEONE RUNNING AWAY FROM HIMSELF.
A BROKEN BOTTLE, BLEEDING.
A WIDOWED PAPER SAILING AROUND A CORNER.
A FREETHINKER PISSING ON THE GRASS,
WHERE TOMORROW THE WELL-DRESSED CHILDREN
WILL PLAY
BESIDE THE DEW.

FAR AWAY SOMETHING SCREAMS, DARK METAL, GENITAL.
ASPHALT AND BLIND STONES, SLEEPING AIR,
DARKNESS, COLD, POLICE, COLD, MORE POLICE.
STREETS, WHORES, DRUNKS, BUILDINGS.
POLICE AGAIN, SOLDIERS, AGAIN POLICE.
THE STATISTICS SAY: FOR EVERY 80,000 OFFICERS OF THE LAW
THERE IS ONE DOCTOR IN GUATEMALA.

THEN UNDERSTAND THE MISERY OF MY COUNTRY,
AND MY PAIN AND EVERYONE'S PAIN!
IF WHEN I SAY: BREAD!
THEY SAY
SHUT UP!
AND WHEN I SAY: LIBERTY!
THEY SAY
DIE!

BUT I DON'T SHUT UP AND I DON'T DIE.
I LIVE
AND FIGHT, MADDENING
THOSE WHO RULE MY COUNTRY.

FOR IF I LIVE
I FIGHT,
AND IF I FIGHT
I CONTRIBUTE TO THE DAWN.
AND SO VICTORY IS BORN
EVEN IN THE BITTEREST HOURS.

— OTTO RENE CASTILLO
(TRANS. MEG RANDALL)

Brown Shoes, November 1968. *Courtesy Special Collections & University Archives, Patricia W. and J. Douglas Perry Library, Old Dominion University, Norfolk, Virginia.*

Unfortunately, the presence of *Brown Shoes* and New Left activity at ODC in the summer of 1968 quickly drew the attention of the FBI Norfolk field office (NFO). In a memo to FBI headquarters dated July 3, 1968, the NFO deplored the fact that ODC administration allowed the Tidewater chapter, clergy and laymen concerned about Vietnam to meet in the Lewis W. Webb Student Center.

"This letter should criticize the ODC Administration for allowing an organization like the SDS to openly operate at a state supported school … helping in the un-American and unpatriotic perversion of the minds of our youths," the memo continued. "The letter should be critical of the school administration for ever allowing the SDS to become active on the campus."

The FBI must have been thrilled when the ODC chapter of the SDS sharply disagreed with its national policy of violent government overthrow and voted to disband on September 21, 1968. It instead embraced an affiliation with Campus Americans for Democratic Action (CADA).

Volume 1, number 2, of *Brown Shoes* appeared on October 18, 1968, with a cover story on an upcoming speech in Norfolk by civil rights activist Dick Gregory, who was on the 1968 Virginia presidential ballot as the Peace and Freedom Party (PFP) nominee.

"The Virginia Peace and Freedom Party…is seeking to offer the voters a clear-cut alternative on the major issues in the campaign," the story reported on the little-known political party and its candidate. PFP picketers in July 1968 forced Norfolk city council to stop conducting closed-door meetings in violation of the Freedom of Information Act.

The second issue also described the progressive ODC Emerson forum as the "most goings-on organization on campus." The Unitarian Universalist Church–sponsored forum was a liberal oasis in the center of a white southern college with a paternalistic president and administration mired in conventional 1950s decorum and sensibilities.

"I remember the dean of women…toward the end of the '60s, wanted to make it a requirement that [female] students had to wear skirts to go into the library," retired professor Dr. Willard Frank said in a 1998 oral history interview. "She found resistance. So her mind was in the '50s when that was considered proper. Students by that time were not accepting this, that kind of *in loco parentis*."

The Emerson Forum kicked off the 1968 school year with a talk by professor and ACLU attorney Dr. Lauren Selden, who criticized the college's recently enacted "riot act" (as described in *Brown Shoes* issue number 1). His presentation was in turn defended by Dr. Webb in a later forum, who quoted a story from *Reader's Digest* describing those "plenty pink" "SDS-ers."

"Somebody's got to say when an emergency arises," Dr. Webb was quoted by the *Norfolk Virginian-Pilot*. "In case there is an emergency the thing would be out of hand immediately, just like Columbia [University]."

Despite the inclusion of national, local and campus coverage, criticism of the paper was swift and withering. "Who are you guys kidding?" wrote Williamsburg reader Mark Edison in a letter to the editor, calling *Brown Shoes* "the biggest joke of the year." "All you need are haircuts and baths but you punks think you're doing something important. Just wait a few years and you'll get the picture."

The fall of 1968 spawned a core group of protestors, who showed their chops on October 2 when presidential candidate Richard Nixon arrived at the Norfolk Municipal Arena for a campaign rally. Many ODC students demonstrated outside the arena, and others told a reporter they were hippies protesting the war in Vietnam.

The FBI was right on top of the demonstration with its inimitable perspective. "In the group which included the hippie element there were observed several young Negroes wearing typical Afro-attire," stated a November 11, 1968 report from the NFO. "The group of demonstrators of which the hippie element was a part was observed to be dirty, unkempt, bearded young people with mustaches and long hair."

At an ODC campus publications panel discussion on November 27, 1968, *Brown Shoes* spokesman Steve Weller said that while the paper was "attempting to reach students at ODC and at Norfolk State," eventually it would seek to serve the nonacademic community as well. Admitting financial difficulties, Weller said the paper's meager finances were derived solely from advertising and sales. He also dispelled a persistent rumor that ODC applied pressure to printers to not print the paper.

The undated volume 1, number 3 (presumed published in late November 1968) contained two big stories: one was a long syndicated piece on the upcoming inauguration of Richard Nixon, but the other was a hard-hitting piece on a Norfolk State student named John Kenyatta who was arrested and indicted of selling marijuana after he bought it from police officer Alfred Fenner, who was caught on tape admitting he trapped Kenyatta into buying from him. "Today it seems no black man is safe from the tricks of the establishment," Kenyatta told *Brown Shoes*.

According to the April 1–15 issue, Kenyatta's appeal was turned down by the Virginia Supreme Court, so he retained civil rights attorney Phillip Hirschkop to take his case to the federal courts, pleading that Kenyatta was the victim of entrapment by the Norfolk Police to force the outspoken black leader out of sight.

Kenyatta's comrades in the Black Liberation Action Council (BLAC) were also detained and frisked on a Norfolk street for two hours after legally obtained and licensed firearms were spotted in their car. BLAC was a nonviolent black liberation group that opened a cooperative market and a school called the "East Ghent Tutorial School for Motivation" in the Ghent area of Norfolk. They rented the building with the proceeds from dues and selling "black-oriented" Christmas cards.

Issue number 3 also contained a column on civil rights progress in the South from former Duke basketball sensation Art Heyman.

The undated issue number 5—now subtitled "Tidewater's Underground Newspaper" and published by the "Norfolk Cooperative Newspaper Project"—was a feisty eight pages and was much more "underground" in its appearance and embrace of advocacy journalism.

The cover story was of an arson attempt at the SSOC collective house at 2000 Hanover Avenue in Richmond, when someone entered through an unlocked basement door and left a burning torch beside the oil furnace.

Page four announced that "a group of Tidewater servicemen opposed to the war, the draft and the injustices of the military establishment" were publishing an underground paper at Fort Eustis called *Rough Draft*.

On page six was part one of an interview conducted and written by Samiel Kenyatta (prime minister of BLAC) with a Norfolk resident and well-known former ODC student Dennis Ciesielski. The next issue, mislabeled volume 1, number 5 (and also undated), continued the Ciesielski interview, titled "We Ain't Marching Anymore!"

Brown Shoes number 6 contained an open call for workers and contributors at its new location at the Unitarian Church center at 902 Grayden Avenue. "If you can write, draw, sell papers or do anything else that will help the paper please come by. *Brown Shoes* belongs to the free community."

Advertisers included Collins New Era clothing at 719 Granby Street and the Folk Ghetto, "Norfolk's only professional coffee house," at West Freemason Street. There were also a handful of classified ads for ODC events.

The FBI noted *Brown Shoes*' move, as it had had the Unitarian Church under surveillance for months. "The Unitarian Church Center of Norfolk has been the center of anti-war, anti-military, and anti-draft activity in the Norfolk area," stated a December 31, 1969 NFO memo. "The Minister, [redacted]…has been identified prominently in this activity. Leads are outstanding to fully identify [redacted] if he has a background of subversive activity."

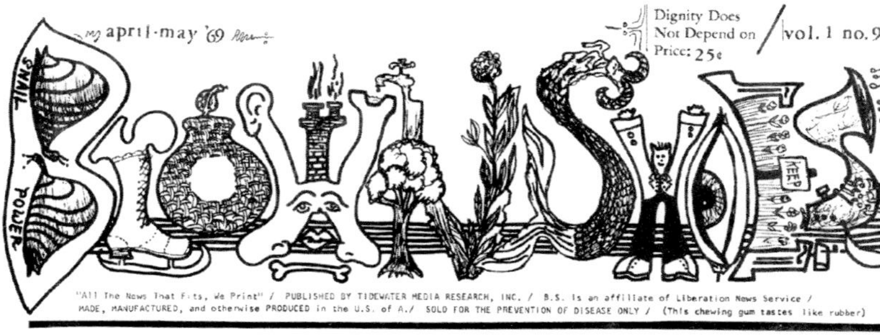

Free the 21 now

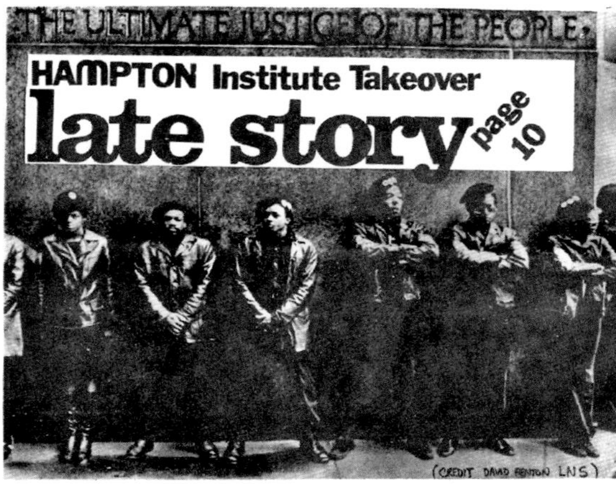

NEW YORK, New York (LNS) -- Shouting "Free the Panther 21; Power to the People," hundreds bearing red banners swarmed across the Chase Manhattan Plaza, and through the streets of New York's financial district during the noon rush on Friday.

The marauders had rushed into the streets (without a permit) from a picket line in front of the Criminal Court Building where a bail reduction hearing was scheduled for 15members of the Black Panther Party who have been arrested on trumped up charges of conspiring to dynamite five Manhattan department stores and the Broax Botannical Gardens. (Six more were indicted, but haven't yet been caught.) The newest phony charges against the Panthers had angered and alarmed radicals in New York, and 1500 of them were picketing the Court Building that morning. About 150 uniformed Black Panthers lined the walls around the steps which lead to the courthouse, chanting, "Fuck the Pigs." The Panthers and families of the defendants packed the courtroom. The ransom for the 21 totals a fantastic TWO MILLION ONE HUNDRED THOUSAND DOLLARS.

District Attorney Frank Hogan has been unsuccessful in completely isolating the Panthers from other groups in the community in spite of his cheap theatrics. Last Tuesday, statements of solidarity from the High School Student Union and the SDS Regional Office were given at a news conference in the Panther's Harlem office.

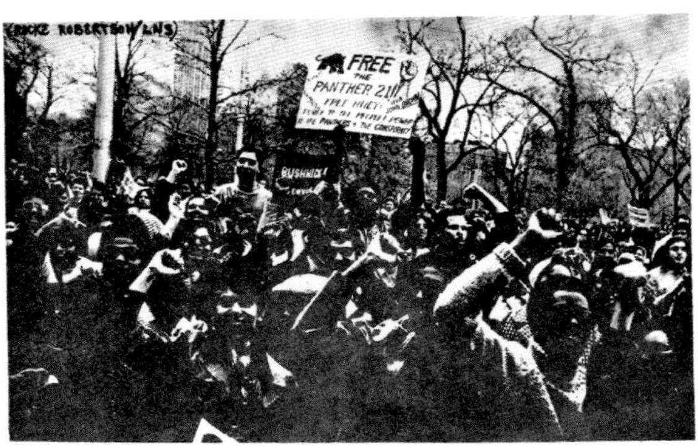

Robbie Newton from the High School Student Union, drew a parallel between the city administration attacks on the Student Union and on the Panthers; "Just as the city wants high school students to believe that the High School Student Union, High School Coalition and the Black Student Union are the cause of the trouble in the schools, they want the working people to believe that the Panthers are the cause of the trouble in the city. And they want the Panthers in jail. Just like they have to put cops in the schools and suspend kids who are demanding a decent education, they have to use force against the people who are working for all of us. Because the bankers, big real estate owners and big corporations who control the Board of Education and the rest of the city don't care about us. Their only interest is to keep things 'running smoothly.'"

One Panther discredited the conspiracy charges quite concisely at a news conference with, "We would not waste dynamite on the blowing up of some jive railway stations and department stores since our primary aim is to organize the people against the demogogue politicians, the avericious businessmen and the racist pig forces and not to murder our own."

Brown Shoes, April–May 1969. *Courtesy Special Collections & University Archives, Patricia W. and J. Douglas Perry Library, Old Dominion University, Norfolk, Virginia.*

On the night of February 24, 1969, some *Brown Shoes* street vendors called the "Squak Squad" were stopped and detained for forty-five minutes by Norfolk police on Boush Street while selling papers to servicemen at a bus stop. The two policemen advised the vendors to provide their names and addresses, which they did, and that they could expect a letter from the city attorney informing them if they had broken any laws. "Mild, to be sure," stated an article on the near bust, "but a hint of things to come because if they hadn't heard of *Brown Shoes* before, they have now."

Volume 1, number 8 of *Brown Shoes*, dated April 1–15, 1969, was two five-page issues in one. The lead story was how Dr. Leland Peterson, the faculty advisor of ODC's literary magazine the *Gadfly*, stepped in a firestorm after a contribution in the March issue titled "Immaculate Deception" told a Christ-like story of a white girl giving birth to a black baby. Virginia governor Mills Godwin received a letter of complaint from "two Black Norfolk ministers" and then shot off a letter to the ODC board of visitors asking for an investigation of the *Gadfly*.

"Down [Godwin] comes like a giant bird of death," *Brown Shoes* said in an editorial. "ODC prexie [*sic*] Lewis Webb holds up Peterson's contract, and some nasty things are said about the *Gadfly* and how federal funds can't be spent for printing this kind of shit, etc."

"No pressure from any person(s) should be able to dictate what is or is not to be published at ODC," said an editorial of the incident in the March 7, 1969 student newspaper the *Mace and Crown*. "If we as students allow this to happen we are cheapening our school and our diplomas."

The controversy died down, however, and on April 11, 1969, Dr. Peterson was awarded his full contract by the ODC board of visitors.

The final issue of *Brown Shoes* was published in May 1969. The lead story was on the back page, placed at the last minute, about how 1,100 students took over the administration building at Hampton University on Wednesday, April 23, over the resignations of two popular sociology professors, George Robertson and Armando de la Torre. Almost unbelievably, the story reported that 100 out of 104 faculty members voted to support the student takeover.

While it was probably floundering finances and a general lack of interest that took down *Brown Shoes*, the FBI Norfolk Office took credit for its demise. "The investigation of the underground newspaper, *Brown Shoes*, apparently disrupted its publication because it has not been published since about May 1969," stated a December 31, 1969 memo from the Norfolk SAC, offering no evidence to support the claim. "The discreet investigation determined that the *Brown Shoes* was being made up at the Unitarian Church Center of Norfolk and possibly under the direction of VISTA workers."

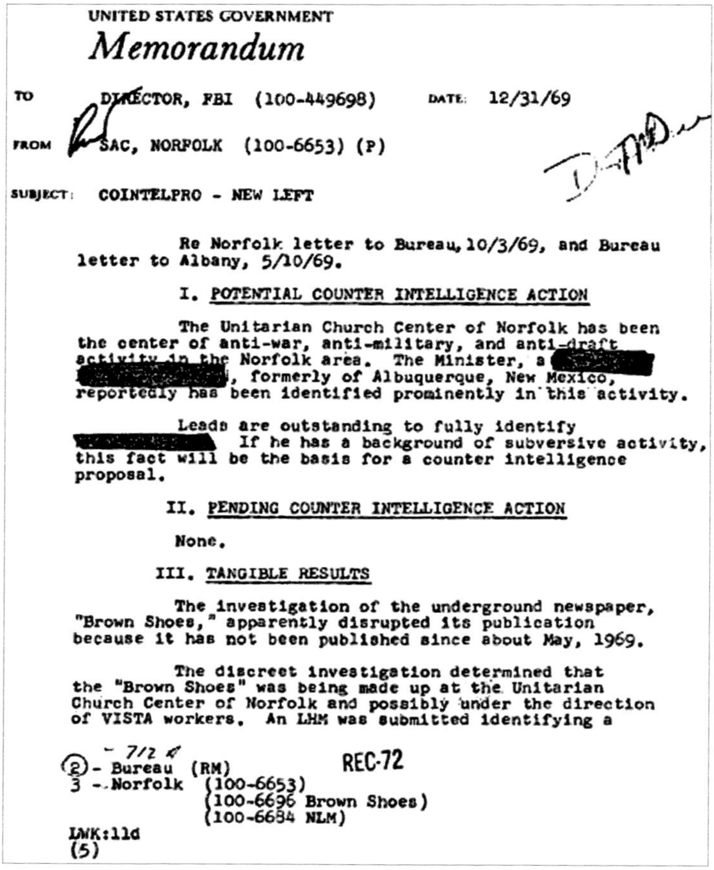

UNITED STATES GOVERNMENT

Memorandum

TO DIRECTOR, FBI (100-449698) DATE: 12/31/69

FROM SAC, NORFOLK (100-6653) (P)

SUBJECT: COINTELPRO - NEW LEFT

Re Norfolk letter to Bureau, 10/3/69, and Bureau letter to Albany, 5/10/69.

I. POTENTIAL COUNTER INTELLIGENCE ACTION

The Unitarian Church Center of Norfolk has been the center of anti-war, anti-military, and anti-draft activity in the Norfolk area. The Minister, a [redacted], formerly of Albuquerque, New Mexico, reportedly has been identified prominently in this activity.

Leads are outstanding to fully identify [redacted]. If he has a background of subversive activity, this fact will be the basis for a counter intelligence proposal.

II. PENDING COUNTER INTELLIGENCE ACTION

None.

III. TANGIBLE RESULTS

The investigation of the underground newspaper, "Brown Shoes," apparently disrupted its publication because it has not been published since about May, 1969.

The discreet investigation determined that the "Brown Shoes" was being made up at the Unitarian Church Center of Norfolk and possibly under the direction of VISTA workers. An LHM was submitted identifying a

2 - Bureau (RM)
3 - Norfolk (100-6653)
(100-6696 Brown Shoes)
(100-6684 NLM)

REC-72

LWK:lld
(5)

A memo from the FBI Norfolk field office to the director updating their investigation into the Norfolk Unitarian Church and *Brown Shoes*, December 31, 1969. *Courtesy the author.*

Retiring educator and former *Brown Shoes* staff member Steve Delzell expressed the attitude of not just *Brown Shoes* but many '60s underground publishers in his address to the 2014 graduating class of Wilton High School in Wilton, Connecticut, after more than thirty years of teaching. "When I was eighteen, I thought the world was doomed," he told the graduates. "I knew about environmental degradation, nuclear war threatened, and we were getting embroiled in a bitter war in Vietnam…I had hopes that my generation could 'save the world.' We were full of hope, righteous indignation and naiveté."

5
VIRGINIA'S GI UNDERGROUND PRESS

1968–72

THE FORGOTTEN ANTIWAR MOVEMENT

Around 1967, military underground newspapers became a bold and visible manifestation of growing dissent inside America's armed forces. Papers were clandestinely created and published near bases, ships and military installations across the country and then tucked inside newspapers sold at nearby newsstands, pinned on bulletin boards, left on bus stop benches or shoved under doors.

As the number of publications grew, so did persecution by the military establishment. A September 12, 1969 Defense Department directive stated that "while publication of 'underground' newspapers by military personnel off-post, on their own time and with their own money and equipment, is not prohibited, if such a publication contains language the utterance of which is punishable under federal law, those involved in the printing, publication or distribution may be disciplined for such infractions."

The Defense Department reported that at their peak in 1970, almost 245 underground presses published at least one edition on America's military bases, with no fewer than 12 titles appearing at least once on D.C. and Virginia bases.

Open Sights
Fort Belvoir, Fairfax County, Virginia

By even underground newspaper standards, military antiwar papers were shaky operations. There was virtually no advertising and no guaranteed circulation, and the staffs swelled and shrank unpredictably as members were transferred or sent to Southeast Asia. The creators risked cease-and-desist orders and court-martials. The papers were sometimes assembled in a hurry, with a wide variety of typefaces and typographical errors.

"I've seen them," an unnamed Pentagon spokesman told *Washington Post* writer Stanford Ungar in March 1969, "and I think they're crude—a bunch of kids letting off steam."

That dismissive attitude didn't stop a group of soldiers that same month from publishing Fort Belvoir's first underground paper, *Open Sights*. The first edition of the ten-page offset-printed publication appeared the weekend of March 8–9, 1969, at Forts Belvoir and Myer in Virginia, Fort Meade in Maryland and the marine installation in Arlington. Volume 1, number 2 appeared the weekend of March 22, in a press run of 4,000 copies, although the *Washington Post* reported only 950 were "earmarked for military installations."

While there was no official regulation preventing a soldier from possessing *Open Sights*, base commanders could prohibit on-base circulation of any material they considered to be in "bad taste, subversive, or detrimental to discipline."

The front page of *Open Sights* declared, "This paper is your personal property. It cannot legally be taken from you. If anybody tries, demand a signed receipt from your C.O."

The identities of the estimated sixty soldiers producing the paper were kept secret. A civilian volunteer told reporter Kevin Klose in August 1969 that the group was more or less evenly divided between black soldiers and whites, who maintained "separate but equal operations."

Articles in *Open Sights* dealt with such topics as the legal ramifications of participating in an antiwar rally; efforts at other military bases to form antiwar organizations, such as the "GIs United Against the War in Vietnam"; and the situation at the Presidio stockade in San Francisco, where a young soldier named Ralph Bunch died while in custody.

In the fall of 1969, *Open Sights* broadened its fire, denouncing "scab labor" servicemen called to help sort and deliver mail during a postal strike. Editor Patrick Ruta admitted, however, that navy charges against the editor of *OM: The Servicemen's Newletter*, Roger Priest, forced his staff to temper their outrage. "Articles are written more carefully now," Ruta told the *Washington*

OPEN SIGHTS

BY GI'S FOR GI'S

Vol. III No. 4 | MAY DAY STARSHIP ISSUE | Apr. – May 1971

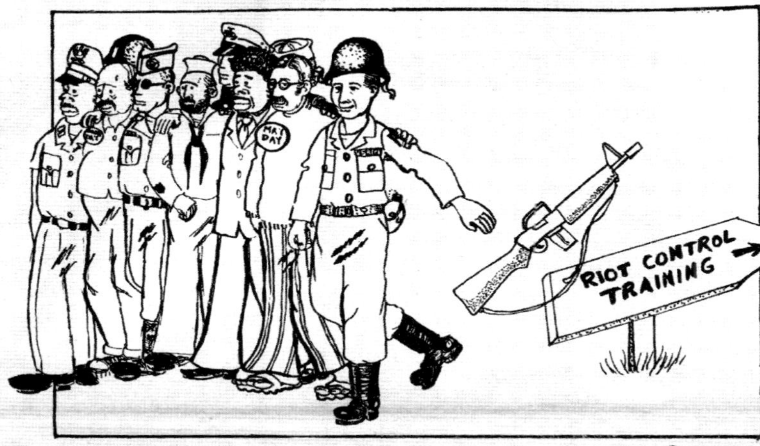

GI SWITCHBOARD OPENS

GI's have a long history of being used to put down foreign and domestic revolutions. In the last ten years we have been used in an attempt to suppress the drive of the people of Indochina for self-determination, peace, and independence. Domestically, the war in Indochina has deepened the inequalities and injustices in America and thus has set off a movement to completely change the social, political and economic structure of America. We have been used many times in attempts to squash this movement. We all know this, but what isn't so well known is that GI's have in many ways resisted being used to repress legitimate movements for change here and abroad. It is becoming clearer to many of us in the service (especially Black, Brown, and working class enlisted men and women) that these movements are in our interests and that we must support them, not repress them.

Nobody knows how to fuck up the army better than a GI. In the past, GI's sent to D.C. have ripped off government typewriters, screwed up files, called their friend all across the country on government phones, gone on sick call, rapped with the demonstrators, and some GI's have even refused orders.

We are well aware that the Pentagon plans to try once again to use us against our brothers and sisters who are against the war, racism, and repression.

✱ If you want to get it together with other GI's at your base for the Spring Offensive Against Riot Duty, call the DMZ at **737-3250**

✱ If you have information on your unit's riot training, equipment, plans, and morale, please call the DMZ at **737-3250**

✱ If you need legal help, information on this Spring's demonstrations, leaflets, or whatever call the DMZ at

737-3250

GI SWITCHBOARD

fuck riot control

Ω

CID in the STREET

Soon the troops will be in D.C. to stop the people who are opposed to the war. Along with them will come the Army's (and probably the Navy's and the Marine Corps') CID boys. They will be there to make sure there is violence and that GI's will get angry at demonstrators.

It seems that the civilian antiwar movement has really begun to realize that GI's are against the war as much as they are. At last civilians understand that GI's hate riot duty. So, protesters will not be hassling GI's because the GI Movement and the civilian movement are allies.

Of course for the Army the last thing they want to see is GI's shaking hands with civilian protesters, so the Army will have CID out in the streets, looking like "hippies" and provoking the GI's on riot duty. If the Army's trick works, their agents will spark violence on the part of civilians, and pig baiting of GI's will get troops uptight. The result will be violence, smashed windows and injured people - maybe some of them GI's. If CID is successful, we may even have people killed as at Kent State.

Demonstrators will be told about these CID pigs and will try to deal with them on the spot where they crop up. But GI's should be watchful too and not let CID spoil a beautiful thing.

Open Sights, "Mayday Starship Issue," April–May 1971. *Courtesy Bonnie Atwood and the VCU Cabell Library Special Collections, Richmond, Virginia.*

Post, so no one could accuse them of "enticing desertion or sedition," the two most serious charges leveled against Priest.

It was estimated that the half million people attending the antiwar protest in D.C. on November 15, 1969, were led by GIs associated with *Open Sights*.

In July 1970, staff members of *Open Sights* joined with a discharged conscientious objector named Bob Rix and seven others to open the DMZ, the Washington area's first GI coffeehouse, in a former movie theater at 918 Ninth Street Northwest.

Coffeehouses were enormously popular around military bases, serving as "military-free and hassle-free" zones where soldiers could relax away from military discipline. "Abandon all rank ye who enter here" read a sign over the DMZ front door.

While the army's May 1968 "Guidance on Dissent" stated that a coffeehouse should not be declared off-limits "unless…activities in the coffee house include counseling soldiers to refuse to perform duty or to desert or to otherwise involve themselves in illegal acts," many still ran afoul of military brass and local ordinances. The civilian operators of the UFO Coffeehouse near Fort Jackson, South Carolina, were charged with "operating and maintaining a public nuisance." In February 1970, a coffeehouse near Fort Dix, New Jersey, was firebombed. Two bombs were also thrown through the window of the Fort Knox coffeehouse in Muldraugh, Kentucky, causing minor damage.

The FBI even mailed fraudulent letters—ostensibly written by "concerned citizens"—to parents of student employees at a coffeehouse in Killeen, Texas, named the Oleo Strut. The bogus letters stated their children were "living in a commune and attending pot parties" as well as engaging in antiwar indoctrination of soldiers stationed at nearby Fort Hood.

Open Sights published fairly consistently until mid-1971, when it abruptly stopped, about the time another group of soldiers briefly published another paper called *Liberated Castle*.

OM: The Servicemen's Newsletter
Pentagon, Washington Navy Yard, Washington, D.C.

The only underground paper published by someone who worked inside the Pentagon, and one of the few such papers to use the creator's real name, *OM: The Servicemen's Newsletter* (later changed to *OM: The Liberation Newsletter*) was the brainchild of U.S. Navy journalist Seaman Apprentice Roger L.

LINK

THE SERVICEMAN'S LINK TO PEACE
1029 Vermont Avenue NW, Room 200
Washington D.C. 20005 (202) 638-4126

OM

THE BEST & THE WORST

25¢ Donation | July 1969 | Washington, D.C. | Free to Servicemen

A CALL TO RESIST ILLEGITIMATE AUTHORITY
AN INDICTMENT AGAINST THE U.S. GOVERNMENT, THE ARMED SERVICES AND ITS INDUSTRIAL ALLIES

By Roger Priest, U.S. Navy

WASHINGTON, D.C. -- As a U.S. citizen and as a human being I wish to expose the illegality and immorality of the unnecessary war in Vietnam. I specifically charge the U. S. government, the Armed Services and its industrial allies collectively and individually with the crime of waging aggressive war crimes against humanity, and with specific violations of the laws of war.

Article VI of the Constitution states that the Constitution and treaties made under the Authority of the United States shall be the Supreme law of the land. Therefore if members of the U.S. government, the Armed Services and its industrial allies have broken any international law, then they are liable to prosecution by U.S. courts under Article VI of the Constitution. I charge that the U.S. government, the Armed Services and its industrial allies have broken international laws and established personal responsibility for these criminal actions.

The Nuremberg Principles define a "crime against peace" as the "planning, preparation, initiation or waging of a war of aggression or a war in violation of international treaties, agreements or assurances." A state of war exists in Vietnam where Vietnamese and Americans are killed almost everyday in armed conflict. The war in Vietnam is a war of aggression on the part of the U.S. government, the Armed Services and its industrial allies. Article 51 of the United Nations Charter states that members of the United Nations have the right of individual or collective self-defense if an armed attack occurs against a member of the United Nations. All other acts of war are acts of aggression. This means that the United States would have the legal right to intervene in Vietnam if there was an armed attack upon Vietnam by military forces that crossed an international boundary. This is the only justification for armed intervention.

The United States government has accused the government of Ho Chi Minh of aggression against the government of South Vietnam. For these actions if they did exist, to be defined as aggressive actions, North and South Vietnam must exist as separate countries. North and South Vietnam have never existed as separate countries. The current separation is the result of temporary zoning of the two belligerents of France and the Vietminh after the French-Indochinese War as of 1954. The zoning was only to be temporary. The two zones were to be reunited in 1956 pending elections. Elections the U.S. government never allowed, because Ho Chi Minh had become so popular a national hero that he would win free elections by a big margin (80 per cent, President Eisenhower estimated in his memoirs). The war in Vietnam, then is a civil war, a war between two belligerents indigenous to the same country. Therefore North Vietnam cannot be guilty of acts of aggression against South Vietnam as defined by the United Nations Charter because "armed attack" has never been carried across international boundaries.

There is no way to peace. Peace is the way.

OM, "The Best and the Worst" issue, July 1969. *Courtesy Alderman Library microfilm collection, University of Virginia, Charlottesville, Virginia.*

Priest. Priest entered the navy in October 1967 and was transferred to the Pentagon's office of navy information in January 1968.

"I was anti-Vietnam before I got into the service," Priest told *Washington Post* writer Nicholas von Hoffman. "I thought I could live this lie…and I'm not even killing, I'm just shuffling papers."

Throughout 1968, Priest became more dismayed with America's role in Southeast Asia. "How many more women and children must be burned before the people of the United States realize the horrendous crime they are committing against a peasant people?" he wrote.

About one thousand copies of the first mimeographed issue of *OM* appeared on April 1, 1969. On April 2, within ninety minutes of arriving at his desk, Priest was reassigned to the Navy and Marines Exhibit Center at the Washington Navy Yard. "I don't care if they send me to the North Pole," Priest told the *Washington Post*. "I'll write my stuff on ice cubes if I have to."

Exercising his first amendment rights while knowing full well he was placing himself in U.S. Navy crosshairs, Priest published a second edition of *OM* on May 1, then a third one on June 1, each with a press run of one thousand copies.

Priest also raised the ire of the navy when he made an antiwar group the beneficiary of his service life insurance and urged other soldiers to do the same. In his case, if the Viet Cong in Southeast Asia killed him, the War Resistor's League would receive his $10,000 payout.

OM was unabashedly blunt. "Today's Pigs Are Tomorrow's Bacon," stated one headline in issue number 2 that described Joint Chiefs chairman General Earl Wheeler. *OM* called Secretary of Defense Melvin Laird "People's enemy no. 1" and "a practicing prostitute and a pimp."

Other statements appearing in the paper that crossed the navy included, "Our goal is liberation … by any means necessary," and "Shoot a pig!"

On June 12, 1969, Priest was interrogated about *OM* by the Office of Naval Intelligence (ONI). Three days later, fourteen official charges were lodged against him, including soliciting fellow soldiers to desert, urging insubordination, making statements disloyal to the United States, using "contemptuous words" against South Carolina representative L. Mendel Rivers and, worse, not stating in the paper that his statements were his own opinions and not those of the U.S. Navy.

Von Hoffmann wrote on June 25, 1969, that Priest was accused of "everything that's happened to the Navy except perhaps stealing the [USS] *Pueblo*." Priest also noticed he was being followed around by civilians in Ford Fairlanes and Plymouth Valiants.

"This whole thing hinges on free speech, freedom of the press," Priest told von Hoffman. "They're not talking about my military behavior…they're talking about what I do on my own free time, outside of the Navy, in my own apartment…as an American citizen."

In July, Priest published a special "Best & Worst" issue of *OM* in conjunction with a defense fund called LINK, "The Servicemen's Link to Peace." On July 21, Priest—holding a sign that read "My crime is speech"—led a demonstration of about one hundred people in front of the National Archives building. The next day, an Article 32 pre-court-martial investigation convened at the Naval Air Station in Anacostia.

About 102 members of the Navy Ceremonial Guard armed with M-1 rifles, live ammo and gas masks stood watch as navy aviator Commander Norman Mills conducted the proceedings. Priest was represented without fee by Washington attorney David Rein.

"If I can be put away for a number of years in prison for the mere writing of words—an act so basic to the founding of this country that it finds its basis in the First Amendment of the Constitution—then my crime is speech," Priest said in his opening statement. "But let me tell you this: *OM* will go on, for others will take up the pen where I leave off."

During this trial, testimony proved that twenty-five naval intelligence agents had been assigned to follow and harass Priest. Furthermore, when a letter found in Priest's trash was introduced as evidence, ONI special agent Robert Howard testified that the Washington, D.C. department of sanitation provided a truck for special trash pickup at Priest's apartment building.

Attorney Rein said that this activity alone "brought more discredit on the armed services than anything Roger Priest has done." Infuriated, D.C. mayor Walter Washington promised a "full and complete investigation" of the sanitation department when Director William Roeder was quoted as saying, "If the police ask us to do this, we cooperate with them." He later denied making the statement.

"City Denies Trash Spying" trumpeted the *Washington Post*.

Despite the disorganization of the proceedings, Priest was ordered to appear before a general court-martial on charges that he solicited members of the military to desert and commit sedition and that he published statements "urging insubordination, disloyalty and refusal of duty by members of the military and naval forces with intent to impair loyalty, morale and discipline." The combined charges carried a maximum sentence of thirty-nine years in prison and dishonorable discharge.

During this time, Priest kept a low profile at his navy job, obeying orders and being careful not to break a single regulation. His strategy was to force the navy to court-martial him only for *OM*'s contents and not on some extraneous charge that disguised the political nature of his battle.

Not to be held down, Priest published "The Court-Martial Edition" of *OM* in October 1969. "ONI left no stone unturned or garbage can unmolested, nor did they mind to stoop to entrapment in trying to deny the constitutional rights of free speech and free press to Seaman Roger Priest."

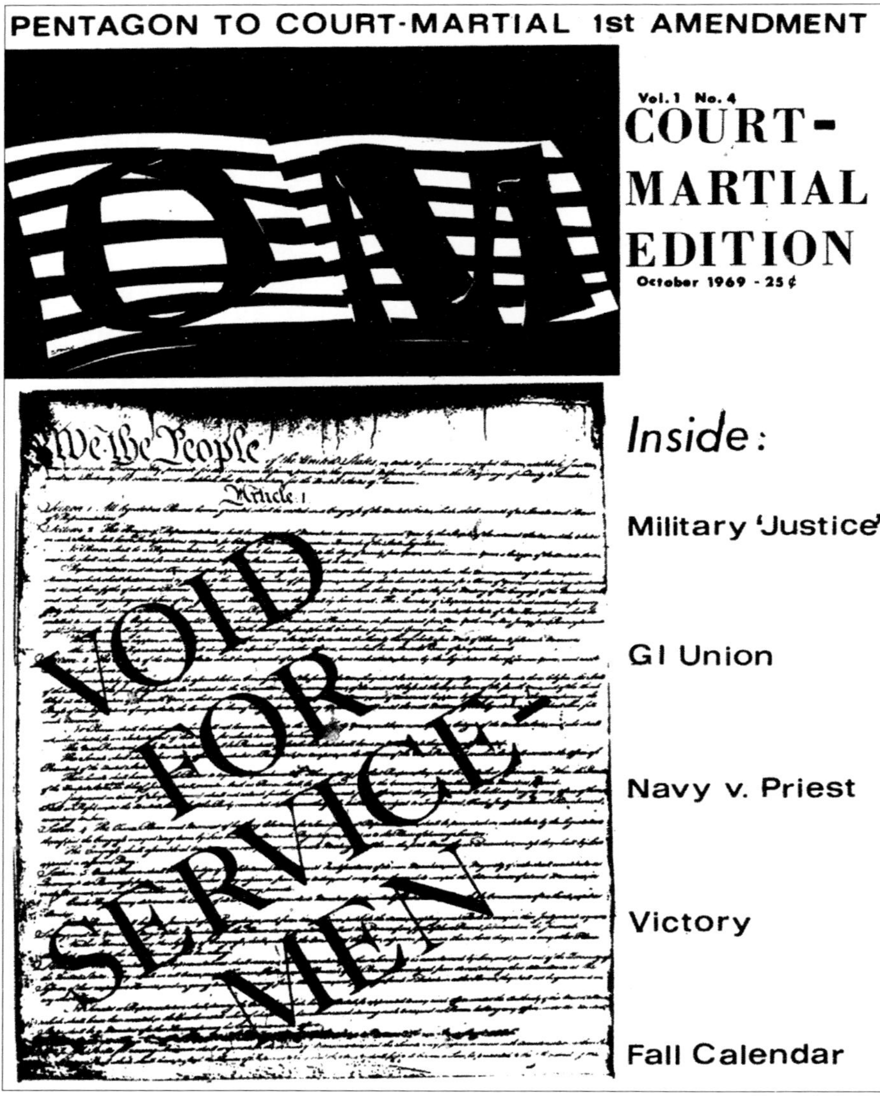

OM, "Court-Martial Edition," October 1969. *Courtesy Alderman Library microfilm collection, University of Virginia, Charlottesville, Virginia.*

By April, Priest had become a hero to other like-minded servicemen across the country. LINK director Carl Rogers estimated his organization spent over $17,000 in buttons, posters, postage and travel expenses for Priest's speaking engagements.

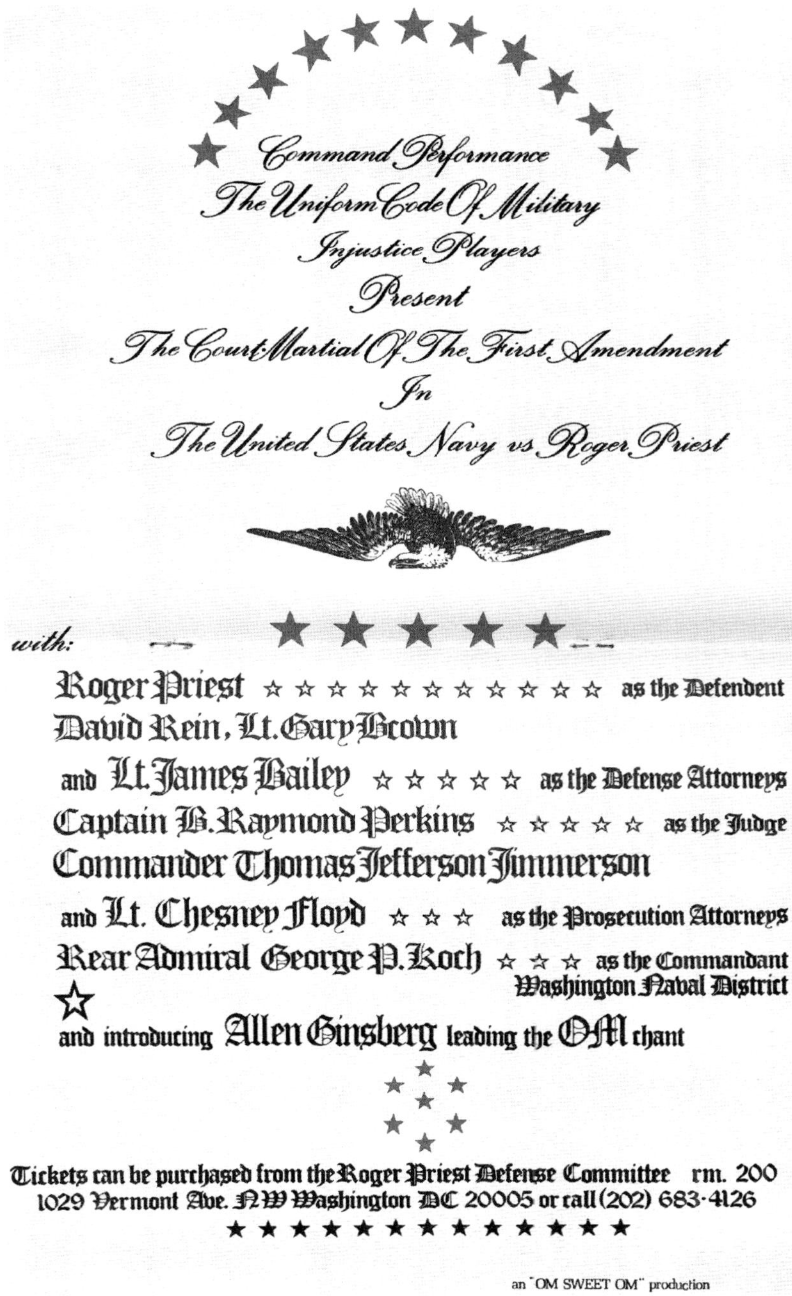

Court-martial announcement from *OM*, "Court-Martial Edition," October 1969.
Courtesy Bonnie Atwood and the VCU Cabell Library Special Collections, Richmond, Virginia.

"No group like ours," Rogers said, "can begin to counter the resources and the manpower of the Pentagon…to harass and oppress dissenters." Rogers also estimated that about ten thousand souvenir reprints of *OM* (far more than the original press run of one thousand) and ten thousand "OM" buttons had been distributed since the summer.

Priest gained an unlikely ally with New York senator Charles Goodell, who issued a statement on September 5 that said, in part, "When Roger Priest enlisted in the Navy, he accepted certain well-defined responsibilities as a soldier. He did not, however, forfeit his constitutional rights as a citizen of the United States."

During the court-martial, it was disclosed that the wife of the commander of the submarine USS *Nautilus* helped distribute copies of *OM*. Winifred Davis Cockfield, who was active in progressive causes for many years, testified that the Vietnam War was "a terrible mistake" and that she had invited Priest to her Arlington home to "talk philosophy."

"My God, I told her not to talk about that," her visibly aggravated father, retired vice admiral William Davis Jr., told a *Washington Post* reporter. Cockfield said she gave copies of *OM* to friends, officers and anyone who asked for one.

The court-martial board convicted Priest only on two minor counts of promoting "disloyalty and disaffection among members of the armed forces." They recommended Priest be reprimanded, reduced to the lowest pay grade and receive a bad conduct discharge, but no jail time. Thrilled with the outcome, Attorney Rein said he would still appeal the bad conduct discharge.

On February 11, 1971, a panel of navy appeals judges reversed that conviction and awarded Priest an honorable discharge, citing the grounds of reversal on a "technical error" by Judge Raymond Perkins. Also, the reprimand was dropped by Rear Admiral George Koch, commandant of the Washington Naval District, on review of the case.

Priest's case presented a conundrum regarding military dissent: how does a country impress young men into the army to fight a war they ideologically oppose or even outright despise? Can men so profoundly disaffected be reliable soldiers?

An anonymous columnist proposed a somewhat cynical solution off record to von Hoffman: "You can't fight imperialist wars [anymore] with conscript armies. You have to use mercenaries."

Rough Draft
Fort Eustis, Williamsburg, Virginia

A milestone in the GI antiwar movement and military underground publishing was reached at Williamsburg's Fort Eustis in August 1969 when, after nearly four months of dogged effort, the antiwar paper *Rough Draft* won headquarters approval to be openly distributed on base. The victory set a precedent across the United States, and soon more antiwar papers gained permission for on-base distribution, thanks to *Rough Draft*.

Founded by PFC Carlos Barcena, *Rough Draft* appeared in late February 1969. "From a meeting of servicemen in the Tidewater area representing all the branches of the armed Forces comes this newspaper," stated page two. The mission was four-fold: to expose those in authority who abuse their power; to strive for liberty, justice and equality for servicemen and women; to be a forum and rallying point for dissent; and to destroy negativity and encourage servicemen to stand for their rights.

Volume 1, number 1 of *Rough Draft* was a robust six pages, neatly typed and mimeographed in the standard two-column format on legal-size paper. It was "free to servicemen," but a ten-cent donation was asked.

A long article titled "Life in the Military" signed by "J.S." from Norfolk described his inequities of military life. Another article described the advantages of joining the American Servicemen's Union (ASU) and the eight demands its "growing membership" was working for, including "an end to the saluting and sir-ing of officers"; "racial equity"; a federal minimum wage; and especially, the right to disobey illegal orders—"like orders to go and fight in an illegal war in Vietnam."

There were also numerous short articles on the legal problems faced by other military dissenters in bases around the country, such as navy nurse Susan Schnall, who was court-martialed in San Francisco for marching in uniform in a peace parade.

Volume 1, number 2 included a two-page spread on the horrific situation in San Francisco with the "Presidio 27"—a group of military prisoners facing court-martials for staging a sit-down strike at the infamous stockade in protest of the fatal shooting of prisoner Ralph Bunch on October 11, 1968 (Bunch was diagnosed manic depressive and was shot by a guard as he ran from him). The spread urged readers to write their congressmen and send contributions to the "Committee for the 27."

"By handing out these stiff sentences and getting more visious [*sic*] the Brass think they can scare us. It won't work," stated a letter to *Rough Draft*

THE MISSION

*To expose those in authority who have betrayed the trust of the American people by using their power to deprive men of their Constitutional rights and, by exposure, to act as a deterrent to such abuse.
*To strive for Liberty, Justice and Equality for the men and women of the Armed Forces.
*To be a forum and a rally point for dissent.
*To destroy the negative influence of apathy among the servicemen of the Armed Forces and encourage them to stand for their rights.

ROUGH DRAFT

Tidewater Servicemen's Newspaper

No. 1 10¢ donation FEB - MAR 1969 Free to Servicemen

LIFE IN THE AMERICAN MILITARY

Today there is a great controversy over conscription and the American military. Only recently, the Navy has been embarrassed to a great degree by the Pueblo incident. Testimony from high ranking naval officers has shown that the men of the Pueblo were told that they had a backup force which, in reality, naver existed. They were lied to so that they would do a hazardous job with fewer reservations. This situation is not unique with the Navy. Those sort of white lies are found throughout the military, and they are allowed to be perpetuated because the civilian public does not know what goes on in the military. That is the purpose of this article; to give anyone who will read it a factual account of life in the American military.

Before I continue, let me say that I am not any type of anarchist, kook or wierdo. I was honorably discharged from the U.S. Marine Corps when I returned from Viet Nam last August. I am now a student at Old Dominion College, and I hope to become an English teacher. This article is not meant to be inflammatory; it merely points out the basic faults in the American military in the hope that people will think a little before plunging headlong into a despotic and unfair organization.

When you sign an enlistment contract, you are automatically relinquishing your right of assembly, free speech, and the pursuit of happiness. In the military, once you make your feelings know, i.e., "I don't care for Gunny Jones," you have made an enemy who will try to make life miserable for you. You will be given an unfair load of duties and work details. Your free time will be encroached upon, and you will be harrassed constantly, all in an effort to push you over the brink. After you reach the breaking point, good Old Gunny Jones is right there to railroad you to a courts-martial. There, you are automatically guilty.

(con't on page 3)

COLUMN LEFT: RIOT CONTROL

"I DON'T ASK QUESTIONS, I JUST FOLLOW ORDERS. IF PEOPLE RIOT, I SHOOT."

Black soldier; "Oh, man, get off it. People have been put up tight for too long; They're cheated and poor."
White soldier: We defend America.
BS: What about here, man? What are we defending here? Liquor stores?
WS: Well, maybe we shouldn't be here, but we get sent into other countries when governments ask us to come.
BS: You know those people looting on 14th St? What if they asked the Chinese to help them fight and the Chinese came in and fought us. They would say Americans asked them in. Well, maybe that's what we do in other countries. I just came back from Vietnam and I bet that's what happened there. I don't understand it there.
WS: I just follow orders.
BS: You should be in Nazi Germany. Hitler would like you.
(To the reporter:)
BS: There aren't many guys like him in the Army. He volunteered to go to Vietnam four times but they wouldn't take him. He kept saying he wanted to kill people. He thinks he's John Wayne. They've kept him here. He's nuts. Other guys don't like it.
*from an interview with National Guards by a WASHINGTON FREE PRESS reporter during the rebellion in D.C. after King was murdered.

If your unit is anything like mine, it has a so-called "Emergency Operation" SOP. In it is probably a plan to mobilize the guys in the unit to quell local "civil disturbances." In it, too,is probably contained the inference, at least, that all strikes, civil disturbances, etc. are started by the "enemy," that is, those evil-eyed communists with the pointed ears you hear so much about in Character Guidance. I guess they're talking about the VC or something.

(con't on page 5)

TH IS YOUR PAPER - - - IT CANNOT BE LEGALLY TAKEN FROM YOU!

Rough Draft, "Tidewater Servicemen's Newspaper," number 1, February–March 1969. *Courtesy the author.*

signed "Seaman USN Atlantic fleet." "The servicemen resistance movement is too big and too angry."

Distribution was the biggest roadblock in *Rough Draft*'s quest to reach as many servicemen as possible. The Virginia Shore Patrol was stymied as to how copies kept getting left in its Norfolk headquarters until finally someone

THE MISSION

•TO EXPOSE THOSE IN AUTHORITY WHO HAVE BETRAYED THE TRUST OF THE AMERICAN PEOPLE BY USING THEIR POWER TO DEPRIVE MEN OF THEIR CONSTITUTIONAL RIGHTS, AND BY EXPOSURE, TO ACT AS A DETERRENT TO SUCH ABUSE.

•TO STRIVE FOR LIBERTY, JUSTICE AND EQUALITY FOR THE MEN AND WOMEN OF THE ARMED FORCES.

•TO BE A FORUM AND A RALLY POINT FOR DISSENT.

•TO DESTROY THE NEGATIVE INFLUENCE OF APATHY AMONG THE SERVICEMEN OF THE ARMED FORCES AND ENCOURAGE THEM TO STAND FOR THEIR RIGHTS

Rough Draft

Tidewater Servicemens Newspaper

NO. 5 10¢ DONATION AUGUST 1969 FREE TO SERVICEMEN

AT FT. EUSTIS·

'Rough Draft' ~~Asks For~~ Distribution DEMANDS

The Fort Eustis brass is understandably worried about Fort Eustis GI's digging our paper. Since the Rough Draft is one of the GI's few alternatives to official Army and mass media propaganda, it can be likened to a gnat who's stinger is long enough to pierce the armor of the Army's indoctrination machine. All GI's are made aware of this machine from their first individuality-destroying Army haircut to their re-up interview.

If the Eustis brass didn't see our paper as a threat to their positions and to their post-retirement cushy jobs with huge corporations, they wouldn't have seen to it that GI's caught distributing the Rough Draft got every kind of harassment in the Army itinerary.

Because of this harassment of our distributors at Eustis, we decided to find out what the channels were for gaining legal status for the Rough Draft at Eustis and use them. As you can see from the following chronological summation, our correspondence with Eustis has had its interesting turns: our utilization of legal channels seems to have shocked the Eustis brass, and they made up the rules as they went along.

21 Apr 69 – Rough Draft's first letter to Eustis requesting permission to make the paper available to Eustis personnel, citing the Constitutional rights of freedom of speech and press as our qualifications.

23 Apr – letter received from Col. Reed A. Booth (Eustis Adjutant General) requesting a brief description of the method, time, and place of distribution...prior to any official action being taken on the application. Booth's letter refers to Fort Eustis regulation 210-23, which is dated 13 May 69, three weeks after our initial request for distribution privileges. 210-23 regulates the distribution of publications on Ft. Eustis.

18 May – The Rough Draft supplies the information requested in Booth's letter of 23 April.

26 May – the Rough Draft receives acknowledgement of our letter of 18 May to Eustis.

12 June – Ft. Eustis command requests specific times and places for, and frequency of distribution desired on post, the number of copies to be distributed and the identity of the distributors, the publisher and editors of Rough Draft.

(continued page 8)

Rough Draft, August 1969. *Courtesy Alderman Library microfilm collection, University of Virginia, Charlottesville, Virginia.*

pinned one to the bulletin board with a note that read "Desire to know when and where distributed."

On April 21, 1969, *Rough Draft* representative Dennis Ciesielski requested permission from Fort Eustis to make the paper available to base personnel, citing freedom of speech and of the press. Thus began a restless and frustrating back-and-forth between the paper and an intractable Eustis brass. On June 12, fort command finally requested the specific times, places and frequency of planned distribution and the identities of the distributors, as well as the publisher and the editor. The paper at first refused, responding that the request would expose those people to disciplinary action, but one active duty soldier, his wife and one recently discharged soldier gave permission to be named as base distributors.

"Eustis Brass! Here's issue #5 of *The Rough Draft*!" wrote Private Tom Libby in the August 1969 issue. "The decision is now yours as to whether it gets into the hands of Fort Eustis GIs legally or illegally."

In the midst of this correspondence, in June, a special edition of *Rough Draft* appeared, reporting that *Rough Draft* publisher Barcena was given one month of hard labor and confinement for missing two hours of extra duty after a legal battle during his "special court martial" on June 2.

Despite the sentence, on the week of August 25, Fort Eustis commander Major General Howard Schiltz permitted *Rough Draft* to be distributed on base. "Dissident GI Paper Gets OK to Peddle Issue at Ft. Eustis" stated a front-page headline on the August 27, 1969 issue of the Newport News, Virginia *Daily Press*. Another headline read "*Rough Draft* Distribution at Ft. Eustis Pleases Editors, Astonishes Some GIs."

"This action cannot be construed in any way as an official endorsement of the contents of the newspaper," an army spokesman told the Associated Press. "Freedom of speech and freedom of the press are among rights granted under our constitution…to soldiers as well as civilians."

Technically no longer "underground," *Rough Draft* continued its monthly publishing schedule with fewer hassles after that, and in the fall of 1971, its precedent opened the doors to another on-base antiwar paper called *Square Wheel*, which published a few issues until February 1972.

Spartacus
Fort Lee, Petersburg, Virginia

GI Harold Muskat, an activist at New Jersey's Fort Dix, was court-martialed for publishing an antiwar paper there called *Shakedown*. On May 4, 1969, he was shipped into the relative obscurity of Petersburg's Fort Lee, where he wasted no time finding like-minded GIs who also wanted to "free their minds from the involuntary servitude of the military machine." Using off-base facilities in their free time, they then began putting together the first issue of *Spartacus*, Fort Lee's first underground paper, which appeared on Memorial Day weekend in 1969.

"We at *Spartacus* know that there are a large number of servicemen at Fort Lee who dread the thought of becoming involved in the war in Vietnam," stated an article in volume 1, number 2. "One of our goals is to encourage men to take a stand rather than demean themselves to becoming tools of the military machine."

"Fort Lee didn't have an antiwar newspaper so I thought I'd find a group of GI's to help put one together," wrote Muskat in 2014. "It was that simple."

Muskat found out quickly that Fort Lee brass were not forgiving either when he was caught by Petersburg police and turned over to MPs for handing out copies of *Spartacus* ("with massive civilian help") at the city bus terminal a mere four days after its publication. Unable to prosecute Muskat since he was off base, Fort Lee instead transferred him back to Fort Dix on June 2—less than one month after arriving. Back at Fort Dix, Muskat wrote that he "continued [his] involvement in *Shakedown* and the Fort Dix Coffeehouse."

Muskat's departure chilled the other contributors to *Spartacus*. Still, during that summer, other servicemen stepped forward and, maintaining strict anonymity, published a second edition on August 4. "In the true spirit of *Spartacus*, we present, against what may be called difficult odds, our second edition," stated the masthead of volume 1, number 2.

Another article in that issue expressed hope that the military was starting to tolerate some dissent; for example, *Spartacus* announced that the Pentagon directed the commanding officers of all U.S. posts to "handle with care" GIs who engage in dissenting activities off-post during off-duty hours. "These concessions have been won through struggle," *Spartacus* declared, "and we must continue the struggle to keep these concessions and to win full citizenship (the rights and freedoms that civilians have)."

Spartacus led to the creation in mid-1970 of another paper at Fort Lee called the *Paper Bag*, "A Free Press for GIs and the Draft Weary."

While little information is available on this paper, according to the website sirnosir.com in volume 3, number 3, a first sergeant associated with the Quartermaster Brigade notified his company that those apprehended with a copy of the *Paper Bag* were subject to Article 15 punishment. Perhaps Fort Lee had softened little in its attitude toward those papers after all.

OTHER VIRGINIA GI ANTIWAR PAPERS

The *COM Newsletter* and *COM Mon Sense* were published by the Concerned Officer's Movement in Washington, D.C., in April 1970. The Concerned Officer's Movement (COM) differed in that it was made up of active duty officers (rather than GIs) who expressed dissent on the Indochina war, according to the stated mission on issue number 3. A total of four issues were published.

A paper called the *Oppressed* was published out of Walter Reed Army Medical Center. Issue number 1 appeared on April 1, 1971.

Grapes of Wrath, first published in 1968 by the Norfolk, Virginia defense committee, was co-founded by Phil Wilayto, who now publishes the *Virginia Defender* in Richmond. A paper called *On the Beach* also appeared around the Norfolk Naval Base in mid-1970. Bolling Air Force Base was the home of a short-lived paper published in late 1971 into early 1972 by Sergeant Gordon Youngs called the *Bolling Other*.

New Mobilizer, AntiWarrior and *Left Face* 1969

Published by the Washington, D.C.–based Student Mobilization Committee to End the War (MOBE)

New Mobilizer was first published on September 5, 1969, at 1029 Vermont Avenue in Washington, D.C., to bring attention to "offensives" planned by the New Mobilization committee in the fall. "The week of September 15, New MOBE traveling teams met with more than 5,000 people in 50 cities to launch the fall offensive to end the war in Vietnam," stated the lead story in issue number 2, published on September 25. Four issues were published, with the last appearing on October 28, 1969.

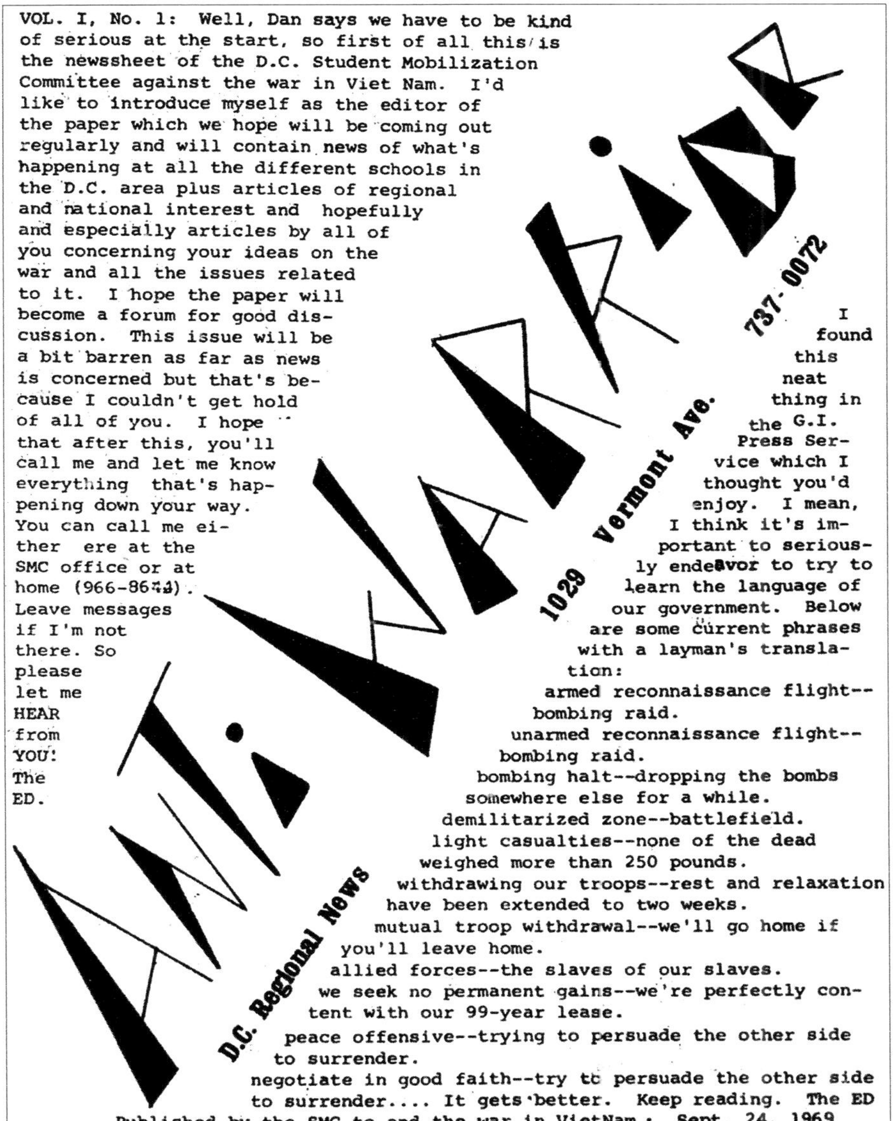
AntiWarrior

1029 Vermont Ave. 737-0072

D.C. Regional News

VOL. I, No. 1: Well, Dan says we have to be kind of serious at the start, so first of all this is the newssheet of the D.C. Student Mobilization Committee against the war in Viet Nam. I'd like to introduce myself as the editor of the paper which we hope will be coming out regularly and will contain news of what's happening at all the different schools in the D.C. area plus articles of regional and national interest and hopefully and especially articles by all of you concerning your ideas on the war and all the issues related to it. I hope the paper will become a forum for good discussion. This issue will be a bit barren as far as news is concerned but that's because I couldn't get hold of all of you. I hope that after this, you'll call me and let me know everything that's happening down your way. You can call me either ere at the SMC office or at home (966-86[illegible]). Leave messages if I'm not there. So please let me HEAR from YOU! The ED.

I found this neat thing in the G.I. Press Service which I thought you'd enjoy. I mean, I think it's important to seriously endeavor to try to learn the language of our government. Below are some current phrases with a layman's translation:

armed reconnaissance flight--bombing raid.
unarmed reconnaissance flight--bombing raid.
bombing halt--dropping the bombs somewhere else for a while.
demilitarized zone--battlefield.
light casualties--none of the dead weighed more than 250 pounds.
withdrawing our troops--rest and relaxation have been extended to two weeks.
mutual troop withdrawal--we'll go home if you'll leave home.
allied forces--the slaves of our slaves.
we seek no permanent gains--we're perfectly content with our 99-year lease.
peace offensive--trying to persuade the other side to surrender.
negotiate in good faith--try to persuade the other side to surrender.... It gets better. Keep reading. The ED

Published by the SMC to end the war in VietNam : Sept. 24, 1969

AntiWarrior, volume 1, number 1, September 24, 1969. *Courtesy Alderman Library microfilm collection, University of Virginia, Charlottesville, Virginia.*

AntiWarrior was first published on September 24, 1969, by the D.C. Student Mobilization Committee against the war (SMC). "The Student Mobilization Committee is the anti-war organization that mobilizes high school and college

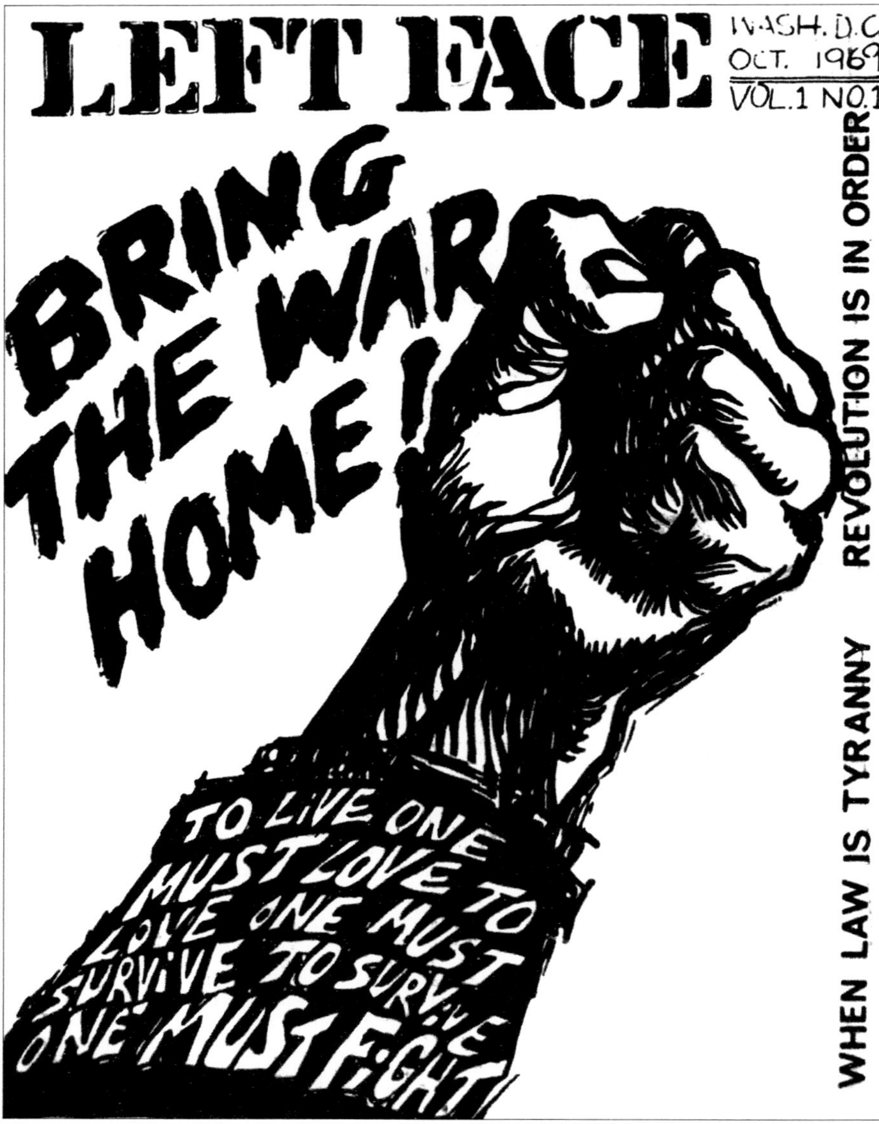

Left Face, volume 1, number 1, October 1, 1969. *Courtesy Alderman Library microfilm collection, University of Virginia, Charlottesville, Virginia.*

youth," stated the mission presumably written by editor Alice Feathers on page seven of the first issue. "The SMC brings together individuals and members of different groups who unite in actions around one issue—to end the war in Vietnam and bring ALL the troops home NOW."

Left Face—appearing in October 1969—was more emotionally antagonistic than *AntiWarrior* and *New Mobilizer*, angrily calling for revolution in its four pages, with long screeds that vaguely recalled messages published by Roger Priest in *OM* earlier that year.

"Now is the time for revolution on all fronts from racism to imperialism," the anonymous creator wrote on page four. "The people of the world are fighting back, we must too. Don't let yourself down. Dare to struggle, dare to win."

EPILOGUE

NOW WHAT?

Today's American mainstream press may recall the underground press of the '60s and early '70s as a temporary deviation, choosing to emphasize the divisions of the free press papers while deemphasizing their successes. Because of the relatively short lifespans of the underground press publications, many national mainstream writers have eulogized them as having failed prematurely due to narrow target audience appeal, factional infighting, sectarianism and fickle political trends. It is true that staffs were mostly held together by collective friendships rather than corporate policy; therefore, political and even personal disputes translated into organizational crises that threatened their stability.

But this is a false eulogy. The underground press forced the mainstream media to confront and address social issues they may have blown off as not newsworthy, fleeting or threatening to the established order. Free press writers, artists and photographers with little or no journalistic experience other than an undying passion for the revolution rallied support against an unpopular war, assailed orthodoxy and challenged those in power, sometimes in admittedly capricious, tasteless ways, but never in dreary or monotonous ones. The underground press achieved its purpose of giving a voice to radical criticism and social change, and the legacy passed on by those gritty early papers is the dozens of alternative weeklies that rose up in the mid-'70s and still continue today.

The civil rights and antiwar activism of the '60s also produced a proliferation of community-based movements and groups that embodied the idealism of the earlier period, but with considerably more focus; the women's liberation, gay rights, Chicano, organic foods and antinuclear movements of the '70s and '80s are examples. Women's shelters, public law centers, food and child care co-ops and free health clinics are still today visible reminders of the social idealism of the '60s New Left movement.

But did the underground press have a long-term editorial impact on the mainstream press? "Stories I would have done for the underground press I'm now doing for the daily papers," former '60s freelance writer Tom Miller said about writing for the mainstream press in the '80s.

"So either I'm slowing down or they're catching up."

BIBLIOGRAPHY

WASHINGTON, D.C., AND NORTHERN VIRGINIA

Aarons, Leroy. "Militants Find New Legal Breed in 'Collectives.'" *Washington Post*, February 8, 1970.

Anderson, Jack. "Revolutionary Fugitives Stymie FBI." *Washington Post*, May 3, 1971.

Avakov, Aleksandr V. *Plato's Dreams Realized: Surveillance and Citizen Rights from KGB to FBI*. New York: Algora, 2006.

Baker, Ross. "How Weathermen Keep on Bombing." *Washington Post*, November 15, 1970.

———. "ZAP! No More Underground Press." *Washington Post*, April 8, 1973.

Baltimore Sun. "Ex-Army Agents Describe Break-in by FBI in 1969." May 31, 1973.

———. "Freedom of Which Press?" March 11, 1969.

———. "*Free Press* Loses Plea." May 29, 1969.

Barker, Karlyn. "Divisions Slow Women's Lib Drive." *Washington Post*, November 14, 1971.

———. "New D.C. Biweekly Takes on Press." *Washington Post*, October 28, 1971.

Barnes, Bart. "Girl Arrested as Witness in Capitol Blast." *Washington Post*, April 29, 1971.

Bart, Peter. "Bohemian Newspapers Spread Across Country." *New York Times*, August 1, 1966.

Beckerman, Seth. "Free Press Cartoon Ruled Obscene." (George Washington University) *Hatchet*, April 14, 1969.

Bercovici, Liza. "*Quicksilver*: Paper of Politics and Barred Doors." *Washington Post*, August 11, 1970.

Bernstein, Carl. "Communes: A New Way of Life in District." *Washington Post*, July 6, 1969.

———. "D.C. Becoming Haven for Teen-Aged Runaways." *Washington Post*, January 25, 1970.

———. "*Free Press* Is Dead After 3 Years." *Washington Post*, March 9, 1970.

———. "Rennie Davis: Make Clear...We Failed." *Washington Post*, May 4, 1971.

———. "Staff Dispute Closes *Quicksilver*." *Washington Post*, April 19, 1970.

———. "U.S. Court Dilutes Ober Law." *Washington Post*, February 7, 1970.

Blum, William. *West-Bloc Dissident: A Cold War Memoir*. New York: Soft Skull Press, 2002.

Brown, Rita Mae. *Rita Will: Memoir of a Literary Rabble-Raiser*. New York: Bantam, 1997.

Burner, David. *Making Peace with the Sixties*. Princeton, NJ: Princeton University Press, 1996.

Capra, Jim. "Intra-University Paper to Publish for D.C. Area." (Washington, D.C.) *Hoya*, March 17, 1966.

Carter, Philip. "Underground Paper Features Sex and Culture." *Washington Post*, September 3, 1969.

Churchill, Ward, and Jim Vander Wall. *The COINTELPRO Papers: Documents from the FBI's Secret Wars against Domestic Dissent*. Boston: South End, 1990.

Crewdson, John M. "Documents Show F.B.I. Harassed Foes of War." *New York Times*, June 25, 1975.

Diamond, Stephen. *What the Trees Said: Life on a New Age Farm*. New York: Delacorte Press, 1971.

Eagle (Washington, D.C.). American University Digital Archives.

Evslin, Bernard. *The Furies*. New York: Chelsea House, 1989.

Federal Bureau of Investigation. *Counterintelligence Program: Internal Security, Disruption of the New Left. Washington, D.C.* U.S. government declassified memorandums. Washington, D.C.: FBI, 1968–1969.

Goodman, Mitchell. *The Movement Toward a New America: The Beginnings of a Long Revolution*. New York: Knopf, 1970.

Halley, Jean. "FBI Is Accused of Terrorism." *Washington Post*, March 11, 1971.

Henold, Mary J. *Catholic and Feminist: The Surprising History of the American Catholic Feminist Movement*. Chapel Hill: University of North Carolina Press, 2008.

Hersh, Seymour. "F.B.I. Was Given Key for Search in 1969." *New York Times*, June 2, 1973.

Jeffers, Philip. "This Generation Hippie Papers." *Baltimore Sun*, October 24, 1967.

Kernan, Michael. "Radical Press Underground Energy." *Washington Post*, July 6, 1970.

Leo, John. "Politics Is Now the Focus of Underground Press." *New York Times*, September 4, 1968.

Levey, Robert, and Jean Halley. "10-Day Protest to Begin." *Washington Post*, April 26, 1971.

Los Angeles Indymedia: Activist News. "*Quicksilver Times*: A Study in the Infiltration and Manipulation of Alternative Media." May 10, 2007. http://la.indymedia.org/news/2007/05/198569_comment.php.

Mackenzie, Angus. "Sabotaging the Dissident Press." *Columbia Journalism Review* (March 1981): 57–63.

———. *Secrets: The CIA's War at Home*. Los Angeles: University of California Press, 1997.

MacPherson, Myra. "Battle of the Sexes Becomes a Word War." *Washington Post*, August 27, 1970.

McMillian, John Campbell. *Smoking Typewriters: The Sixties Underground Press and the Rise of Alternative Media in America*. New York: Oxford University Press, 2011.

McNees, James. "ACLU to Sue Authorities on Behalf of *Free Press*." *Baltimore Sun*, June 11, 1969.
Medsger, Betty, and Ken Clawson. "FBI Secretly Prods Colleges on New Left." *Washington Post*, April 6, 1971.
Newmeyer, Barbara. "*Quicksilver Times* Back on D.C. Streets." *Washington Post*, May 10, 1970.
Quinn, Sally. "A Roast Pig at the Benefit." *Washington Post*, February 4, 1972.
Rainbow History Project Digital Collections.
Ross, Nancy. "Homosexual Revolution." *Washington Post*, October 25, 1969.
Sales, Kirkpatrick. *SDS*. New York: Random House, 1973.
Scharfenberg, Kirk. "Dillingham Gets 6 Months in Obscenity Case." *Washington Post*, July 3, 1969.
———. "Grand Jury to Probe Underground Paper." *Washington Post*, March 4, 1969.
———. "Obscenity Conviction Reversed." *Washington Post*, July 16, 1970.
Smyth, Jeannette. "A *Quicksilver* Farewell." *Washington Post*. August 2, 1972.
Stewart, Sean. *On the Ground: An Illustrated Anecdotal History of the Sixties Underground Press in the U.S.* Oakland, CA: PM, 2011.
Time. "The Hippies." July 7, 1967.
U.S. Congress. Senate Judiciary Committee. *The Weather Underground*. 94th Cong., 1st sess. S. Rept. 0-200-898.
———. Senate Rep. No. 94-94-755 (1976).
U.S. Court of Appeals. District of Columbia Circuit. *Colonial Times, Inc., D.b.a. the Daily Rag, Petitioner, v. Honorable Oliver Gasch, United States District Judge*. January 3, 1975. Law.justia.com.
———. *Hobson v. Wilson*. June 20, 1984. Scholar.google.com.
Valentine, Paul. "Informers for Police Exposed." *Washington Post*, October 7, 1973.
———. "John Rees: Newsletter Supplied Data on Anti-war Activists." *Washington Post*, June 27, 1976.
———. "Post Office Intercepts 'Obscene' D.C. Tabloid." *Washington Post*, December 1, 1972.
———. "Protesters Threaten Massive City Tie-Up." *Washington Post*, April 22, 1971.
Valk, Anne. *Radical Sisters: Second-Wave Feminism and Black Liberation in Washington, D.C.* Urbana: University of Illinois Press, 2008.
Wachsberger, Ken. *Insider Histories of the Vietnam Era Underground Press, Part 1*. Lansing: Michigan State University Press, 2011.
Washington Post. "All Phones Cut Off, Protesters Protest." April 30, 1971.
———. "Charges Dropped Against 14 in Raid on Newspaper." July 11, 1970.
———. "County Official's Son Arrested Selling Papers." February 8, 1969.
———. "Court Dismisses Most of 2,000 Protest Cases." May 19, 1971.
———. "Editor of Free Press Given Fine, Sentence." February 20, 1969.
———. "'Hippie' Reporter Arrested." September 21, 1968.
———. "Three Newsmen Start Political Weekly Here." October 12, 1968.
———. "Two Charged in Sale of D.C. Paper." August 5, 1967.
———. "The 'Underground' Press: An Old Tradition." Editorial. August 5, 1970.
———. "Women With or Without a Wild Streak." September 11, 1969.

———. "Youths Protest 'Repression.'" April 15, 1969.

Wiegers, Mary. "Beneath Those Charred Bras Revolution Smolders." *Washington Post*, March 8, 1970.

———. "Lib Sees Women's Limited Roles." *Washington Post*, March 10, 1970.

———. "Women's Lib: 'Only Active Radicals in Town.'" *Washington Post*, March 11, 1970.

Charlottesville and Central Virginia

Carson, Clayborne. *In Struggle: SNCC and the Black Awakening of the 1960's*. Cambridge, MA: Harvard University Press, 1981.

Crowe, Dallas Randall. *Desegregation of Charlottesville, Virginia, Public Schools, 1954–1969: A Case Study*. N.p., 1971.

Dyas, Richard W. *Censorship and Dean Runk, 1963–1967*. http://www.cdalumni.org.

Gardner, Thomas, and Al Long. *A Radical View of the University*. Charlottesville, VA: Radical Student Union, 1969.

Hanna, Thomas M. "'Shut It Down, Open It Up': A History of the New Left at the University of Virginia, Charlottesville." VCU thesis, 2007.

Hartford, Bruce. "Civil Rights Movement." Civil Rights Movement Veterans. http://www.crmvet.org.

Hartman, David. "Remembering Sheldon Vanauken." *The Imaginative Conservative*. http://www.theimaginativeconservative.org.

Michel, Gregg L. *Struggle for a Better South: The Southern Student Organizing Committee, 1964–1969*. New York: Palgrave Macmillan, 2004.

Social Movements Collection, 9430-f. University of Virginia Special Collections Library.

Southern Student Organizing Committee Additional Papers, 11192-a, 11192-e, 11192-f. University of Virginia Special Collections Library.

SSOC Bylaws. Report. Nashville, TN: SSOC, 1965.

Tal, Kali. *The Sixties Project*. Advanced Technology in the Humanities, University of Virginia, January 28, 1999. http://www2.iath.virginia.edu/sixties/HTML_docs/Sixties.html.

U.S. Supreme Court. *Bigelow v. Virginia*. June 16, 1975. Find Law. http://caselaw.lp.findlaw.com/scripts/getcase.pl?court=US&vol=421&invol=809.

The Shenandoah Valley and Southwest Virginia

Ackler, Bryan. "*Alice*: The Study of a Free Press." Unpublished manuscript. 1969. Newman Library Special Collections, Virginia Polytechnic Institute and State University, Blacksburg, Virginia.

"The Bluestone." *1970 James Madison College Yearbook*. Archive.org. https://archive.org/details/bluestone197062jame.

Breeze. Archives and Special Collections. James Madison University Carrier Library, James Madison University, Harrisonburg, Virginia.

Charles Knox Martin official papers. Radford University Archives, McConnell Library, Radford University, Radford Virginia.
Fisher, Michael. "Dr. Martin Discusses Policies." *Radford News Journal*, August 22, 1968.
———. "Spring Fever." *Radford News Journal*, April 14, 1967.
Grapurchat. Archives and Special Collections. Radford University Archives, McConnell Library, Radford, Virginia.
Horton, David. "A Narrative History of Radford University." Archives and Special Collections. Radford University Archives, McConnell Library, Radford, Virginia.
Johnson v. Commonwealth. Supreme Court of Virginia. January 17, 1972. Justia U.S. Law. http://law.justia.com/cases/virginia/supreme-court/1972/7749-1.html.
Mihal, Colleen. "Democracy, Citizens' Media, and Resistance: A Study of the *New River Free Press.*" 2004. Virginia Polytechnic Institute and State University. http://scholar.lib.vt.edu/theses/available/etd-07262004-140609/unrestricted/ETD.pdf.
Rainey, Jay. G. "Madison College Student Protest, April 1970." Oral interview with Jeremy Turner. 1998. http://catalog.lib.jmu.edu/record=b1626325.

TIDEWATER

Federal Bureau of Investigation. *Counterintelligence Program: Internal Security, Disruption of the New Left. Norfolk, VA.* U.S. government declassified memorandums. Norfolk, VA: FBI, 1968.
Frank, Willard. Oral interview with Jay Gaidmore, May 7, 1998. Special Collections and University Archives, Patricia W. and J. Douglas Perry Library, Old Dominion University Libraries, Norfolk, Virginia.
Mace and Crown. March 7, 1969. Special Collections and University Archives, Patricia W. and J. Douglas Perry Library, Old Dominion University Libraries, Norfolk, Virginia.

VIRGINIA'S GI UNDERGROUND PRESS

Cook, Adrienne, and Tom O'Brian. "The GI Movement and the 'DMZ.'" *Washington Post.*
Cortright, David. *Soldiers in Revolt: GI Resistance during the Vietnam War.* Chicago: Haymarket, 2005.
GI Press Service. "GI Resistance 1965–1973." Sir! No Sir! Digital Collections. http://militarylies.typepad.com/gi_resistance_19651972.
———. "*Rough Draft* Wins." Vol. 1, no. 7. Sir! No Sir! Digital Collections. http://www.sirnosir.com/archives_and_resources/library/articles/GI_press_service_07.html.
Klose, Kevin. "Ft. Belvoir GIs Start Anti-war Paper." *Washington Post*, March 25, 1969.
Lewes, James. *Protest and Survive: Underground GI Newspapers during the Vietnam War.* Westport, CT: Praeger, 2003.

Liberation News Service. "Army Man Charged After Telling Truth about Pig." July 3, 1969.
Luebke, Barbara. "GI Underground Press a Stubborn Bloom." *Washington Post*, December 27, 1970.
Ungar, Stanford. "Anti-war Seaman Cleared on Appeal." *Washington Post*, February 12, 1971.
———. "Underground Papers Flourish Among GIs." *Washington Post*, August 3, 1970.
Valentine, Paul. "Many Rally to Aid Anti-war Seaman." *Washington Post*, April 9, 1970.
Von Hoffman, Nicholas. "Giving Up the Ship." *Washington Post*, March 24, 1969.
Weil, Martin. "Lawyer Defends Navy Man Against Disloyalty Charge." *Washington Post*, July 24, 1969.
Zieger, David. *Sir! No Sir!* DVD. Displaced Films, 2005.
Zito, Tom. "Coffeehouse Seeks GIs Outside DMZ." *Washington Post*, September 7, 1970.

INDEX

A

Ackler, Bryan 141, 143, 146, 152
Adams-Morgan 80
Adkins, Warren 23, 84
Agee, Philip 50, 66
Agitator, The 115
Alice 140, 141, 143, 144, 145, 146, 147, 149, 151, 152
Amazing Grace 80
American Civil Liberties Union (ACLU) 15, 106, 126, 127, 147, 149, 158, 159, 167
American Servicemen's Union (ASU) 15, 183
American University (AU) 15, 17, 18, 20, 22, 23, 39, 52, 91, 93, 94, 95, 96, 97, 98, 99
Anderson, Jack 50, 66, 77, 106
Ant Hill, The 133, 135, 137, 139, 140, 152
AntiWarrior 188, 189, 191
Armageddon News 96
Associated Press (AP) 15, 186
Atwood, Bonnie 13, 68

B

banana hoax 29
Beatles 34, 36, 37, 49
Beattie, Ann 18, 21, 91
Becker, Terry 47, 51, 58
Bercovici, Liza 62
Berkeley Barb 149
Berlet, Chip 65, 66, 108
Bernstein, Carl 28, 44, 45, 46
Bigelow, Jeffrey 130, 131
Biren, Joan 13, 79, 80, 83
Black Liberation Action Council (BLAC) 15, 169
Black Panther 8, 45, 87, 92, 102, 119, 130
Blacksburg 140, 141, 144, 146, 149, 151, 152
Blacksburg Free Press 141
Bloom, Marshall 30, 33, 37
Blum, William 13, 27, 28, 30, 34, 36, 37, 45, 46, 49, 50, 52, 53, 62, 66
Boggs, Thomas Hale 100
Bolling Other, The 188
Boston Globe 61
Boudin, Kathy 36
Bread Box 90
Breeze, The 152, 155, 159

Brown, James "Rat" 125
Brown, Rita Mae 79, 82
Brown Shoes 164, 165, 167, 168, 169, 171, 172
Bunch, Charlotte 79

C

Cambodia 54, 127
Catholic University 22, 95
Cavalier Daily 120, 121, 123
Central Intelligence Agency (CIA) 11, 15, 25, 49, 50, 52, 53, 56, 57, 58, 60, 62, 65, 66, 76, 93
Charlottesville 78, 111, 115, 117, 119, 125, 126, 131
Charlottesville Daily Progress 127
Chavez, Cesar 103
Chevara News 95, 96
Chicago 7 44, 50, 60, 141, 149
Chicago Seed 149, 158
Church Committee hearings 100, 101
Ciesielski, Dennis 164, 169, 186
Citizen's Commission to Investigate the FBI 100
civil rights 8, 20, 27, 37, 72, 80, 87, 93, 102, 110, 111, 114, 115, 119, 123, 133, 149, 161, 167, 168, 169, 193
COINTELPRO 15, 45, 72, 91, 92, 93, 94, 100, 101, 102
College News Service 65, 108
Collinge, Paul 13, 76, 78
Colonial Times 103, 104
Columbia University 11, 33, 74, 93, 168
COM Mon Sense 188
Community Bookstore 76, 78, 106
COM Newsletter 188
Concerned Officer's Movement 188
counter-inauguration 38, 101
Country Joe and the Fish 29
Crumb, R. 36, 43, 45

D

Daily Rag 103, 104, 106, 108, 109
Danky, James 13, 96
Davis, Rennie 44, 60, 61
D.C. Gay Liberation Front 90
De Baggio, Joyce 13, 17, 18, 21, 38
De Baggio, Thomas 17, 21, 24, 25
Dedrick, Donald 17, 20
Deevey, Sharon 79
Dellinger, David 34, 44
Democratic Presidential Convention 44
Dillingham, Brint 41, 42, 43, 46, 47
DMZ, the 176
Doran, Tom 130
Dreyer, Thorne 36

E

Eagle, The 17, 20, 21, 39, 52, 91, 94, 97, 98
East Village Other 34, 91

F

Fairfax 38, 43, 104, 174
Featherstone, Ralph 110
Federal Bureau of Investigation (FBI) 15, 16, 23, 25, 33, 38, 45, 49, 50, 52, 53, 56, 58, 63, 72, 76, 77, 78, 84, 91, 92, 93, 94, 96, 98, 99, 100, 101, 106, 126, 130, 167, 168, 169, 171, 176
Ferrera, Sal 49, 50, 51, 52, 53, 60, 61, 62, 65, 66
Firestone, Shulamith 70
Fixer, The 152, 153, 155, 156, 158, 159
Flouride, Stan 13, 50, 52
Foley, Bob 111
Fonda, Jane 158, 159
Forcade, Tom 58
Forer, Joseph 41, 42, 43
Fort Belvoir 174
Fort Dix 176, 187
Fort Eustis 164, 169, 183, 186
Fort Lee 187, 188
Frank, Willard 20, 127, 155, 161, 163, 164, 167
FREE! Blacksburg Underground Newsletter 141

Friedan, Betty 68, 75
Friedman, Ken 23
Furies, the (collective) 76, 79, 80, 82, 83
Furies, The (paper) 76, 79, 80, 82, 83

G

Gadfly, The 171
Galloway, Will 165
Gardner, Thomas 13, 121, 123, 126, 131
Gay Activists Alliance 90
Gay Blade, The 8, 84, 85, 87, 90
Georgetown 24, 31, 41, 49, 51, 52, 87
Georgetown University 25, 95
George Washington University (GWU) 15, 42, 49, 95
Gold, Theodore 36
Grapes of Wrath 188
Grapurchat 135, 137, 139
Great Speckled Bird 111, 158
Gregory, Dick 31, 98, 167
Grimaldi, Gerald T. 101
Grosman, Art 27
Grossman, Michael 27, 28, 34
Guardian 54
Guss, Steven 47

H

Hagerhorst, John 47
Hahn, Thomas M., Jr. 152
Haight-Ashbury 7, 23, 29
Hammond, Les 153, 155
Hampton, Fred 8, 45
Harambee 153, 158
Hard Times 8, 102, 103, 117
Harrisonburg 151, 152, 155, 158
Harrisonburg Daily News-Record 158
Hawthorne, Nathaniel 111, 114, 115
Heck, Patti 50, 66
Helms, Richard 56, 62
Hess, Karl 50, 52
Hirschkop, Philip 123, 159, 168
Hoffman, Abbie 9, 44, 50, 119
Hogg, Everett 141, 143
Hoover, J. Edgar 56, 91, 92, 93, 94, 96, 100, 102
Houbolt, Jan 22
Howard University 22, 27
Hurwitt, Robert 18, 21, 23
Hutton, Bobbie 8

I

Iconoclast, The 119, 121
Information Digest 76
in loco parentis 153, 159, 167
Inman, Will 23
Irresponsible Sensationalist, The (*IS*) 114, 161, 165
It Ain't Me Babe 74

J

Jackson State 8
James Madison University. *See* Madison College
Joint Possession 43, 75
Jones, Courtland J. 101

K

Kameny, Frank 23, 84, 90
Kenbridge Post 114
Kennedy, Robert 125
Kent State 8, 54, 127, 151, 158
Kenyatta, John 168, 169
King, Martin Luther, Jr. 36, 37, 92, 94, 125, 143
Kirk, Grayson 11
Kopkind, Andrew 102, 103
Koppelman, Dorothy 13, 21
Krassner, Paul 47
Ku Klux Klan (KKK) 93, 113
Kunstler, William 50, 123, 127

L

Lanier Place 38, 51, 52, 60
Lebovit, Suzanne 27
Left Face 188, 191
Liberated Castle 176

Liberation News Service (LNS) 8, 15, 28, 30, 31, 33, 34, 36, 37, 63, 72, 109, 110, 117, 144, 149, 155, 158
Life magazine 11
Loeb, Dr. Louis 98
Longhorn Tale 96
LSD 24, 29, 125, 149
Lynchburg College 115

M

Mace and Crown 171
Mackenzie, Angus 50, 57, 60
Madison College 151, 152, 158
Madison College Free Press 153
Mad magazine 11, 29
Magic Quilt 70
Mailer, Norman 34
Martin, Charles K., Jr. 133
Maryland 25, 31, 38, 39, 41, 42, 43, 44, 45, 46, 49, 53, 87, 110, 174
Mattachine Foundation 84
Mattachine Society 23, 84
Mayday 60, 61, 62, 65, 76, 102, 103, 106
Merhige, Robert, Jr. 123
Merritt, Earl Robert 77, 106, 108
Miller, George Tyler 22, 23, 155, 156, 158
Morgan, Robin 68
Mungo, Ray 27, 28, 30, 31, 33, 37
Muskat, Harold 13, 187

N

Nader, Ralph 102
National Liberation Front 54
National Organization of Women (NOW) 15
National Peace Action Coalition (NPAC) 15, 60, 106
New Left Notes 54
New Mobilizer 188, 191
New River Free Press 152
Newton, Huey 130
New Virginia, The 111, 113, 114
Nichols, Jack, Jr. 23, 84, 85, 87
Nixon, Richard 37, 38, 54, 56, 58, 61, 62, 70, 82, 102, 103, 108, 119, 127, 168
Nordlinger, Gary 13, 91, 98
Norfolk 114, 131, 165, 167, 168, 169, 171, 183, 185, 188
Norfolk State University 163
Norfolk Virginian-Pilot 168
Northern Virginia Free Press 109
NOW 68, 75, 79

O

Ober Law 39, 46
Ober, Richard 57
ODC Free Press 161, 164, 165
Office of Naval Intelligence (ONI) 15, 178
Off Our Backs (*OOB*) 8, 15, 66, 68, 72, 73, 74, 75, 76, 78, 80, 82, 104
Old Dominion College (ODC) 15, 114, 161, 165
OM: The Servicemen's Newsletter 174, 176, 178, 179, 182, 191
On the Beach 188
Open Sights 8, 174, 176
Operation Bent Penny 61
Operation CHAOS 56, 58, 93
Operation Resistance 11
Oppressed, The 188
Osawatomie's Soul (*OS*) 115, 117
Oughton, Diana 36

P

Paper Bag, The 187, 188
Payne, William 110
Peace and Freedom Party (PFP) 167
Peck, Abe 37
Peeples, Edward H. 13, 115
Pentagon 33, 34, 36, 65, 125, 174, 176, 182, 187
Poor People's Campaign 95, 144
Presidio 174, 183
Price, Pat 90
Priest, Roger 76, 109, 174, 176, 177, 178, 179, 180, 182, 191

Progressive labor 54
Project MERRIMAC 93
Project RESISTANCE 93
Pugh, James 39, 40, 41, 42, 46

Q

Quicksilver Times (*QT*) 8, 16, 23, 47, 50, 53, 54, 56, 60, 63, 65, 103, 109

R

Radford College 133, 134, 135, 139, 140, 149
Radford News-Journal 135
Radicalesbians 79
Radical Feminists 28 83
Radical Student Union (RSU) 126
Rainey, Jay Garland 153, 156, 158
Ramparts 50, 57, 102, 103
Rational Observer 91, 96, 97, 98, 100, 101
Rat Subterranean News 68, 74
Realist, The 47
Red House 76, 77, 78, 106
Rees, John 76, 77, 78
Richmond 12, 53, 61, 115, 126, 131, 144, 169, 188
Richmond Afro-American 117
Richmond Chronicle 7, 8, 9, 72, 111, 117, 144
Richmond Times-Dispatch 128
Ridgeway, James 102, 103
Robbins, Terry 36
Rolling Stone 65
Romaine, Howard 13, 111, 121
Rough Draft 164, 169, 183, 185, 186
Rubenstein, Rachel 27
Rubin, Jerry 44, 50, 119, 127, 141
Rudd, Mark 93
Ryan, Sheila 37

S

Sabaroff, Nina. ***See*** Taylor, Katya Sabaroff
Sally Hemings, The 128
San Francisco Oracle 23
Saunders, Thomas 141, 143, 146, 147
SCOPE project 111
Scott, Jim Lee 115, 117
Seale, Bobby 110
Selden, Lauren 164, 167
Shaefer, Bill 13, 38, 51, 52, 53, 63
Shakedown 187
Shales, Tom 20, 91
Shannon, Edgar 127, 128
Shapiro, David 11, 12
Shenandoah Valley 133
Sherrill, Robert 102
Smith, Bruce 13, 53, 111, 117, 119, 144
Sojourner Truth Press 80
Southern Students Organizing Committee (SSOC) 16, 53, 110, 111, 115, 117, 119, 121, 123, 125, 126, 144, 169
Spartacus 187
Speltz, Ann 27
Speltz, Frank 27, 30, 33
Square Wheel 186
Stamberg, Marjorie 27, 72
Steamtunnel, The 152
Stone, I.F. 102
Stonewall Inn 85
Student Mobilization Committee (SMC) 16, 38, 60, 96, 99, 100, 189
Student Mobilization Committee to End the War (MOBE) 188
Student Nonviolent Coordinating Committee (SNCC) 16, 28, 110, 125
Students for a Democratic Society (SDS) 16, 31, 36, 42, 50, 51, 54, 70, 92, 93, 94, 95, 96, 102, 108, 115, 164, 167, 168
Sumner, Robert 13, 50

T

Taylor, Katya Sabaroff 7, 8, 13, 30, 37, 44, 117
Thrasher, Sue 110

Tichy, Susan 13, 50, 51
Tucker, Nancy 77, 87, 90

U

Underground 17, 18, 20, 21, 22, 23, 24, 38
Unicorn Times 65
United Farm Workers 119
University of Virginia 119, 121, 123, 125, 126, 127, 130

V

Vanauken, Sheldon 115, 117
Venceremos Brigade 7, 74
Victoria 113, 114
Vietnam 7, 11, 16, 18, 22, 27, 28, 30, 33, 34, 56, 60, 62, 82, 93, 94, 98, 110, 114, 121, 123, 134, 135, 137, 139, 141, 146, 147, 149, 151, 155, 158, 159, 161, 164, 167, 168, 172, 174, 177, 182, 183, 187, 188, 190
Village Voice 34, 49, 75, 87, 103
Virginia Defender 188
Virginia Polytechnic Institute (VPI) 16, 135, 140, 141, 144, 146, 147, 149, 151, 152
Virginia Progressive Party (VPP) 126
Virginia Students' Civil Rights Committee (VSCRC) 16, 111, 120
Virginia Tech, The 141
Virginia Weekly 111, 119, 121, 123, 125, 126, 128, 130, 131
Voice from the Mother Country 56
von Hoffman, Nicholas 44, 177, 178, 182

W

Wallace, George 103, 127
Washington Blade 90
Washington Daily News 53
Washington, D.C. 7, 17, 23, 33, 43, 49, 63, 77, 84, 91, 104, 106, 146, 176, 179, 188
Washington Evening Star 41, 73
Washington Free Community 27, 30, 39
Washington Free Press (*WFP*) 16, 23, 25, 41, 45, 47, 75, 93, 101, 149
Washington Independent Publishing Company 50
Washington Post 28, 31, 39, 43, 45, 49, 51, 58, 61, 62, 63, 65, 75, 76, 79, 90, 102, 104, 126, 174, 176, 177, 178, 179
Weathermen. *See* Weather Underground
Weather Underground 36, 54, 56, 78
Webb, Lewis W. 161, 167
Webb, Marilyn 13, 68, 70, 72, 74, 75, 78
Wenger, Bart 87
Whalen, Robert 13, 54, 62
Wilayto, Phil 188
Wilkerson, Cathy 36, 56
Wilson, Dagmar 34
Women's International Terrorist Conspiracy from Hell (WITCH) 70
women's liberation 66, 68, 70, 72, 73, 74, 79, 80, 82, 104, 140, 149, 151, 155, 158, 194
Women Strike for Peace 34, 101
Woodstock 149
Woodwind 65
Workshop, The 95

Y

yippie 16, 50, 119, 127
Young, Allen 13, 28, 30, 37

Z

Zappa, Frank 165

ABOUT THE AUTHOR

Dale Brumfield just received his MFA at age fifty-five at Virginia Commonwealth University and is the author of seven books. His 2013 book *Richmond Independent Press: A History of the Underground Zine Scene* was nominated for a Library of Virginia Literary Award in nonfiction. He has also won numerous state and national awards for his work in Richmond's *Style Weekly* magazine.

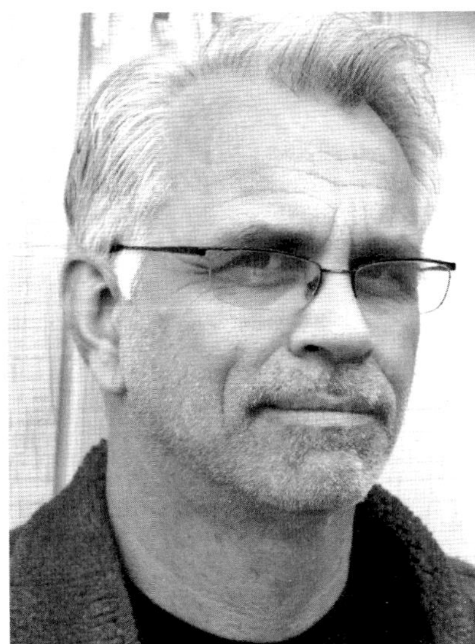

Dale lives in Doswell, Virginia, with his wife, Susan. Their three children live in Richmond.